Morality and American Foreign Policy

Morality and American Foreign Policy

THE ROLE OF ETHICS IN INTERNATIONAL AFFAIRS

Robert W. McElroy

PRINCETON UNIVERSITY PRESS

PRINCETON, NEW JERSEY

Copyright © 1992 by Princeton University Press
Published by Princeton University Press, 41 William Street,
Princeton, New Jersey 08540
In the United Kingdom: Princeton University Press, Oxford

Library of Congress Cataloging-in-Publication Data

McElroy, Robert W.
Morality and American foreign policy : the role of
ethics in international affairs / Robert W. McElroy.
p. cm.
Includes bibliographical references and index.
1. United States—Foreign relations—
20th century—Moral and ethical aspects.
2. International relations—
Moral and ethical aspects. I. Title.
JX1417.M37 1992 172'.4—dc20   91–25337 CIP

ISBN 0-691-08621-4

This book has been composed in Linotron Primer

Princeton University Press books are printed on acid-free paper,
and meet the guidelines for permanence and durability
of the Committee on Production Guidelines for Book Longevity
of the Council on Library Resources

Printed in the United States of America

1   3   5   7   9   10   8   6   4   2

For my family

———————————————

CONTENTS

TABLES

ACKNOWLEDGMENTS

THIS WORK grew out of my doctoral dissertation in political science at Stanford University, and I wish to thank first and foremost all those in the Stanford community who helped make it possible. To Judith Goldstein, who was willing to undertake the direction of a doctoral dissertation even as she was beginning a two-year sabbatical, I offer my thanks for creative suggestions, careful scrutiny, and the constant challenge to think broadly and coherently. To Alexander George, who helped me to grapple with the thorny issue of how to approach productively the relationship of morality and foreign policy at the earliest stages of my work, I offer thanks for wise counsel and constant encouragement. To Stephen Krasner, who never let a sloppy thought go by unchallenged, I give thanks for penetrating questions and for the care that lay behind them. I also want to thank Nina Halpern and Jack Rakove, whose presence at my oral examinations made them a far more fruitful experience, as well as David Abernathy, David Holloway, and John Ferejohn for their assistance during the past three years. No academic department can function well without a committed support staff, and the political science department at Stanford has one of the best; thus I would offer my gratitude to Arlee Ellis, Jean Lee, Dorothy Blake, Elizabeth Rafferty, and Juni Kim for all of the many kindnesses that they have provided to me.

My Stanford experience was an enjoyable and productive one in large part because of the companionship and stimulation offered by my fellow graduate students. To Jane Holl, whose comments and suggestions improved every chapter of this work, I express my heartfelt gratitude. To Rose McDermott, who contributed not only a proofreader's fine eye but also her expansive knowledge of the social sciences, I want to express my thanks. And to my other classmates, who made the study of political science a far more provocative and intriguing enterprise, I offer thanks for three years of friendship and good times: Marty Finnemore, Kevin Cunningham, Ken Roberts, Jendayi Fraser, Alfonso Lara, Chuck Shipan, Dan Abbasi, Steve Fish, and Kurt Weyland.

There are also thanks which I owe to many non-Stanford friends: to my family, who have always provided me with love and encouragement; to Archbishop John Quinn, who has supported my study of ethics and politics in every possible way; and to Bruce Dreier, Ray Sacca, Jim McKay, Pete Armstrong, Barbara von Emster, Gerry Coleman, Jack Penebsky, Chris Luvisi, Rita Carroll, Clementina Tracy, Tom Madden, Bill Brady, Bruce Koty, Greg Sandman, and Joe Ocuto. To all these, I offer my deepest thanks for their friendship and support.

Finally, I want to thank Michael Doyle of Princeton University for his immensely beneficial comments on my manuscript; and especially Malcolm DeBevoise of Princeton University Press and Nancy Trotic, for their kind assistance at every step of the publication process.

Morality and American Foreign Policy

Chapter One

THE DEBATE ON MORALITY AND
INTERNATIONAL RELATIONS

FOR THE FIRST sixty years of this century, the question of what role morality plays in the formulation of foreign policy lay at the very heart of the scientific study of international relations. But during the past quarter century, in contrast, the role of morality in international affairs has been banished to the periphery of the field. Leading scholars may reject the charge that their scientific approaches to international relations lead to amoral conclusions, but they do not dedicate serious attention to investigating the influence of moral values on the conduct of nations.[1]

There are two major reasons for this transposition of the question of morality in the field of international relations. The first stems from the desire to establish the independence of the study of international affairs from all ethical and philosophical presuppositions, to construct a value-free science "consisting of formal models in which the preferences of the actors are treated as givens and in which attempts are made at quantifying the multiple unponderables of international affairs."[2] The second reason for the vanishing interest in the role of morality flows from the massive impact that realism has had in the field of international affairs. The realist tradition, which has remained the dominant paradigm in the study of international relations almost without interruption for the past thirty years, stresses the roles of necessity and anarchy in the politics of nations. In such a world of intense competition among nations, there is little room for meaningful choice on the part of state decision makers, and even less room for the choice of moral values that conflict with the national interest.

But if the role of morality in the formulation of foreign policy has come to occupy a peripheral place in the field of international relations, it has become an ever more prominent part of the field of applied

[1] Joseph Nye and Stanley Hoffmann are two notable exceptions to this generalization. See Nye, *Nuclear Ethics* (New York: The Free Press, 1986); and Hoffmann, *Duties beyond Borders: On the Limits and Possibilities of Ethical International Politics* (Syracuse: Syracuse University Press, 1981).

[2] Stanley Hoffmann, *The Political Ethics of International Relations* (New York: Carnegie Council on Ethics and International Affairs, 1988), p. 8.

ethics. There has arisen in the past decade a vast new literature that investigates the moral choices inherent in foreign-policy decision making and offers prescriptions for ethical conduct in foreign affairs. In part, this literature has focused upon specific moral questions such as the deployment and use of nuclear weapons or the inequality in the distribution of resources among nations.[3] But there has also appeared a series of more general theoretical treatments of the role of morality in foreign policy, treatments that grapple with the realist analysis of international relations and offer substantive non-normative criticisms of the realist worldview. Such writers as Charles Beitz, Marshall Cohen, and J. E. Hare have challenged the realist paradigm by arguing that all political action is goal-oriented activity, that there are substantive moral principles that meaningfully address questions of international affairs, and that the formulation of foreign policy is intrinsically a domain of moral choice.[4]

The result of this resurgence in normative treatments of international relations has not been a substantive dialogue between empirical students of international affairs and ethical thinkers. Rather, there have emerged two separate scholarly communities, each operating from a different worldview, using different languages, and arriving at different conclusions about the essential nature of the politics among nations. This was not what Hans Morgenthau had in mind when he wrote *Politics among Nations* in 1948. For Morgenthau saw in the realist enterprise an effort to build a bridge between normative and empirical thinkers in the field of international relations, so that the leaders of nations could erect their foreign policies upon foundations that were both ethically sound and realistically conceived.[5]

This study is an effort to assist in building such a bridge. Speaking from an empirical rather than a normative perspective, it seeks to identify concrete ways in which moral norms can substantively influence foreign-policy decision making.

The first step in this process is to review the efforts that previous authors have made to identify the role that morality plays in the formulation of foreign policy. While realist thought remains the most important body of commentary on the question of morality and international relations, realism comes in many shades, and authors who

[3] See, for example, *Ethics* 95 (April 1985).

[4] Charles Beitz, *Political Theory and International Relations* (Princeton: Princeton University Press, 1979); Marshall Cohen, "Moral Skepticism and International Relations," *Philosophy and Public Affairs* 13 (Fall 1984): 299–346; and J. E. Hare and Carey Joynt, *Ethics and International Affairs* (London: Macmillan Press, 1982).

[5] Hans Morgenthau, Introduction to *Ethics and United States Foreign Policy*, by Ernest Lefever (Cleveland: Meridien Books, 1967), p. ix.

would consider themselves to be in the realist tradition dramatically disagree with one another on important issues in the debate. These differences, as well as the common theoretical core that unites all realists in sharply delimiting the role of morality in international affairs, are crucial to understanding how a bridge between the empirical and normative communities can begin. Equally crucial are the criticisms that ethical thinkers and political theorists have leveled against the realist school in recent years; for in locating weaknesses in the realist definition of morality and how it functions in human action, these normative authors have effectively challenged the notion of "political man" that lies at the heart of the realist critique. But before examining either the proponents of realism or their critics, it is necessary to begin in the interwar period, with the liberal internationalist thought that dominated the field of international relations from 1918 to 1945 and formed the background against which the debate on morality and foreign policy has been waged.

THE CREED OF THE INTERNATIONALISTS

The liberal internationalists were a group of English-speaking commentators on international relations who wrote in the interwar period and maintained that the era ushered in by the Treaty of Versailles marked a watershed in the relations among nation-states. A distinguished company that included most of the pioneers of the academic study of international relations, the liberal internationalists were led by Alfred Zimmern, the first professor of international relations at Oxford University; Gilbert Murray, the president of the League of Nations Union; Nicholas Murray Butler, the president of Columbia University; and James T. Shotwell, the first Carnegie professor of international relations and the architect of the Kellogg-Briand Pact.[6] What bound these thinkers together was their belief that the postwar world could be made more stable, more just, and more peaceful than any previous epoch in human history. The internationalists believed firmly in the notion of human progress, and they contended that the

[6] Liberal internationalism was not confined to the academic study of international affairs; rather, it constituted a mind-set that was quite prevalent in the cultural, business, and political elites of the interwar period and counted among its adherents Charles Beard, Herbert Croly, Raymond Fosdick, George Louis Beer, and David Davies. The Council on Foreign Relations, which was founded in 1921, was not exclusively composed of liberal internationalists, but the liberal impulse was the guiding spirit for much of the early work of the Council. See Robert Divine, *Second Chance: The Triumph of Internationalism in America during World War II* (New York: Atheneum, 1967), chap. 1; and Michael Joseph Smith, *Realist Thought from Weber to Kissinger* (Baton Rouge: Louisiana State University Press, 1986), pp. 54–67.

twentieth century held the promise of fundamentally transforming the politics among nations to give it a more cooperative and transnational cast.

The formative event for the proponents of internationalist thought was World War I. This cataclysmic event, which rent both the political and social fabric of Europe, was seen as the ultimate indictment of the power politics that had governed European interstate relations since the Napoleonic Wars. The "balancing of power with power" that was supposed to have checked the ambitions of every major power was revealed to be an unreliable restraint, and even before the war had ended, students of international relations were searching for new approaches to the politics among nations. "The great adventure of our day," wrote Shotwell, "is the uprooting of barbarism in international relations."[7]

Crucial to this endeavor was the notion that war arose not from the nature of the human person, but rather from patterns of state interaction that could be altered through moral education and the collective action of the peoples of the world. Gilbert Murray exemplified this internationalistic mind-set when he wrote in 1929:

> The apologists for war . . . get their minds badly confused because they continue to speak of war as if it were an element of human nature, like strife or fear or ambition. . . . The war which is formally renounced in the Pact of Paris and practically guarded against in the covenant of the League of Nations is not an instinct, it is a form of state action. It is not an element in human nature, it is part of a political programme. It is no more an instinct, or an element in human nature, than the adoption of the income tax.[8]

Since war was part of a political program, that program had to be changed. What needed to be stressed was the common interest that all nations had in preserving peace and in creating a stable and just international order. The internationalist writers did not believe by any means that this would be an easy task, for they recognized that war is an all-too-alluring tool of state policy. But they believed that the trauma of the Great War had created a situation of revolutionary potential, in which "the will to peace is paramount in the civilized world."[9]

This "revolutionary potential" of the postwar era, according to the

[7] James Shotwell, *War as an Instrument of National Policy* (New York: Harcourt, Brace, 1929), p. 88.

[8] Gilbert Murray, *The Ordeal of This Generation* (New York: Harper and Brothers, 1929), p. 29.

[9] Shotwell, *War as an Instrument*, p. vii.

internationalists, arose not merely because World War I had revealed the bankruptcy of the Old Order, but also because the growing economic, technological, political, and cultural interdependence among nations in the late nineteenth and early twentieth centuries had created the beginnings of a genuine international society. Alfred Zimmern noted in his inaugural lectures at Oxford the profound implications of this reality: "The Industrial Revolution and the consequent interdependence of the parts and peoples of mankind have already changed the conditions of political activity. The problems of the modern world are no longer local, but large-scale, no longer concerned with the broils and prejudices of neighbors, but with forces which, in the vast sweep of their influence, affect millions of men in all parts of the globe."[10] Such forces of interdependence ranged from commercial policy to raw-material networks to issues of public health, and while they certainly had not eliminated the enormous importance of state boundaries, they had created new conditions for the interaction of states. Most importantly, as Murray noted, they had changed the way in which individuals looked at the boundaries of their world:

If you look back at history, you find at every epoch or in every society that there is a set of precincts within which the world is understood or is at least understandable, and outside of which rage the unknown heathen. There was the Hellenic world, within which there were doubtless many wicked and hateful persons, but they were still Hellenes and had customs upon which you could calculate. . . . To the men of the Middle Ages, the precinct was Christendom, within which reigned, ideally at least, the law of Christ. . . . It is that fence which [modern conditions] have, I will say, not merely broken down, but as far as human beings are concerned, removed the edges off the map of the world.[11]

To the internationalists, the central change in the relations among states in the era following World War I arose from the fact that human beings in all parts of the world shared a destiny that was increasingly interconnected on the economic, political, cultural, and technological planes.

But the mere fact that relations among nations and national societies were growing more complex with every passing year was less important than the question of what form those relations would take in the years following 1918. As Zimmern noted, "We have reached a stage in world development when the common affairs of the world can

[10] Alfred Zimmern, *The Prospects of Democracy* (Freeport, N.Y.: Books for Library Press, 1929), p. 101.
[11] Gilbert Murray, *Tradition and Progress* (Boston: Houghton Mifflin, 1922), pp. 187–189.

and will be organized. The only question is whether they will be organized in the interests of mankind."[12] This was both a moral and a political question, and its affirmative answer would require action on both the moral and political planes. The internationalists found significant hope that such a moral renewal in foreign policy was possible, and they looked to recent history for support for their position. "I think we must recognize," Murray wrote, "the influence of moral advances made by civilized man in the nineteenth century, the awakening of his social conscience and the ever-widening range of his imaginative sympathy, as shown by the great humanitarian efforts to relieve suffering."[13] All of these advances, the internationalists claimed, were signs that moral parochialism was breaking down among the nations of the world, and that principles of an incipient genuine international morality could be discerned.[14]

The internationalists were quick to point out that only the *beginnings* of an international morality could be detected in the years following World War I, and that "the public opinion of mankind is not yet ripe for a permanent written constitution which [would] regulate its political activities."[15] There were still many issues with moral overtones on which there was no international consensus. But in the growing support for the peaceful resolution of conflicts, for joint efforts to carry out humanitarian aid to countries stricken by plague or natural disaster, and for the erection of a commercial regime that would attempt to embody just rules for international trade, the liberal internationalists perceived the emerging tenets of a true international morality that would grow more detailed and more cohesive as the twentieth century progressed.

Even if there *were* emerging standards of international morality that governed the politics among nations, the question remained: how could such standards be brought to bear upon the formulation of foreign policy? The internationalists proposed that there were three channels through which morality could influence international relations; none of these channels offered a consistent or foolproof way of incorporating moral principles into the relations of nation-states, but each of them provided an opportunity to make foreign policy significantly more moral than it had been before.

Domestic public opinion was the first channel through which morality could influence the making of foreign policy. No longer was

[12] Zimmern, *Prospects of Democracy*, p. 125.
[13] Gilbert Murray, *Liberality and Civilization* (London: George Allen and Unwin, 1938), p. 60.
[14] Murray, *Tradition and Progress*, p. 189.
[15] Zimmern, *Prospects of Democracy*, p. 172.

statecraft to be solely the province of diplomats and heads of state, for the democratization of Europe had created a situation in which the mass public of each nation would enjoy an ever-larger role in the politics among nations. Nicholas Murray Butler spoke for the internationalists when he maintained that

> at no time in history has there ever been so widespread and grave a questioning of the underlying principles of the political, the economic, and social order of mankind. From the time when the Greek philosophers began their classical examination of those questions, down, perhaps, to the middle of the nineteenth century, these discussions were confined to what might be called the leaders of opinion, the intellectual classes, and those who, by reason of circumstance or capacity, were guiding the affairs of their several peoples. In our time, however, this constituency has been broadened and extended by the principles of democracy, until it includes substantially the entire mass of mankind. Men and women everywhere, in America, in Europe, in Africa, in Asia, and in Australia, are now in a position of authority with respect to the formation and guidance of public opinion and through it, to the control of the conduct and policies of government.[16]

The first results of this broad-based reexamination of the international social, economic, and political order could be found in the increasing commitment of the peoples of the world to the peaceful resolution of conflict, the desire to establish just commercial relations among nations, and the acceptance of international responsibility for humanitarian relief. As a result, domestic public opinion in each nation-state could be expected to periodically hold in check actions of state leaders that contradicted these principles of the emerging international morality.

It is important to emphasize that the internationalists did not blindly believe in the uprightness of public opinion; nor did they ignore the role that public opinion had played in fomenting war throughout the early twentieth century. As Zimmern noted in his classic treatment on the League of Nations and the rule of law:

> Not only can the general public never become as familiar with [international] problems in detail as with the ordinary issues of domestic politics; there is the added difficulty that the conditions involved are generally so remote from the experience of the "average man in the street" that he has no easy means of bringing his healthy common sense to bear upon them. Thus it is easy for him to divest himself, unconsciously, of his sav-

[16] Nicholas Murray Butler, *The Family of Nations* (New York: Charles Scribner's Sons, 1938), p. 151.

ing realism and to fall a victim either to the well-meaning appeals of the ignorant sentimentalist or to the artful wiles of the unscrupulous propagandist. . . . The remedy here is not to mobilize sentiment against sentiment or propaganda against propaganda, but to deepen and strengthen the foundations of general education.[17]

Such a process of education would be slow and arduous; it meant strengthening the moral and political outlooks of the mass publics of Europe and the United States so that they would never again support leaders who advanced bellicose or imperialist aims.[18] In order to accomplish this task, the clear moral principles of the international order—self-determination, the peaceful resolution of conflict, and the unity of all nations—would have to be stressed at every level of the educational process and through the media.[19] If such a campaign of moral education were carried out, the internationalists believed, domestic public opinion in the world's most powerful nations could become an ever more effective constraint on the actions of belligerent leaders and nations, and the politics of nations could come to bear a clear, if not consistent, moral imprint.

The second channel that the internationalists believed could bring morality into the formulation of foreign policy lay in the "courtroom of world opinion" represented by the League of Nations. The liberal internationalists recognized that sanctions and collective action would at times be required at the League if peace was to be preserved. But they argued that the more normal, and in general the most effective, international force for establishing just and pacific relations among states was the organized opinion of humankind:

[17] Alfred Zimmern, *The League of Nations and the Rule of Law: 1918–1935* (London: Macmillan and Company, 1939), pp. 27–28.

[18] Alfred Zimmern, *America and Europe* (New York: Oxford University Press, 1929), p. 191.

[19] Harold Josephson, *James T. Shotwell and the Rise of Internationalism in America* (London: Associated Press, 1975), pp. 196–199. One indication of the impact that the internationalists believed domestic public opinion could have on foreign policy lies in the work that Murray, Butler, and Shotwell expended in organizing mass education programs to bring moral values in international affairs to the grass-roots level. Murray was vice-chair of the Committee for Intellectual Cooperation (which included Albert Einstein, Henri Bergson, and Marie Curie) and attempted to devise a mass curriculum for education on cooperation and morality in international relations. Shotwell worked with the Carnegie Endowment to devise a similar program for use in the United States and helped to organize scholars' symposiums to speak to mass audiences across the United States on the importance of peace, stability, and morality in foreign policy. And Butler used his presidency of Columbia and his trusteeship of the Carnegie Endowment to bring the message of international liberalism not only into the boardrooms of America and Europe, but also into the living rooms and classrooms.

The world has not yet sounded or measured the immense power of mere publicity. I do not mean advertisement in newspapers; I mean the knowledge that your actions are to be known and discussed, and particularly that you will have to answer questions about them face to face with your questioner. Publicity is the only new weapon which the League possesses, but if properly used it may well prove to be about the most powerful weapon that exists in human affairs.[20]

The internationalists believed that nations cared about their reputations and about their standings in the community of nations; and they believed that as a result international condemnation did carry enormous political weight apart from any other sanctions that might be imposed. Thus it was important to mold international public opinion in order to make it as cohesive as possible, and as reflective as possible of the moral principles that stood at the heart of the League Covenant.

In the view of most liberal internationalists, the whole of world public opinion could be mobilized only rarely, such as in cases of outright aggression or a gross flouting of the most basic moral standards of humanity. But this did not mean that international public opinion could not be a continuing and effective check on the morality of international relations. For the growth of interdependence in the economic, political, technological, and cultural spheres had generated a series of international networks of "interested publics" that could be brought to bear effectively upon state actions that less glaringly violated international moral standards. What was necessary was that there be "a healthy flow of public opinion in each domain" of international affairs so that these more specialized sectors of international public opinion could constructively monitor the actions of states within their interest areas and call upon states to conform with international moral standards.[21]

The final channel through which morality could influence the formulation of foreign policy, according to the internationalists, lay in the consciences of individual national leaders. While skeptical of the prewar diplomacy that had made foreign-policy decision making largely the private preserve of an exclusive elite, the liberal internationalists did believe that state leaders and diplomats would at times follow international moral standards not merely because of domestic public opinion or a fear of international condemnation, but because in conscience they believed such standards to be right.[22] Woodrow Wilson stood for the internationalists as the prime example of a statesman

[20] Murray, *Tradition and Progress*, p. 199.
[21] Zimmern, *America and Europe*, p. 201.
[22] Murray, *Ordeal of This Generation*, p. 88.

living by moral principle, and Zimmern, Murray, and Butler sought to encourage future national leaders to see their roles as Wilson had seen his, using moral standards as a guide for action in the international arena. As Zimmern wrote in his commentary on "politics as an idealistic career":

> What we are concerned with . . . is not the kind of politics which seize hold of the mind like a religious revival. . . . On the contrary, it is the political activity which is diametrically opposed to this type of obsession— the steady and persistent effort of those who have their own sure personal standards of belief and are seeking to apply them to a subject matter of peculiar importance and complexity.[23]

The liberal internationalists believed that the years after 1918 provided a fertile opportunity for just such political leaders to reshape the character of international affairs and to bring their personal moral standards firmly to bear upon the making of foreign policy.

It is sometimes said of the liberal internationalists that they were so idealistic in their conception of the role that morality could play in foreign affairs that their writings have little to offer to a contemporary investigation of international relations.[24] But such analyses overlook the many passages in the internationalist writings that underscore the difficulties inherent in trying to bring moral principles into the arena of international affairs. Gilbert Murray spoke for the internationalists when he pointed out that political and moral conflicts are worked out in a parallelogram of conflicting forces in which neither morality nor self-interest is entirely victorious, while Zimmern cautioned that there was a constant need to channel ideals through "a trained sense of the scope and limitations of political action."[25] The internationalists may have pointed to a world in which international moral standards took on a far greater role than they had enjoyed in previous generations, but internationalist thought never regarded the effort to moralize the conduct of nations as anything but a complex, challenging, and very gradual process.

The internationalists of the interwar period made four important claims, for the purposes of this study, about the role of morality in foreign policy. They claimed that relatively clear international moral norms existed that could guide state decision makers in pursuing just policies. They argued that domestic public opinion could serve as an effective moral constraint upon the actions of state decision makers.

[23] *Prospects of Democracy*, p. 266.

[24] Smith, *Realist Thought*, p. 67.

[25] Murray, *Tradition and Progress*, pp. 188–189; Zimmern, *America and Europe*, p. 96.

The internationalists advanced a view of human nature that stressed rationality and community, rather than conflict and the drive for power. And they believed that World War I and the democratization of the West had created a radically new situation for international relations in which morally based precepts of state action could be effectively enforced by international public opinion and the community of nations. The politics of nations was for the internationalists a malleable thing that was capable of being patterned, albeit imperfectly, according to an effective moral order.

THE REALIST PRELUDE

It is ironic that a tradition such as realism, which seeks to advance a scientific theory of international relations, should trace its intellectual heritage to a theologically based conception of the human person. But it was Reinhold Niebuhr's theological anthropology that undergirded the realist attack upon liberal internationalism in the period after World War II.[26] As a consequence, an understanding of Niebuhr's thought is essential for comprehending the flow and meaning of the twentieth-century debate upon the role of morality in international life.

Niebuhr's anthropology echoes Martin Luther's stress upon the sinfulness of humanity and the human desire to deny that sinfulness. In Niebuhr's view, men and women comprehend their limitations and yet seek to deny them; while capable of self-transcendence because of their spiritual identity, they are nonetheless burdened by their creatureliness. As a consequence, women and men stand in a position of ambiguity; they are unwilling to accept the dependency and insecurity that is their lot. From this unwillingness flows the will to power that taints all human interrelationships:

> Man is insecure and involved in natural contingency; he seeks to overcome his insecurity by a will-to-power which overreaches the limits of human creatureliness. Man is ignorant and involved in the limitations of a finite mind; but he pretends that he is not limited. He assumes that he can gradually transcend finite limitation until his mind becomes identical with the universal mind. All of his intellectual and cultural pursuits,

[26] This irony is heightened by Niebuhr's critical stance toward all attempts at constructing a scientific theory of human behavior. See Kenneth Thompson, "The Political Philosophy of Reinhold Niebuhr," in *Reinhold Niebuhr: His Religious, Social, and Political Thought*, ed. Charles Kegley (New York: Pilgrim Press, 1984), pp. 224–228.

therefore, become infected with the sin of pride. Man's pride and will-to-power disturb the harmony of creation.[27]

Thus the same drive for self-transcendence that is capable of uniting the human person with God is also the cause of human sinfulness. Such is the ultimate ambiguity of human existence.[28]

Human pride and the will for power express themselves on three distinct planes, according to Niebuhr. The first is the search for security, which leads to a desire for domination over others. Because such domination can never allow men and women to truly break through the bonds of their finitude, the search for security is never-ending. For those who have attained great power and wealth there is a perpetual fear of losing it, and for those who have not yet attained a modicum of wealth and power there is a deep sense of deprivation and a desire for redress.[29] The search for security transforms all human relations into relations of power and domination; only through self-sacrificial love can the taint of domination be overcome, and self-sacrificial love is an all-too-rare commodity.

The second plane on which human pride expresses itself, according to Niebuhr, is the intellectual plane. Blind to the fact that all human thought is by nature limited, philosophers and social movements have raised finite insights to the status of all-encompassing worldviews that claim to transcend history.

> All human knowledge is tainted with an "ideological" taint. It pretends to be more true than it is. It is finite knowledge, gained from a particular perspective; but it pretends to be final and ultimate knowledge. Exactly analogous to the cruder pride of power, the pride of intellect is derived on the one hand from ignorance of the finiteness of the human mind and on the other hand from an attempt to obscure the known conditioned character of human knowledge and the taint of self-interest in human truth.[30]

The most threatening of these ideologies, in Niebuhr's view, is Marxism; for Marxism correctly locates the shortcomings in all competing ideologies but then proclaims its own freedom from the limitations of human understanding. As a consequence, it is an ideology of unprecedented power and demonic force.[31]

---

[27] Reinhold Niebuhr, *The Nature and Destiny of Man: Human Nature* (New York: Charles Scribner and Sons, 1943), pp. 178–179.

[28] For an incisive interpretation of Niebuhr's conception of the human person, see Edward Wolf, "Niebuhr's Doctrine of Man," in Kegley and Bretall, *Reinhold Niebuhr*, pp. 229–250.

[29] Niebuhr, *Nature and Destiny of Man*, pp. 188–194.

[30] Ibid., pp. 194–195.

[31] Niebuhr's criticism of Marxism grew more intense during the 1950s, but it had

The final plane on which human pride is expressed is the moral plane. Because the human person stands in a continual position of ambiguity and sinfulness, human moral standards must always be seen as provisional and flawed. Moral pride denies this reality and claims that "man's highly conditioned virtue is the final righteousness and that his very relative moral standards are absolute."[32] As a result of moral pride, hypocrisy rules human moral evaluation and further distorts the human search for self-transcendence. This hypocrisy fails to recognize either the overwhelming complexity of moral problems or the inherent sinfulness in every human act.

In translating his anthropology to the political sphere, Niebuhr accentuates the will for power and security. Since men and women are frustrated in their search for individual security, they seek to fulfill this search vicariously by projecting their drive for power to a collective plane. Thus they pledge their loyalty to the nation-state in order to attain some sense of security and domination. As a result, "society . . . merely cumulates the egoism of individuals and transmutes their individual altruism into collective egoism so that the egoism of the group has a double force. For this reason no group acts from purely unselfish or even mutual intent and politics is therefore bound to be a contest of power."[33]

The restraining power that love exerts upon human relationships at the level of family and friendship is almost totally vitiated in the political world. For "love, which depends upon emotion, . . . is baffled by the more intricate social relations in which the highest ethical attitudes are achieved only by careful calculation. If love cannot find an immediate object, it has difficulties in expressing itself."[34] The politics of nations is for Niebuhr a fight for power and security in which altruism is almost totally absent; only a balancing of power with power can bring some semblance of harmony in the international system.

Reinhold Niebuhr transformed the debate on morality and interna-

---

always been present in his thought because of Marxism's claim to provide an ultimate referent in society. By 1948, Niebuhr had concluded that "the deepest tragedy of our age . . . is that the alternative to capitalism has turned out to be worse than the disease which it was meant to cure." (Reinhold Niebuhr, Editorial, *Radical Religion* 13, no. 4 [Autumn 1948]: 5)

[32] Niebuhr, *Nature and Destiny of Man*, p. 199.

[33] Reinhold Niebuhr, "Human Nature and Social Change," *Christian Century* 50 (1933): 363, quoted in Thompson, "Political Philosophy of Reinhold Niebuhr," p. 240.

[34] Reinhold Niebuhr, *Moral Man and Immoral Society* (New York: Charles Scribner's Sons, 1960), p. 74. In the 1940s, Niebuhr gave greater nuance to this argument by proposing that the difference between individual and social men and women is a difference of degree rather than a difference of kind. But it is an enormous difference of degree. See Niebuhr, *Nature and Destiny of Man*, pp. 208–213.

tional relations because he advanced a compelling conception of human nature that destroyed the foundations of the internationalist argument. As Hans Morgenthau wrote in 1962:

> It is this kind of optimistic denial of the intrinsic relationship of the lust for power and its social upshot—the political sphere—which Reinhold Niebuhr has destroyed, and he has restored the idea which was basic both to the Biblical and ancient Greek and Roman conception of man: that the lust for power and the social configurations to which lust gives rise is an intrinsic element, an intrinsic quality of human nature itself.[35]

But Niebuhr did more than rebut the idealist notion that human nature was not intrinsically warlike and lustful for power. For in his argument about the hypocrisy and contingent nature of all human moral prescriptions, Niebuhr undercut the idealist assertion that there were clear international moral norms that, if applied consistently, would gradually transform the international system into a more humane and ethical world. In Niebuhr's view, morality could not triumph in international relations both because men and women seek power vicariously through their national loyalties and because international politics is inherently too complex for any human ethical standards to address effectively.

But if Niebuhr despaired of the triumph of morality in international relations, he did not believe that moral norms had no place in determining the actions of statesmen. For Niebuhr argued that even in international politics there is a residual capacity for justice that tempers the competition among nations. "Politics will, to the end of history, be an area where conscience and power meet, where the ethical and coercive factors of human life will interpenetrate and work out their tentative and uneasy compromises."[36] The problem with this stance, and with the manner in which Niebuhr developed it in his writings on international relations, is that while it is easy to project from Niebuhr's anthropology how severely morality is circumscribed in the international field, it is difficult to project how justice takes on a substantive role. The "tentative and uneasy compromises" that Niebuhr envisions have emerged in the tradition of realism not as real compromises between power and morality, but as decisions in which moral values play only the most residual role.

If Reinhold Niebuhr provided the anthropology that fueled the realist critique of international morality, E. H. Carr provided the incisive

[35] Hans Morgenthau, "The Influence of Reinhold Niebuhr in American Political Life and Thought," in *Reinhold Niebuhr: A Prophetic Voice in Our Time*, ed. Harold Landon (Greenwich, Conn.: Seabury Press, 1962), p. 100.

[36] *Moral Man*, p. 4.

reflections of a veteran diplomat on the shortcomings of the internationalist worldview. The first target of Carr's attack was the centerpiece of the internationalist argument: the assertion that it was in the interest of every nation to ban warfare from the face of the earth. In Carr's view, such an assertion was no more than the projection by predominantly British and American scholars of their hope that Anglo-American dominance could be maintained without the necessity of war; it completely ignored the fact that such a dominance was decidedly hostile to the interests of Germany and other ascendent nations:

> The utopian assumption that there is a world interest in peace which is identifiable with the interest of each individual nation helped politicians and political writers everywhere to evade the unpalatable fact of a fundamental divergence of interest between nations desirous of maintaining the status quo and nations desirous of changing it. . . . the fact of divergent interests was disguised and falsified by the platitude of a general desire to avoid conflict.[37]

This divergence of interests characterized not only the issue of war and peace in international affairs, but also the issues of free trade, colonialism, and cultural intercourse. Once this reality was recognized, it was possible to see how illusory the internationalist agenda was. For the idealists had argued that it was in the rational interest of every nation to pursue peace, economic cooperation, and greater social intercourse. The observance of international moral norms was a logical outcome of the mutually reinforcing interests of nations; ethical conduct was self-interestedly rational conduct. In pointing to the divergence of national interest between nations favoring the status quo and ascendent powers, Carr showed the fallacy of this reasoning. "Internationally, it is no longer possible to deduce virtue from right reasoning, because it is no longer seriously possible to believe that every state, by pursuing the greatest good of the whole world, is pursuing the greatest good of its own citizens, and vice versa."[38]

Carr accepted the existence of an international community, and he accepted the fact that at times nations would act out of moral motivations. But he believed that the role of morality in international relations was severely circumscribed by the difficulty of applying the principle of equality in the international system and by the unwillingness of nations to act upon the principle that the good of the whole (in this case the community of nations) should take precedence over the good

---

[37] E. H. Carr, *The Twenty Years' Crisis: 1919–1939* (London: Macmillan and Company, 1956), p. 53.
[38] Ibid., p. 62.

of the individual nation. The equality of nations, Carr argued, is a principle of great importance in international dialogue and debate. But it is not a reality in the international system. For the gross disparities in power and resources among nations render it almost impossible to establish a comprehensive and realistic set of egalitarian rights and obligations for nation-states. These difficulties flowing from the inequality of nations are compounded by the general unwillingness of nations to undertake costly actions in service to the common good of the international community; the allegiance of most citizens to the world community is so minimal that they are seldom willing to sacrifice their national interests in order to pursue a more inclusive interest.[39] As a consequence, Carr argues, it is "a dangerous illusion to suppose that this hypothetical world community possesses the unity and coherence of communities of more limited size up to and including the state."[40] And without this unity and coherence, morality can play only a minimal role in the politics of nations.

One of the chief reasons that the international community does not exert a stronger claim upon the citizens of all nations, in Carr's view, is the susceptibility of public opinion to mass propaganda and state control. The internationalists had recognized the ease with which mass publics could fall prey to nationalist slogans; but they believed that mass education and the growing democratization of the West could lead to a new age of moral international relations. Carr called this optimistic estimate into serious question:

> The same economic and social conditions which have made mass opinion supremely important in politics have also created instruments of unparalleled range and efficiency to mold and direct it. . . . The mass production of opinion is the corollary of the mass-production of goods. Just as the nineteenth century conception of political freedom was rendered illusory for large masses of the population by the growth and concentration of economic power, so the nineteenth century conception of freedom of thought is being fundamentally modified by the development of these new and extremely powerful instruments of power over opinion. . . . The nationalization of opinion has proceeded everywhere *pari passu* with the nationalization of industry.[41]

Watching from the vantage point of 1939, when the Fascist and Nazi systems had managed to bring nationalistic propaganda to a new level of sophistication and control, Carr regarded with extreme skepticism

[39] Ibid., pp. 162–169.
[40] Ibid., p. 162.
[41] Ibid., p. 134.

the internationalists' faith in the power of moral education to instill in mass publics an enduring sense of moral rectitude in the conduct of international affairs.

The Twenty Years' Crisis is a response to the dominance of internationalist thought in the field of foreign affairs. As such, it accentuates the role of power in the world of diplomacy: "In the international order, the role of power is greater and that of morality less."[42] But strong as Carr's critique of idealism is, he does not deny an important and enduring role to morality in the shaping of international affairs. Explicitly quoting Niebuhr's ultimate dictum on the relationship of morality and foreign policy, Carr concludes that

> "politics will, to the end of history, be an area where conscience and power meet, where the ethical and coercive factors of human life will interpenetrate and work out their tentative and uneasy compromises." The compromises, like solutions of other human problems, will remain uneasy and tentative. But it is an essential part of any compromise that both factors shall be taken into account.[43]

The brilliance and subtlety of Carr's thought was to mount an effective critique of the internationalist approach while still asserting the empirical importance of morality in international affairs. The major shortcoming of Carr's thought was its inability to explain how morality exercised this important role in the world of power and conflict that he described so well. Thus the empirical bridge between morality and foreign policy cannot be identified from the work of E. H. Carr.

HANS MORGENTHAU AND THE DEBATE ON MORALITY AND FOREIGN POLICY

Hans Morgenthau's *Politics Among Nations*, published in 1948, has set the terms for the debate on morality and international relations for the past forty years. Indeed, it is little exaggeration to say that every contribution to the postwar literature dealing with the role of morality in foreign policy is essentially either an elaboration of, or a response to, themes presented by Morgenthau. Writing at the zenith of American hegemony, Morgenthau compellingly undercut the moral foundations of American foreign policy by pointing to the complexity of the moral problems involved in international affairs and by emphasizing that all politics, and especially international politics, is a struggle for power: "Dominant elements in Western Culture, and American cul-

---

[42] Ibid., p. 168.
[43] Ibid., pp. 100–101.

ture in particular, have consistently misunderstood the nature of foreign policy and they have done so in the name of morality. In the process, our culture has deformed its understanding of morality and corrupted its moral judgment as well."[44] Morgenthau argued that there is an inherent contradiction between power and ethics, and that theories of international morality that failed to grasp this antinomy of human existence would lead to policies that were both ethically unsound and diplomatically dangerous.

The foundation for Morgenthau's analysis lies in Niebuhr's theological anthropology. But whereas Niebuhr saw the drive for self-transcendence in the human person as leading both to selfishness and to justice, Morgenthau sees the drive for transcendence leading only to selfishness and the lust for power. Writing in *Scientific Man versus Power Politics*, Morgenthau asserts that

> the lust for power manifests itself as the desire to maintain the range of one's own person with regard to others, to increase it, or to demonstrate it. . . . Centered as it is upon the person of the actor in relation to others, the desire for power is closely related to the selfishness of which we have spoken, but it is not identical with it. For the typical goals of selfishness, such as food, shelter, security, and the means by which they are obtained have an objective relation to the vital needs of the individual. . . . The desire for power, on the other hand, concerns itself not with the individual's survival but with his position among his fellows once his survival has been secured. Consequently, the selfishness of man has limits; his will to power has none.[45]

As a result of this unsatiable drive for power, every human action is tinged with evil, and no human action is truly unselfish. Morgenthau did believe that on the level of family life and in human friendships, the drive for power is somewhat mitigated by the bonds of community. But in the political realm, there is no such mitigation; for it is the nature of politics to unleash the drive for domination in all of its fury:

> To the degree in which the essence and aim of politics is power over man, politics is evil; for it is to this degree that it degrades man to a means for other men. It follows that the prototype of this corruption through power is to be found on the political scene. For here the *animus dominandi* is not merely blended with dominant aims of a different kind, but is the very essence of the intention, the very life-blood of the action, the constitutive principle of politics as a distinct sphere of human activity. Politics is a

---

[44] Introduction to Lefever, *Ethics and United States Foreign Policy*, p. xv.

[45] Hans Morgenthau, *Scientific Man versus Power Politics* (Chicago: University of Chicago Press, 1962), pp. 192–193.

struggle for power over men, and whatever its ultimate aim may be, power is its immediate goal and the modes of acquiring, maintaining, and demonstrating it determine the technique of political action.[46]

But how can a person act ethically in the political sphere, if all political action is inherently corrupted by the drive for power? The answer lies in the clear recognition of the role of power and in the choice of the lesser evil in every concrete human situation:

> Neither science nor ethics nor politics can resolve the conflict between politics and ethics into harmony. We have no choice between power and the common good. To act successfully, that is according to the rules of the political art, is political wisdom. To know with despair that the political act is inevitably evil, and to act nevertheless, is moral courage. To choose among several expedient actions the least evil one is moral judgment. In the combination of political wisdom, moral courage, and moral judgment, man reconciles his political nature with his moral destiny.[47]

The Destruction of International Morality

Despite his stress on the intrinsic lust for power in all political action, Hans Morgenthau believed that an effective international morality had existed in the nineteenth century and had constrained the drive for power on the European continent. But Morgenthau argued that this constraining influence had been possible only because the international morality of the nineteenth century had reflected a European-wide moral and intellectual consensus: "It is this consensus, both child and father, as it were, of common moral standards and a common civilization as well as common interests, which kept in check the limitless desire for power, potentially inherent, as we know, in all imperialisms, and prevented it from becoming a political actuality."[48]

The end of World War I shattered this international moral consensus, in Morgenthau's mind, and transformed international affairs from a preserve of the European aristocracy to a sphere in which competing mass-based nationalisms fought for universal supremacy. As a consequence, the moral limitations that had previously constrained states in their search for power were no longer operative; even the restraints upon total war that had been a hallmark of European civilization for over a thousand years were abandoned in the unrestrained search for power:

[46] Ibid., p. 195.
[47] Ibid., p. 203.
[48] Hans Morgenthau, *Politics among Nations* (New York: Alfred A. Knopf, 1956), p. 200.

The deterioration of moral limitations in international politics which has occurred in recent years with regard to the protection of life is only a special instance of a general and for the purposes of this discussion, much more far-reaching dissolution of an ethical system which in the past imposed its restraints upon the day-to-day operations of the foreign offices, but does so no longer. Two factors have brought about this dissolution: the substitution of democratic for aristocratic responsibility in foreign affairs and the substitution of nationalistic standards of action for universal ones.[49]

Thus while the internationalists saw in the rise of mass democracy an opportunity to build a more moral world reinforced by educated popular opinion, Morgenthau saw in the democratization of international relations the destruction of the moral strictures that had civilized international affairs in the past.

The key to Morgenthau's despair about effective international moral standards after World War I was his belief that democratization and nationalism had destroyed the aristocratic nature of the international society that had existed before 1918. When the diplomatic corps was filled with nobles who knew one another and would retain their posts for long periods, there was both an incentive for diplomats to take personal moral responsibility and a code of moral responsibility to follow. In the era of democratic diplomacy, on the other hand, where politicians came in and out of office and owed their allegiance only to their national public, there was no such incentive. Moreover, there was no consensual moral code, since the breakdown of the nineteenth-century international society left a vacuum in the very notions of justice and equality that lie at the heart of any substantive international morality:

What justice means in the U.S. can within wide limits be objectively ascertained; for interests and convictions, experiences of life and institutionalized traditions have in large measure created a consensus concerning what justice means under the conditions of American society. No such circumstance exists in the relations among nations. For above the national society there exists no international society so integrated so as to be able to define for them the concrete meaning of justice or equality, as national societies do for their individual members.[50]

Morgenthau believed that a substantive international morality can exist only to the degree that an international society provides consensual

[49] Ibid., p. 220–221.
[50] Hans Morgenthau, *In Defense of the National Interest* (Washington: University Press of America, 1982), p. 34.

moral standards that are universally accepted. In the twentieth century, he concluded, both that society and those standards were absent.

But even though Morgenthau concluded that no consensual international morality existed in the postwar world, he did not believe that moral issues and moral language were unimportant in the formulation of foreign policy. On the contrary, Morgenthau argued that morality touched international affairs in three critically important ways: (1) as an ideological justification of the self-interested actions of states; (2) as a one-dimensional moral calculus that distorts foreign policy in destructive ways; and (3) in the moral dignity of the national interest. Because these three categories have basically framed the debate on morality and international relations in the years since Morgenthau wrote, it will be helpful to review each of them in turn.

Ethical Ideology

Just as Morgenthau's anthropology formed the basis for his definition of politics, so too it forms the basis for his approach to the role of morality in international relations.

> We have learned from our discussions . . . that in the mind of the individual the aspirations for power of others bear the stigma of immorality. While this moral depreciation has one of its roots in the desire of the prospective victim of the power of others to defend his freedom against this threat, the other root stems from the attempt of society as a whole to suppress and keep in bounds individual aspirations for power.[51]

This depreciation of the drive for power leads to ethical ideology, that is, the manufacturing of moral justifications for actions taken out of self-interest. By dressing its foreign-policy aspirations in moral garb, Morgenthau argued, the nation resolves for its citizens the tension between moral claims and national loyalty. The citizen, too wedded to the concept of morality to give it up altogether, now sees national loyalty and moral identity not only as not in tension, but as coextensive. Ethical ideology brings many benefits to a leader and to a nation: it unites the citizenry in a bond of moral purpose; it raises national morale and energy, and it can be an effective weapon against opponents, both foreign and domestic.[52]

Modern realist writers have generally endorsed Morgenthau's argument that ethical ideology has been a frequent ingredient in inter-

---

[51] Ibid., p. 37.
[52] Morgenthau, *Politics among Nations*, pp. 81–82.

national affairs during the twentieth century.[53] And no observer of international affairs could doubt the basic claim that moral language and slogans have often functioned to legitimate, rather than critically evaluate or affect, foreign-policy undertakings. At the same time, it is important to note that just because moral language is frequently used as a tool of legitimation, it does not mean that morality is always a tool of policy legitimation. Morgenthau comes very close to saying that all moral evaluation of foreign-policy actions constitutes ideology; but he makes this judgment on the basis of his definition that all politics is intrinsically the search for power.[54] Thus his judgment is a definitionally tautological one. If one does not assume from the outset that all politics is consumed by the search for power, then one can readily admit that morality has often functioned to legitimate foreign-policy decisions made on nonmoral grounds, and yet still maintain that moral judgment is not always ideological.

Moral Absolutism

Morgenthau believed that the American people had historically allowed moral language and moral norms to influence the formation of foreign policy in a way that went beyond the usual ideological uses of morality in international affairs. He labeled this tendency "sentimentalism" and argued that it constituted the misguided efforts of the people of the United States to pursue single moral values such as "democracy" and "liberty" at the expense of the American national interest.

> What distinguishes this sentimental approach to foreign policy from the common and well-nigh inevitable ideological justification of political action, domestic and international, is the fact that we are here not in the

[53] See, for example, Lefever, *Ethics and United States Foreign Policy*, p. 5; George Kennan, *American Diplomacy: 1900–1950* (Chicago: University of Chicago Press, 1951), pp. 91ff.; and J. D. B. Miller, "Morality, Interests, and Rationalization," in *Moral Claims in World Affairs*, ed. Ralph Pettmann (New York: St. Martin's Press, 1979), pp. 36–51.

[54] Hare and Joynt vehemently reject Morgenthau's argument on this point: "[Morgenthau lets] his philosophical objections get in the way. For to say this is to rely on a black and white picture of human nature. People and nations are rarely moved by unmixed altruism or unmixed self-interest. . . . There are many ways in which morality and prudence or morality and 'ideology' can be mixed together. Morgenthau makes it true by definition that no action can be truly 'moral' unless it is totally sacrificial; and that no action can be truly 'political' unless it is motivated entirely by the struggle for power. But ordinary usage is not so restrictive. If we do restrict the words in these ways, we will simply have to invent new ones with more inclusive senses." *Ethics and International Affairs*, p. 39.

presence of a mere ideology, superimposed upon the actual motives and objectives of political action, which, unaffected by it, follows its own pragmatic course. The American people have not used their moral principles as mere ideologies, that is, for the exclusive purpose of deceiving themselves and others. They have taken them seriously, devoted themselves to them, and in not a few instances have been ready to shed their blood, to spend their treasure, to jeopardize the very existence of the country, in order to make these political principles prevail on the international scene. In one word, they have allowed them, nay required them to influence political action itself.[55]

This sentimentalist streak was not limited to the mass public in American society. Rather, the attachment to the advancement of particular moral values reached to the highest levels of the American government and continued to influence American foreign policy even as the United States took on the role of a superpower in the postwar world.

One objection that Morgenthau had to "sentimentalism" in American foreign policy was that it tended to obfuscate the nature of politics as a quest for power. But Morgenthau's deeper reservations about the "sentimentalist" strain in American foreign policy arose from its tendency to focus on the realization of a single moral value and to ignore all of the negative moral consequences that flowed from pursuing that single moral value. On this issue, Morgenthau stood firmly in the tradition of Reinhold Niebuhr: there are no absolute moral values to which all else can be sacrificed; thus to act in single-minded devotion to a solitary moral value, rather than by prudentially weighing the full consequences and the conflicting moral duties inherent in all political action, is to court disaster on both the level of morality and the level of national interest.[56]

The normative literature has been largely sympathetic with Morgenthau's attack upon moral absolutism in foreign policy, since ethicists and political theorists are just as interested as the realists are in eradicating one-dimensional and absolutist approaches to the complex issues of international affairs.[57] But the normative literature sharply attacks the assumption implicit in much of the commentary of Morgenthau and his disciples that because blind adhesion to a single

[55] *National Interest*, p. 114.

[56] Ibid., pp. 35–39. Morgenthau's disciples have generally endorsed this view, arguing that sentimentalism often created a crusading mentality in American foreign policy that was morally harmful in the long run. See Arthur Schlesinger, Jr., "National Interests and Moral Absolutes," in *Ethics and World Politics*, ed. Ernest Lefever (Baltimore: The Johns Hopkins University Press, 1972), pp. 26–27; and Lefever, *Ethics and United States Foreign Policy*, p. 16.

[57] See Cohen, "Moral Skepticism."

moral precept leads to tragic consequences, all moral reasoning in international affairs leads to such tragedy. As Charles Beitz notes, realism often points out that

> we are likely to make mistaken foreign policy choices if we take an excessively moralistic attitude toward them. This might mean either of two things. Perhaps it means that a steadfast commitment to a moral principle that is inappropriate to some situation is likely to move us to make immoral or imprudent decisions about it. Or it might mean that an idealistic or overzealous commitment even to an appropriate principle might cause us to overlook some salient facts and make bad decisions as a result. Each of these recommends reasonable circumspection in making moral judgments about international relations. But neither implies that it is wrong to make such judgments at all. What is being said is that the moral reasoning regarding some decision is flawed: either an inappropriate moral principle is being applied, or an appropriate principle is being incorrectly applied. It does not follow that it is wrong even to attempt to apply moral principles to foreign affairs.[58]

Treatments of morality and international affairs that condemn all moral reasoning merely because moral simplism is counterproductive are no more valid than treatments that condemn all power politics because simpleminded power politics is counterproductive. Yet commentaries on morality and international relations have often cited the poor use of moral reasoning to argue that a substantive and effective morality is impossible in the international arena.

The National Interest

Morgenthau was convinced that ethical ideology and moral absolutism had skewed international relations and subjected the world to a series of bloody conflicts that could have been avoided—if only the nations engaged in them had fashioned their policies in terms of their genuine national interests. "The national interest of a peace-loving nation can only be defined in terms of national security, and national security must be defined as integrity of the national territory and of its institutions."[59] Morgenthau argued that this "rational core" of a nation's interests could be objectively defined, and that scientific analysis was capable of "pruning down overweening ambitions to available resources," so that the entire national leadership would consistently

[58] *Political Theory and International Relations*, p. 21. See also Hare and Joynt, *Ethics and International Affairs*, pp. 35, 45.
[59] Morgenthau, *Politics among Nations*, p. 528.

formulate its foreign-policy objectives in strict conformity to the nation's integrity and institutions.[60] The obligation to follow the national
interest in formulating foreign policy is not only a practical dictum of
successful politics, according to Morgenthau; it is a moral obligation
founded firmly upon political reality. There are two roots of this obligation. The first flows from the obligation that all nations have to protect their own citizens from harm. Since the international system is a
world of conflict and competition in which any nation that practices
altruism does so at the expense of its own citizens, altruism by nation-
states is an immoral act that violates the trust that their citizens put
in them.[61] The second root of the moral obligation to follow the national interest arises from the fact that the mutual pursuit of the national interest by nations is the only genuine way of promoting peace
and order within the international system: "In the absence of an integrated international society, the attainment of a modicum of order
and the realization of a minimum of moral values are predicated upon
the existence of national communities capable of preserving order and
realizing moral values within the limits of their power."[62]

The duty to pursue the "national interest" has become a central
tenet of realist thought. But the nature of this duty seems very con-
fused. In 1985, George Kennan argued that there is no moral dimension at all in the national interest: "The interests of the national society for which government has to concern itself are basically those of
its military security, the integrity of its political life, and the well-being
of its people. These needs have no moral quality."[63] But in earlier
works, Kennan has spoken of the moral dignity of the American national interest that from the fact that the values underlying that national interest are democratic and liberal in character. He has pointed
to the moral power that America can exercise through its example of
freedom and popular government, a power that can influence even
societies as hostile as the Soviet Union.[64] And Kennan has stated that
America has an obligation "as a political society to our own national
ideals, and through these ideals to the wider human community of
which we are in ever increasing measure a part."[65] Ernest Lefever's

[60] Hans Morgenthau, "The Problem of the National Interest," in *The Decline of Democratic Politics* (Chicago: University of Chicago Press, 1962), pp. 91–102.

[61] *National Interest*, pp. 35–36.

[62] Ibid., p. 38.

[63] George F. Kennan, "Morality and Foreign Policy," *Foreign Affairs* 64 (Winter
1985–86): 206.

[64] *American Diplomacy*, p. 153; and George Kennan, *The Cloud of Danger* (Boston:
Atlantic Monthly Press, 1975), p. 25.

[65] George Kennan, *Realities of American Foreign Policy* (Princeton: Princeton University Press, 1954), p. 120.

description of the national interest shows similar variations. While emphasizing that pursuing the national interest will not result in the extravagant moralistic campaigns that have plagued American diplomatic history, Lefever defines the national interest as "a calculation which attempts to relate moral values and political necessity. . . . America's national purpose, it can be said, is to preserve and improve a society based upon consent and mutual respect and to help to create an international climate in which government by consent can take root and flourish."[66] Once one includes the defense of the national purpose as part of the national interest and then contends that part of America's national purpose is to help to create an international climate that promotes government by consent, it is difficult to see how pursuing the national interest differs from the Wilsonian principles that the realists sought to replace.

The difficulty of establishing the "moral dignity of the national interest" lies in the fact that the national interest purports to be an objective reality and yet wishes to claim moral status. At times, realist proponents wish to emphasize the scientific, objective nature of the national interest, and therefore they define it in cold and narrow terms. At such times, the obligation for a government to pursue its national interest flows from a nation-centric morality in which the pursuit of one's national good outweighs the rights of all competing nations.[67] But such a nation-centric morality is unacceptable to most Americans, and to many proponents of the pursuit of the national interest as well. As a consequence, the *American* national interest is often defined in terms of democratic values and institutions. But once these values and institutions are included in the concept of the national interest, it is difficult to see how it can remain the modest and restraining concept that the realists are seeking. Instead, it becomes a concept of almost unlimited suppleness and incoherence.

Seeking a Bridge

None of the three roles that the realist tradition has identified for morality in the international arena constitutes an empirical bridge upon which a dialogue with the normative community can be established regarding a constructive role for morality in international affairs. The role of morality as ideology fails because it provides no substantial role for morality at all. Morality as the single-minded pursuit of a solitary moral value fails because both the realists and their normative critics

[66] *Ethics and United States Foreign Policy*, p. 16.

[67] For an elaboration on this theme, see Beitz, *Political Theory and International Relations*, pp. 22–24.

agree it is morally simplistic and is destructive in its consequences. And the moral quality of the national interest cannot provide a bridge between normative and empirical analysts because the moral dimensions of the national interest seem to vary all the way from a nation-centric obligation to pursue one's own national aggrandizement to the obligation to create an international environment hospitable to liberal democracy. Thus it is necessary to look beyond these three possibilities in order to establish an empirical bridge to the normative community.

One such bridge lies in the role of international moral norms, on which the internationalist school put so much stress in the interwar period. Certainly the realist critique has established that the idealist dream of a world without war is not a viable approach to the politics of nations. And realist writers have effectively pointed to the divergence in national interests and to the competitive nature of the international system. But despite the modesty that these insights impose on any effort to rehabilitate the idealist approach to international moral norms, several elements of internationalist thought do deserve reexamination. The first is the proposition that certain substantive international moral norms exist and are consensually held by the citizens of most nations. The second is that nations care about their reputations and do not wish to be labeled as "immoral" in the international system. The third is that domestic public opinion at times pressures state decision makers to follow international moral norms. And the fourth is that the state system bears certain characteristics of an international society. Taken together, these four assertions constitute the basis for identifying a meaningful role for morality in the international system, a role that can lead state decision makers to follow international moral norms on significant foreign-policy questions because of (1) considerations of conscience; (2) domestic political support for following the norm; and (3) their desire to maintain a positive reputation for their nation in the state system. It is important to turn now to outlining the theoretical reasons why international moral norms can occupy this role in the international system.

Chapter Two

TOWARD A THEORETICAL UNDERSTANDING
OF THE ROLE OF INTERNATIONAL
MORAL NORMS

THE QUESTION of whether international moral norms influence foreign-policy decision making in a substantial way is ultimately an empirical question that can be answered most effectively through the use
of individual case studies. But there are significant theoretical reasons
for believing that international moral norms do exist, and that they are
capable of influencing international relations through the three mechanisms pointed to by the liberal internationalists: (1) the conscience
of state decision makers; (2) the influence of domestic public opinion;
and (3) international reputational pressures. It is important to investigate at some length these theoretical underpinnings for the liberal
internationalist case before turning to an empirical investigation of the
role of international moral norms. The issues of moral conflict and
moral ambiguity must also be addressed. But first it is necessary to
consider what is distinctive about international moral norms and what
sets them apart from other norms in the international system.

THE CHARACTERISTICS OF MORAL NORMS

In order to distinguish international moral norms from other, nonmoral prescriptions in the international system, it is helpful to utilize
two arguments that are commonly employed in discussions of moral
maxims: (1) the argument that moral norms can be identified by their
universalizability; and (2) the argument that moral norms are distinctive because they demand that an actor take another person's interests
and point of view into account.

Kant is most often associated with the relationship between morality and universalization, but R. M. Hare has most succinctly and
forcefully brought the Kantian insight into contemporary discussions
of morality. Hare argues that "if I maintain that morally I ought to do
X, then I am committed to maintaining that morally anyone else ought

to do X unless there are relevant differences between the other person and myself and/or between his situation and mine."[1]

This requirement of universalizability can guarantee that moral norms are generalized and consistent behavioral rules, but it does not serve to distinguish international moral norms from mere conventions. Thus it is necessary to add W. K. Frankena's requirement that moral norms contain a prescriptive reference to the interests of parties other than the actor: moral norms "concern the relations of one individual . . . to others and involve or call for a consideration of the effects of the actor's actions on others (not necessarily all others), not from the point of view of his own interests or aesthetic enjoyments, but from their own point of view."[2] Seen in this light, a moral norm must be rooted in impartiality to all of the contending parties affected by the norm and in equal benevolence toward all such parties.[3]

Thus the definition of a moral norm that will be utilized throughout this work is: a behavioral prescription that is universal in the claims it makes and that involves a consideration of the effects of the actor's action on others, not from the point of view of the actor's own interests, but from the point of view of the others' interests.[4]

An International Society with International Moral Norms?

The heart of the liberal internationalist argument for moralizing international relations lay in the assertion that there exists an international society capable of generating strong, clear, and consensual moral norms that govern the behavior of states. The internationalists saw in

[1] R. M. Hare, *Freedom and Reason* (Oxford: Oxford University Press, 1963), p. 15. As John Pollock notes in his discussion of the principle of universalizability, a central question not answered by this principle is what features are to be counted as relevant in distinguishing one situation from another. But this problem is more closely related to the issue of discerning the correctness of moral norms than to the issue of defining a norm as moral. See Pollock, "A Theory of Moral Reasoning," *Ethics* 96 (1985–86): 606.

[2] W. K. Frankena, "The Concept of Morality," in *The Meaning of Morality*, ed. by G. Wallace and A. D. M. Walker (London: Methuen and Company, 1970), p. 156.

[3] For a discussion of how this principle is reflected in a series of contending philosophical approaches to ethics, see R. M. Hare, "Rules of War and Moral Reasoning," in *War and Moral Responsibility*, ed. Marshall Cohen, Thomas Nagel, and Thomas Scanlon (Princeton: Princeton University Press, 1974), pp. 46–51.

[4] Charles Beitz offers a complementary approach to moral norms in arguing that "the moral point of view requires us to regard the world from the perspective of one person among many rather than from that of a particular self with particular interests, and to choose courses of action, policies, rules and institutions on grounds that would be acceptable to any agent who was impartial among the competing interests involved." (Charles Beitz, *Political Theory and International Relations* [Princeton: Princeton University Press, 1979], p. 58)

the increasing economic, technological, and cultural interdependence of the world a sign that such an international society was indeed being achieved, and they argued that any effective assessment of the international system would have to take this emerging world culture into account. But from the vantage point of contemporary international relations, how valid is the claim that there exists an international society? And what indications are there that strong, clear, and consensual moral norms exist in the international system?

In answering these questions, it is helpful to consider the issues raised almost two centuries ago by Immanuel Kant in his writings on political obligation, international affairs, and world peace. Kant proposed that the very forces of economic competition and technological change that frequently lay at the root of war were in the long run creating conditions for world peace. For the growing technological and economic interpenetration of nations was creating a situation of mutual dependence among nation-states that would ultimately make war an unacceptably costly enterprise. This technological and economic interpenetration was also sowing the seeds for the development of a world community that, though only in its beginning stages, nonetheless held the promise of creating a world culture and an international morality. "The narrower or wider community of all nations on earth has in fact progressed so far," Kant asserted, "that a violation of law and right in one place is felt in all others."[5] As this integration of states continues and is supported by the ever-growing number of states that construct republican constitutions based on liberal principles, in Kant's view, culture progresses and peoples gradually come closer together toward a "greater agreement" on the bases for peace and understanding.[6]

The moral dimensions of this "greater agreement" would take two forms in the international system.[7] The first of these would be the law of states—rules governing the behavior of nation-states with one another. Kant recognized that just and pacific relations among nations would be impossible unless there developed a more regularized and explicit code specifying what was appropriate and what was inappropriate for states to do in their relationships with one another. He believed that the liberal republican governments of the world would take

[5] Immanuel Kant, "Eternal Peace," in *The Philosophy of Kant*, ed. Carl J. Friedrich (New York: Random House, 1949), p. 448.

[6] Ibid., p. 454.

[7] The increasing moral agreement among nations would also be reflected in a critically important way in domestic politics—in the recognition of the need for liberal republican state constitutions that would protect human rights and provide for the consent of those governed.

the lead in forming a community dedicated to generating and observing such a code of international conduct founded upon principles of fairness and prudence.[8] Kant's second form of international morality, which would complement the law of states, was "cosmopolitan," or "world-citizen's," law. This code would be founded not upon the moral identity of nation-states, but upon the identity of every human person as an equal member of the world community. "Cosmopolitan law" would specify certain rights as the inalienable possessions of every citizen of every nation, and it would signal that these rights could not be violated by either states or individuals.[9] While Kant certainly recognized that the day was far off when a full-blown cosmopolitan morality would be accepted by the nations of the world, he pointed to the increasing force of world culture and argued that "the idea of a cosmopolitan or world law is not a fantastic and utopian way of looking at law, but a necessary completion of the unwritten code of constitutional and international law to make it a public law of mankind."[10]

Kant's dedication to the notion that history is progressive lay at the root of his faith that increasing interdependence and cooperation among nations would produce a true international society. But Kant recognized that such a society was far off, and that the progression toward a genuine international morality reflected in international law

[8] "Eternal Peace," pp. 441–446. Kant is very vague about the nature of this pact among nations, about whether it needs to be institutionalized, and about what its content would be. See Michael Doyle, "Kant, Liberal Legacies, and Foreign Affairs," *Philosophy and Public Affairs* 12 (Winter 1983): 226–227; and Howard Williams, *Kant's Political Philosophy* (New York: St. Martin's Press, 1983), pp. 14–15.

It is important to note that while Kant in "Eternal Peace" uses the term "law" rather than "morality" to speak of the code of conduct among nation-states, this law for Kant has a clearly moral quality. For he argues that the "homage which every state renders the concept of law (at least in words) seems to prove that there exists in man a greater moral quality (although at present a dormant one) to try and master the evil element in him (which he cannot deny) and to hope for this in others." ("Eternal Peace," p. 443) For a fuller exposition of how Kant's notions of the moral and political development of humankind are intertwined, see Williams, *Kant's Political Philosophy*, pp. 261–265.

[9] Kant himself limited the content of "cosmopolitan law" to the precept of hospitality, which demanded that "a foreigner not be treated with hostility when he arrives upon the soil of another." ("Eternal Peace," p. 446) But elsewhere Kant spoke of the formation of a more full-bodied cosmopolitan ethic, in which "the duties of virtue apply to the entire human race" and "the concept of ethical commonwealth is extended ideally to the whole of mankind." (Immanuel Kant, "Religion within the Limits of Reason Alone," in Friedrich, *The Philosophy of Kant*, p. 406) Charles Beitz has used Kant's notion of "cosmopolitan law" in support of Beitz's efforts to identify an international morality that is "concerned with the moral relations of a universal community in which state boundaries have a merely derivative significance." (Beitz, *Political Theory and International Relations*, p. 182)

[10] "Eternal Peace," p. 448.

would encounter many frustrations and reverses along its path. Thus, while Kant pointed to a world of "eternal peace," he recognized that he lived in a world in which neither a finished international society nor a finished international morality existed. Both were projects only partly realized, and while it was legitimate to hope for more in the future, it was not legitimate to claim more for the present.

Kant's reflections on the nature of international society and international morality correctly frame the question of whether an international society exists in the present day. For in contrast to the realist-internationalist debate, which has tended to view as dichotomous the question of whether an international society exists, Kant perceived that such a yes-or-no approach fundamentally skews the complex reality of the international system. There are many elements of international life that reinforce a Hobbesian view of the international system as a set of warring states, each seeking its own national interest and bound by no moral or social or cultural ties that have the power to restrain. But there are other aspects of international life that can best be approached through the interpretive lens of an international society: the increasingly interconnected world economy; the near-universal dispersion of particular forms of educational, cultural, and scientific organization; and the aviation, food, and nuclear-energy regimes.[11] These contradictory elements of life in the international system make it necessary to conclude that an international society exists, as Hedley Bull notes, at certain times and under certain conditions: "A society of States (or international society) exists when a group of states, conscious of certain common interests and values, form a society in the sense that they conceive themselves to be bound by a common set of rules in their relations with one another, and share in the working of common institutions."[12]

[11] See Ronald Dore, "The Prestige Factor in International Affairs," *International Affairs* 51 (April 1975): 407–424; Francisco Ramirez, "Global Patterns of Educational Institutionalization," in *Institutional Structure*, ed. by George Thomas and John Meyer (Newbury Park, Calif.: Sage Publications, 1967), pp. 157–167; John Meyer, "The World Polity and the Authority of the Nation-State," in *Studies of the Modern World System*, ed. by Albert Bergeson (New York: Academic Press, 1980), pp. 109–138; and Donald Pachula and Raymond Hopkins, "International Regimes: Lessons from Inductive Analysis," in *International Regimes*, ed. Stephen Krasner (Ithaca: Cornell University Press, 1983), pp. 84–95. Social, cultural, and economic commerce in the international system is increasingly carried on by international issue networks of specialists who share common values, interests, and perspectives. While the ability of the nation-state to shape the activity of these issue networks is still formidable, the identity of the nation-state system itself has been shaped by the cultural interaction of the state system.

[12] Hedley Bull, *The Anarchical Society: A Study of Order in World Politics* (New York: Columbia University Press, 1977), p. 13.

Thus the notion of an international society rests on three pillars: a shared perception of common interests in the basic goals of social life; rules designed to achieve these goals; and institutions that support the rules and make them effective. At times these three pillars produce regular patterns of interaction among states strong enough to constrain nations and enduring enough to be seen as at least partially independent of changing power configurations. It is at such moments that a genuine international society is operative in the state system. It is certainly important not to overdraw the argument for the existence of a genuine international society in the state system, or to underestimate the degree to which conflict characterizes and structures foreign policy. But it is equally important not to underestimate the webs of culture, values, interests, and institutions that give the international system some characteristics of a true society.

One such web of culture, values, interests, and institutions can be found in the effort that has taken place in the twentieth century to establish a set of discrete moral norms that are binding on all nations. Transnational issue networks of philosophers, lawyers, religious leaders, educators, and government officials have reflected upon the significant conflictual issues of the international system and produced norms that can be characterized as moral because they meet the canons of universalizability and fairness described earlier in this chapter. Such norms include the prohibition against torture, the guarantee of the right to emigrate, the prohibition against territorial colonialism, and rules repelling unjust aggression.[13] Some of these norms, such as the prohibition against territorial colonialism and the rules of warfare, apply principally to conduct among states; thus they would reflect Kant's "law of states." But other norms, such as the prohibition against torture and the guarantee of the right to emigrate, concern not states' relations with one another, but states' internationally sanctioned obligations to their own citizens and the citizens of other nations. These latter norms reflect Kant's notion of "cosmopolitan law": the idea that all persons as citizens of a world community have certain moral claims that must be respected by governments.[14]

[13] For a treatment of the evolution, content, and efficacy of the prohibition against torture and of the entire human-rights regime, see Jack Donnelly, "International Human Rights: Regime Analysis," *International Organization* 40 (Summer 1986): 599–632. For a discussion of the international approaches to the morality of war, see Cohen, Nagel, and Scanlon, *War and Moral Responsibility*. For a discussion of the issue of decolonization in the international system, see United Nations, Department of Political Affairs, *Decolonization* 2, no. 6 (December 1975).

[14] Michael Walzer has noted that there is an inbuilt tension between a morality of states and a morality of individual human rights. The morality of states presumes that "men and women are protected and their interests represented only by their own gov-

The international moral norms described above have been officially accepted by the governments of the world. But these norms are essentially cultural, not governmental, constructs. They are, as Michael Walzer notes, "socially patterned, and the patterning is religious, cultural, and political, as well as legal."[15] What the collective action of states often does contribute to the formation of such international moral prescriptions is clarification, delimitation, and an explicit mutual agreement by states to observe such norms. These are significant elements in the process by which these norms have emerged, but they are not the most important elements.[16]

An example might be helpful to illustrate the process by which international moral prescriptions have emerged. The prohibition of direct killing of noncombatants is a norm that is enshrined in the articles of the Geneva Convention and that has been accepted by the major governments of the world. It emerged from the two-thousand-year-long process of philosophical reflection on the nature of the "just war" that began in the early Roman Empire, continued through the Christian era, and was refined in the writings of Grotius and his international school of lawyers and philosophers. The primary thrust for the formation and recognition of this norm was cultural and transnational: it emerged from the reflection of international issue networks upon the very real moral dilemma of how war should be fought by all nations and who should be spared from being the objects of military attack. The cultural framework in which the norm prohibiting the direct targeting of civilians emerged was a European one, but the principle of preserving noncombatant immunity has been supported by the philosophers, lawyers, educators, and religious leaders of the majority of non-European cultures as well. As a result, there has

---

ernments. Though states are founded for the sake of life and liberty, they cannot be challenged in the name of life and liberty by any other states. The rights of private persons can be recognized in international society, as in the UN Charter of Human Rights, but they cannot be enforced without calling into question the dominant values of that society: the survival and independence of the separate political communities." (Michael Walzer, *Just and Unjust Wars: A Moral Argument with Historical Illustrations* [New York: Basic Books, 1977], p. 61.)

[15] Ibid., pp. 44–45.

[16] It is important to distinguish between customary international law and international moral norms. Customary international law and international moral norms share a common vocabulary, both are concerned with prescribing limits to the actions of states rather than with identifying the proper ends of state action, and both seek to take into account the interests of all states. But customary international law differs from international moral norms because it arises from the judgments of a much more limited set of specialists, and it is heavily influenced by the notion of positive law. See Terry Nardin, *Law, Morality, and the Relations of States* (Princeton: Princeton University Press, 1983), pp. 249–250.

emerged a transnational cultural consensus that war should not extend to the direct targeting of civilians.[17]

Two significant objections can be raised to the foregoing view of international moral norms. The first is that the supposed international consensus about the validity of certain moral norms actually constitutes nothing more than the imposition of Western culture and Western values upon non-Western societies. Louis Henkin has formulated the most compelling response to this objection. Speaking about the international norms regarding human rights, Henkin points out that

> if the human rights idea is Western, so are most other political ideas that are today universal. Ancient traditions and cultures had no recognizable conception of political society; today every society has political forms that necessarily implicate relations between individual and society. For the modern polity human rights is no more foreign than are statehood, sovereignty, international law, plebiscites, or various forms of socialism. In any event, if the idea of rights is modern and Western, the values inherent in the conception of human rights and in the particular rights that have been recognized are not Western. That a human being ought to live, should not suffer torture, arbitrary detention, or fake trials, and should not be allowed to die of hunger, is not an idea exclusive to the West.[18]

Thus the Western origin of many of the moral norms that have become current in the state system does not in any way prevent them from constituting genuine international moral norms supported by an incipient world culture.

A more difficult objection to the notion that genuine international

---

[17] Myers McDougal and Florentino Feliciano have discussed the emergence of this norm of noncombatant immunity in a particularly illuminating fashion. They argue that a genuine transnational consensus concerning the validity of certain international moral norms is possible because all significant cultural groups agree that a substantive human value is at stake and is worth preserving. But this initial agreement that a substantive value is at stake is not enough for an international moral norm to emerge. Such an emergence requires an international cultural network to concretize and legitimate a specific formulation of the basic moral precept at stake. This process of concretization and legitimation can proceed in two fashions: through the dominance of one particular culture or through a cross-cultural process of compromise and dialogue. Often there is a mixture of the two. See Myers McDougal and Florentino Feliciano, *Law and Minimum World Public Order* (New Haven: Yale University Press, 1961), pp. 71–79; see also Louis Henkin, *The Age of Rights* (New York: Columbia University Press, 1990). For treatments of the development of the principle of noncombatant immunity, see James Turner Johnson, *Just-War Tradition and the Restraint of War* (Princeton: Princeton University Press, 1981); Frederick Russell, *The Just War in the Middle Ages* (Cambridge: Cambridge University Press, 1975); and Sydney Bailey, *War and Conscience in the Nuclear Age* (London: Macmillan Press, 1987).

[18] *The Age of Rights*, p. 28.

moral norms exist can be found in the argument that the consensus supposedly underlying such norms is actually merely a surface agreement that masks widely varying interpretations. Stanley Hoffmann echoes a theme from Morgenthau when he proposes that

> there is no single operational international code of behavior. There are competing codes, rival philosophical traditions, clashing conceptions of morality. . . . It is true, as some point out, that all statesmen use the same moral language—they all argue about rights and wrongs, justice and law. And the United Nations Charter, plus a number of quasi universal treaties, seem to provide a common grammar. Unfortunately, from the point of view of moral harmony, this is meaningless. A community of vocabulary is not the same thing as a community of values. When people with very different values use the same vocabulary, it debases both the vocabulary and the values hidden behind the vocabulary. This is what has been happening to notions like self-determination, non-intervention, etc. Behind the common grammar there are competing ideological logics.[19]

Is Hoffmann correct in saying that the cultural diversity of the world automatically means that it is meaningless to speak of a genuine international morality?

Insofar as Hoffmann is arguing that there exists no full-blown international morality, his objection is a valid one. A complete morality must not only include isolated behavioral prescriptions, but also set forth a comprehensive and systematic set of behavioral prescriptions that assist in guiding all human action. In addition, a complete morality must speak to the issues of the nature and ends of the human person. The areas of moral consensus in the international system fall far short of meeting either of these demands. There is a set of moral norms touching upon state action that have been formally accepted by the nations of the world. But these do not form an integrated morality, nor do they address even the majority of state actions that have a moral dimension. Thus Hoffmann is correct in stating that "there is no single operational international code of behavior." Kant's vision of a world where peace was insured by agreement among states on fair and prudent rules for the conduct of states still remains today a vision far from being realized.

But insofar as Hoffmann is asserting that the formation of specific moral norms of state behavior through transnational cultural networks, and the formal acceptance of these norms by the governments of the world, is meaningless, he takes his argument far past the point

---

[19] Stanley Hoffmann, *Duties beyond Borders: On the Limits and Possibilities of Ethical International Politics* (Syracuse: Syracuse University Press, 1981), pp. 19–20.

where it is warranted. For as Charles Beitz has noted in his comments on the issue of cultural relativism and international morality, "considerations of cultural diversity enter our thinking as data that may require revisions of particular principles; they do not undermine the possibility of normative theory itself."[20] The fact that there are significant divergences among various national societies about the priority and meaning of certain moral values does not, in principle, mean that there cannot be meaningful international moral norms that have a particular and substantive ethical content. Thus the issue Hoffmann raises should be seen not as a philosophical question, but as an empirical one. Do there exist specific international moral norms that have been patterned by an incipient world culture, that have been formally accepted by the governments of the world, and that have a definitive and specific ethical content that is consistently interpreted by the diverse nations of the world?

This question can best be answered by observing how the moral prescriptions that have been ratified by the nations of the world are interpreted in concrete situations where it is in a nation's interest to violate those norms. For the liberal internationalist argument that international moral norms influence foreign policy through the channels of conscience, domestic public opinion, and international reputational pressures rests firmly upon the assumption that those norms can be readily and consistently interpreted by state decision makers, domestic publics, and international public opinion. One of the chief goals of this work is to investigate significant cases of foreign-policy decision making in which international moral norms are relevant to see whether these norms are readily and consistently interpreted by all participating actors. Only when such empirical work is done will it be possible to say with any confidence whether international moral norms can have the definitiveness, specificity, and universally shared meaning ascribed to them by the liberal internationalists.

PATHWAYS FROM MORAL NORMS TO FOREIGN POLICY

Even if it is determined that there are moral norms with a specified ethical content that are consensually accepted as valid in the international system, the question still remains: do these norms influence foreign-policy decision making in any substantial way? Again, this is ultimately an empirical question. But there are strong theoretical grounds for concluding that moral norms can make a difference in international affairs through the three pathways identified by the in-

[20] *Political Theory and International Relations*, p. 18.

ternationalists: the conscience of state decision makers, domestic
public opinion, and international reputational pressures. Before an
empirical investigation of the role of international moral norms is possible, it is necessary to present this theoretical case in support of the
liberal internationalist argument; for the theoretical case not only
lends credence to the internationalist claims, but also indicates more
precisely how the channels of conscience, domestic public opinion,
and international reputational pressures can operate.

The Conscience of State Decision Makers

In his essay "Eternal Peace," Kant contrasts "the moral politician"
with "the political moralist." The moral politician is a state leader who
"employs the principles of political prudence in such a way that they
can coexist with morals"; while the political moralist is one "who
would concoct a system of morals such as the advantage of the statesman may find convenient."[21] Most importantly, for our purposes, the
moral politician is willing to at times sacrifice state interests, even very
important state interests, out of a sense of moral obligation. In Kant's
view, the overriding duty of the moral politician is to recognize that
"the natural right of men must be held sacred, regardless of how
much sacrifice is required of the powers that be. [For] it is impossible
to figure out a middle road, such as a pragmatically conditional right,
between right and utility."[22]

But does Kant's "moral politician" exist in the realm of international
affairs? And were the internationalists correct in arguing that statesmen do at times make decisions against their national interest because of international moral norms? In answering these questions, it
is important to look to the findings of contemporary social psychology
about the nature of moral obligation and how it functions in the human mind. There are two leading approaches to issues of morality and
moral action in the field of social psychology—social learning theory
and the cognitive-developmental paradigm—and both of them lead toward an affirmation of the power of conscience to motivate men and
women to follow behavioral moral norms. Social learning theory points
to a process of "self-regulation," in which the internalization of a re-
ward-and-punishment structure leads individuals to praise them-

[21] P. 459.
[22] "Eternal Peace," p. 469. For a more detailed analysis of how this interaction between right and political prudence should function in the mind of "the moral politician,"
see Immanuel Kant, "Theory and Practice: Concerning the Common Saying: This May
Be True in Theory but Does Not Apply in Practice," in Friedrich, *The Philosophy of
Kant*, pp. 412–429.

selves for following socially accepted moral norms and to blame themselves for violating them. Self-regulation constitutes a significant behavioral constraint, not merely on issues of personal interaction, but also on more complex and abstract social issues.[23] The cognitive-developmental paradigm would view the constraints of conscience as the product of stage-structured moral development; but this approach would hold with social learning theory that for most individuals conscience speaks the language of dominant societal moral norms and provides a significant motivation to act in a norm-observant manner. Thus both social learning theory and cognitive-developmental theory support the notion that the presence of international moral norms that are widely disseminated and endorsed by societies and states in the international system would predictably create in the consciences of many state decision makers an inclination to act in favor of those norms. A decision maker will frequently internalize the judgments of international society that torture is wrong, colonialism should be forbidden, and noncombatants should be immune. In such cases, there will be a *prima facie* inclination in the decision maker to avoid torture, colonialism, and the direct targeting of civilians in war.

A critical question for the role of conscience in foreign-policy formulation is whether there are always or almost always competing demands upon state decision makers that overpower the motivation that conscience provides. Two preliminary points must be made in this regard. First of all, the role that decision makers give to moral considerations in general will vary from one individual to another. For some, such as Woodrow Wilson, the motivating power of conscience will provide a very strong incentive for action in favor of an international moral norm. For others, the motivating power of conscience will be weakly felt.[24] Second, the degree to which a specific international

[23] See Augusto Blasi, "Bridging Moral Cognition and Moral Action: A Critical Review of the Literature," *Psychological Bulletin* 88 (1980): 1–45; Walter and Harriet Mischel, "A Cognitive Social-Learning Approach to Morality and Self-Regulation," in *Moral Development and Moral Behavior*, ed. by Thomas Lickona (New York: Holt, Rinehart and Winston, 1976), pp. 84–107; Thomas Wren, "Social Learning Theory," *Ethics* 92 (April 1982): 409–424; J. Philippe Rushton, "Altruism and Society: A Social Learning Perspective," *Ethics* 92 (April 1982): 425–446; and Lawrence Kohlberg, *The Psychology of Moral Development* (San Francisco: Harper and Row, 1984).

[24] This reality is readily understandable in either a social learning or a cognitive-developmental framework. Social learning theory acknowledges that the degree of self-regulation varies from individual to individual; for some people there is a strong and far-reaching structure of internalized rewards and punishments that generate strong feelings of guilt or praise, while for others that structure is weak and ineffective. Similarly, cognitive-developmental theory acknowledges that there are many people whose moral development has stopped on the preconventional level of self-interest; for such

moral norm has been internalized will differ from individual to individual. For example, the moral norm against surprise attack was particularly salient for Robert Kennedy during the Cuban missile crisis because of the American experience of Pearl Harbor. Similarly, the discussions by President Truman's advisors about the morality of dropping the atomic bomb on Hiroshima showed a marked divergence in the salience of the norm of noncombatant immunity among America's top decision makers.[25]

But an even more important question for the role of conscience in the formulation of foreign policy is whether necessity is so dominant in the international system that the motivations of conscience are of little relevance to state decision making. The early realists' picture of the world as a constant struggle for survival and power aggrandizement left little room for the motivations of conscience to provide a significant counterbalance to the dictates of national interest. But as Arnold Wolfers has argued, even important decisions on foreign-policy generally involve not survival, but far lesser objectives: the preservation of outlying bases and possessions, the protection of treaty rights, the reclamation of national honor, or the enhancement of economic advantages.[26] In addition, the configuration of national interests seldom falls uniformly on one side or another of a policy decision. Thus the number of foreign-policy decisions in which conscience-based motivations can potentially come into play is actually quite large, because the sphere of clear and absolute state necessity is relatively small in the universe of significant foreign-policy decisions.

The impact of a decision maker's conscience upon foreign policy making can be seen at two distinct junctures. First of all, the moral relevance of a particular foreign-policy issue can lead a state decision maker to take a particular interest in the issue and thus elevate its place on the nation's foreign-policy agenda. The personal values of decision makers have been shown to be a significant determinant in the formulation of public-policy agendas, and the fact that a particular decision maker sees an issue of foreign policy to be laden with moral significance may lead her to give it greater prominence.[27] Second, the

people there is little motivation to follow what society has designated as the fair and moral course of action.

[25] Barton J. Bernstein and Allen Matusow, eds., *The Truman Administration: A Documentary History* (New York: Harper and Row, 1966), pp. 1–21; and Robert F. Kennedy, *Thirteen Days* (New York: W. W. Norton and Company, 1969).

[26] Arnold Wolfers, *Discord and Collaboration* (Baltimore: The Johns Hopkins University Press, 1962), p. 60.

[27] John Kingdon, *Agendas, Alternatives, and Public Policies* (Boston: Little, Brown and Company, 1984), pp. 116–118. Kingdon found that the value systems of the key decision makers on health care and transportation issues had an immense effect upon

conscience of a state decision maker can lead him to actually decide in favor of a particular policy action at least in part because of its moral significance. There is no reason to believe that the drive of conscience, which leads men and women to sacrifice very significant interests in their personal lives in order to follow moral norms, will not also lead state decision makers to take or reject foreign-policy initiatives because of their moral implications.[28]

Domestic Politics and International Moral Norms

The second pathway from international moral norms to norm-observant state behavior lies in domestic support for international moral norms. At the heart of the liberal internationalist case for the moralization of international affairs lay a belief that the growing democratization of the countries of the world provided a new opportunity for the mass publics of countries to press their leaders to follow international moral norms. More than a century earlier, this faith in the new power of democracy to influence foreign affairs had also lain at the heart of Kant's confidence that a more moral and pacific era in interstate affairs could be achieved.[29] But does a democratic structure allow for greater opportunities to influence foreign policy so that it will conform more fully with international moral norms? A look at how democratic structures can influence foreign policy within the American context can help to answer this question.[30]

Recent studies have shown that there is a significant causal rela-

the attention that they were willing to give to these subjects. Kingdon also found that categorizing the issue of transportation for the handicapped as a moral issue rather than a logistical one led to a tremendous growth in the attention given to this particular policy question.

[28] The early realists, of course, posited a radical discontinuity between individual and state morality. They argued that this radical discontinuity arose from the lack of international moral standards, from the dominance of necessity in the state system, and most of all from moral anthropology, which they viewed as leading to the conclusion that all human collective action is intrinsically power-driven and incapable of significant moral aspirations. Contemporary social psychology offers little support for this anthropologically based argument for discontinuity between individual and societal morality.

[29] See Kant, "Eternal Peace," p. 438.

[30] The institutions referred to in this section are American domestic political structures because this work is intended to investigate the role of international moral norms on American foreign policy as an example of the role of moral norms in international affairs. Because of the focus on American domestic institutions, this section on the pathway of domestic politics is more limited in its applicability than the sections on conscience and international reputation. But even so, many of the points made here could be made, with some modification, in discussions of political systems that are quite different from the American model.

tionship between sustained public and elite preferences on foreign-
policy matters and the making of American foreign policy.[31] These
preferences influence foreign policy because of presidents' concerns
about popularity, reelection, and achievement of policy goals; and because of Congress's concerns about reelection. In addition to this relationship between general public opinion and foreign policy, the decision-making process in international affairs is often influenced by
powerful social institutions such as the media, the military, university
communities, ethnic associations, and public-interest lobbies.[32]

Two factors create especially potent avenues for domestic influence
on behalf of international moral norms. The first is the need for the
president to attain what Alexander George has called "policy legitimacy" for his initiatives in the field of foreign affairs:

> A president can achieve legitimacy for his policy only if he succeeds in
> convincing enough members of his administration, Congress, and the
> public that he indeed does have a policy and that it is soundly conceived.
> This requires two things: first he must convince them that the objectives
> and goals of his policy are desirable and worth pursuing—in other words
> that his policy is consistent with fundamental national values and con-
> tributes to their enhancement. This is the normative or moral component
> of policy legitimacy. Second, the president must convince people that he
> knows how to achieve these desirable long-range objectives.[33]

This process of gaining and keeping normative policy legitimacy provides the necessary quality of "oughtness" to American foreign policy,
and it is a major part of the continuing process of policy formulation
and enactment in the United States.[34] Policies that have strategies or
tactics that violate international moral norms can threaten policy le-

[31] Benjamin Page and Robert Shapiro, "Effects of Public Opinion on Policy," *American Political Science Review* 77 (March 1983): 175–191; and Alan Monroe, "Consistency between Public Preferences and National Policy Decisions," *Political Science
Quarterly* 7 (January 1979): 3–19.

[32] See Thomas E. Cronin, *The State of the Presidency* (Boston: Little, Brown and
Company, 1980); Irving Destler, *Presidents, Bureaucrats, and Foreign Policy* (Princeton: Princeton University Press, 1972); David Mayhew, *Congress: The Electoral Con-
nection* (New Haven: Yale University Press, 1974); and Barry Hughes, *The Domestic
Context of American Foreign Policy* (San Francisco: W. H. Freeman and Company,
1978).

[33] Alexander George, "Domestic Constraints on Regime Change in U.S. Foreign Policy: The Need for Policy Legitimacy," in *Change in the International System*, ed. Ole
Holsti (Boulder, Colo.: Westview Press, 1980), p. 235.

[34] B. Thomas Trout, "Rhetoric Revisited: Political Legitimation and the Cold War,"
International Studies Quarterly 19 (September 1975): 252–253.

gitimacy and thus severely limit support for those policies in Congress, in the media, or within the public at large.

The second factor that provides a special avenue for international moral norms to influence the formulation of foreign policy is the president's desire to remain popular, either because of electoral considerations or because of a thirst to be well remembered in history.[35] Just as the broad acceptance of policy among domestic audiences has a normative dimension, so, too, a president's popularity or place in history can be affected by the public's moral evaluation of that president's foreign policy. Thus a particularly well publicized violation of an international moral norm by a president can harm his public image, while a particularly well publicized instance of a president following an international moral norm can help his public image.

Because of these realities, it is possible for domestic groups to mobilize around an international moral norm and thereby put pressure on a president or Congress to change American foreign policy. There are three steps to such a mobilization process: (1) The mobilizing group uses the fact that an international moral norm has been violated in order to gather other groups into a coalition that will press for change in the existing foreign policy. (2) If sufficient pressure can be generated by this coalition and if the coalition can succeed in framing the issue in the public mind as a violation of an international moral norm, then the administration or Congress will begin to give attention to the issue in dispute.[36] (3) The existence of a strong coalition pressing for a change in policy can provide the president or Congress with political incentives to alter American foreign policy to conform with the international moral norm. This is especially true when such a coalition begins to threaten the legitimacy of important presidential policies or the moral reputation of the president himself. Conversely, the existence of such a coalition offers the president or Congress an opportunity to enhance their reputations for morality by adopting a position consonant with the international moral norm.

Thus the desire of presidents and congressional representatives for reelection and popularity creates a "pathway" from international moral norms to norm-observant state behavior. That pathway can be activated by the efforts of domestic groups to rally support for an in-

[35] For a discussion of how the need for popular support changes over a president's term of office, see William Quandt, "The Electoral Cycle and the Conduct of Foreign Policy," *Political Science Quarterly* 101 (November 1986): 825–837.

[36] John Kingdon argues that the emergence of such a coalition constitutes a "focusing event" for an administration or Congress. Because significant domestic groups have forcefully raised the policy issue in debate, the government must devote attention to that issue. See Kingdon, *Agendas, Alternatives, and Public Policies*, pp. 99ff.

ternational moral norm and thus to threaten a president's policy legit-imacy, personal reputation, or congressional support. Because much of foreign policy is formulated not in crisis situations, but in open and long-term consultative processes that reach deeply into American so-ciety, there is frequently an opportunity for mobilizing around a moral-norm violation.

International Pressure in Support of a Moral Norm

The third pathway linking international moral norms to norm-obser-vant state behavior arises from the role that moral norms play in the international system as reputational indicators. By mobilizing around an international moral norm, states can create significant reputational pressure upon a non-observant nation and thus lead that nation's de-cision makers to adopt a norm-observant course of action. In order to understand how this pathway functions, it is helpful to explore the role of reputation in economic markets, since the structure of the in-ternational system is analogous to the structure of a market system.[37]

The importance of reputation for economics and for international relations arises from the uncertainties that firms or nations have about the intentions of their competitors and potential allies. One crucial

[37] Kenneth Waltz provides a compelling rationale for such a methodological ap-proach: "The problem is this: how to conceive of an order without an order and of or-ganization effects where formal organization is lacking. Because these are difficult questions, I shall answer them through analogy with microeconomic theory. Reasoning by analogy is helpful where one can move from a domain for which theory is well de-veloped to one where it is not. Reasoning by analogy is permissible where different domains are structurally similar." (Kenneth Waltz, *Theory of International Politics* [New York: Random House, 1979], p. 89) See also Robert Gilpin, *War and Change in World Politics* (Cambridge: Cambridge University Press, 1981), pp. ix–x; and Robert Keohane, *After Hegemony: Cooperation and Discord in the World Political Economy* (Princeton: Princeton University Press, 1984), pp. 85–109.

The investigation of microeconomics in this section focuses upon the work of the "new institutional economics," a body of microeconomic analysis that pays particular attention to the myriad forms of market, hierarchical, and quasi-market organization. The notion of transaction costs, which first emerged in the 1930s and is today enjoying a renaissance in the study of economics, is central to the notion of reputation in market economies and in the international system. Transaction-costs analysis "examines the comparative costs of planning, adopting and monitoring task completion under alter-native governance structures." (Oliver Williamson, *The Economic Institutions of Capi-talism* [New York: The Free Press, 1985], p. 2) Transaction-costs analysis focuses on the misunderstandings and conflicts that plague microeconomic interaction in the real world and searches for their causes and solutions. See also Ronald Coase, "The New Institutional Economics," *Journal of Institutional and Theoretical Economics* 140 (March 1984): 229–231.

way for firms and nations to reduce this uncertainty is to utilize the *principle of extrapolation*:

> People extrapolate the behavior of others from past observations, and this extrapolation is self-stabilizing, because it provides an incentive for others to live up to these expectations. This principle of extrapolation drastically reduces the cost of transmission (and therefore in a sense production) of information, in this case information about the future behavior of other people. By observing others' behaviors in the past, one can fairly confidently predict their behavior in the future without incurring further costs.[38]

The principle of extrapolation emerges quite strongly in David Kreps's and Robert Wilson's pathbreaking game-theoretic treatment of reputation, in which the authors conclude that the effort to build a strong reputation can confer immense benefits in a wide variety of fields because of uncertainties about motivation:

> Consider the importance of reputation in contract and labor negotiations; in a firm's employment practices; in a firm's "good name" for its product; in international diplomacy. To each of these contexts our analytical structure can be applied to yield the conclusions: if the situation is repeated, so that it is worthwhile to maintain a reputation, and if there is some uncertainty about the motivations of one or more players, then that uncertainty can substantially affect the play of the game. There need not be much uncertainty for this to happen. The power of the reputation effect depends upon the nature of one's opponents, notably whether they also seek to acquire a reputation.[39]

The structure of the international system has all of the ingredients that Kreps and Wilson found to be necessary for reputation to be important: the number of players is relatively small and thus the players are recognizable; interaction is repeated over time; and there is great uncertainty about the motives of nations. And yet some way must be found for state decision makers to calculate these motives.

The reputation of a firm has different facets that reflect the varying types of relationships that any company must enter into on a continuing basis. Thus a monopoly or oligopolistic firm will find it advantageous to develop a reputation for aggressively fending off the entry of

[38] Christian von Weizsacker, *Barriers to Entry* (New York: Springer-Verlag, 1980), p. 72.

[39] David Kreps and Robert Wilson, "Reputation and Imperfect Information," *Journal of Economic Theory* 27 (August 1982): 275.

all new firms into a field.[40] But that same monopoly or oligopolistic firm will also seek to develop a multitude of interfirm relationships that depend upon a certain degree of trust:

> Since coordinated actions to obtain outcomes of benefit to all parties often depend upon trust, each actor who wants to be a participant in and the beneficiary of such cooperative schemes in the long run, and on a number of separable occasions, has an important stake in erecting and preserving a reputation as a trustworthy partner. By making clear that he defines the situation of choice for himself broadly enough to include a number of future occasions when he will want to be a participant in joint actions requiring trust, an actor can demonstrate that his controlling preference on each particular occasion will be to act so as to preserve his desirability as a partner in transactions requiring trust.[41]

One important element of this notion of trust is captured by the concept of credibility, the willingness to faithfully observe agreed-upon rules.[42] Thus even the most tough-minded monopoly will find it advantageous to develop a reputation for keeping its promises to suppliers and clients.[43] But there is a second type of trust in market behavior that goes beyond the mere observance of agreed-upon rules and that involves a sense of equitableness. This second form of trust arises in those areas of market relations where a cooperative relationship exists, and yet where there are no clear rules that adequately specify the rights and obligations of the cooperative partners. This latter dimension of trust can be termed *equitable trust*, and it is equitable trust that forms the basis for the observance of moral norms in the international system.

The notion of equitable trust has become significant for microeco-

[40] David Kreps and Robert Wilson, "On the Chair-Store Paradox and Predation: Reputation for Toughness" (Research paper prepared for the Graduate School of Business at Stanford University, 1980); and Paul Milgrom and John Roberts, "Predation, Reputation, and Entry Deterrence," *Journal of Economic Theory* 27 (August 1982): 280–312. For an application of this principle to the field of international relations, see James Alt, Randall Calvert, and Brian Humes, "Reputation and Hegemonic Stability," *American Political Science Review* 88 (June 1988): 445–466.

[41] Philip Heyman, "The Problem of Coordination: Bargaining and Rules," *Harvard Law Review* 86 (March 1973): 822.

[42] Svenn Lindskold has called this type of trust "objective credibility." (Svenn Lindskold, "Trust Development, the GRIT Proposal, and the Effects of Conciliatory Acts on Conflict and Cooperation," *Psychological Bulletin* 85 [1978]: 773.)

[43] Williamson, *Economic Institutions of Capitalism*, pp. 167–168; Kenneth Arrow, *The Limits of Organization* (New York: W. W. Norton and Company, 1974), p. 23; and Keohane, *After Hegemony*, pp. 105–106. It is important to note that reputational considerations will not always provide sufficient incentives for observing agreed-upon rules, and thus a firm will not always honor its commitments in a market system.

nomics because it is now apparent that the notion of contracts that has dominated law and classical economics is an inadequate framework for capturing many of the most important continuing cooperative relationships in the marketplace:

> The paradigmatic contract of neoclassical economic and legal analysis is a discrete transaction in which no duties exist between the parties prior to the contract formation and in which the duties of the partners are determined at the formation stage. . . . Relations which are to take place over a long period of time and in which the parties will have to deal with each other regularly over a wide range of issues (many of them unknown in advance) often are forced into this discrete transactional mold both in legal and economic analysis.[44]

Recent work in both law and economics has proposed that such continuing relationships in which critically important duties cannot be adequately specified in advance should be seen not as contracts in the classical sense, but as *relational contracts*.[45] Relational contracts predominate in a host of market relationships, ranging from a producer's obligations to provide quality goods, to a company's long-term duties to nonunionized workers, to a supplier's continuing relationship to a major manufacturing firm.[46] Each of these relationships entails a large number of unspecifiable contingencies in which both parties must rely upon the equitableness of the other, and each of these relationships depends predominantly upon market rather than government mechanisms for the equitable resolution of these contingencies.[47]

[44] Victor Goldberg, "Toward an Expanded Theory of Economic Contract," *Journal of Economic Issues* 10 (March 1976): 49.

[45] Charles Goetz and Robert Scott, "Principles of Relational Contracts," *Virginia Law Review* 67 (September 1981): 1091. Ian Macneil provides a seminal treatment of relational contracts in "Contracts: Adjustment of Long-Term Economic Relationships under Classical, Neoclassical, and Relational Contract Law," *Northwestern University Law Review* 72 (1977–78): 854–906.

[46] Benjamin Klein and Keith Leffler, "The Role of Market Forces in Assuring Contractual Performance," *Journal of Political Economy* 89 (1981): 618; H. Lorne Carmichael, "Reputations in the Labor Market," *American Economic Review* 74 (September 1984): 723; and Williamson, *Economic Institutions of Capitalism*, pp. 71–77.

[47] All three of the works cited in the preceding note argue that the primary enforcement mechanisms in relational contracts arise from market mechanisms rather than government enforcement. This would seem logical, since the unspecifiability of the duties and obligations of a relational contract *ex ante* makes contract enforcement through the court system extremely difficult. The fact that relational contracts rely so heavily upon market rather than governmental enforcement mechanisms makes them significantly more applicable as analogues to cooperative relationships in the international system.

Reputations take on importance in relational-contract situations because they act as a check upon opportunism and exploitative conduct. In most relational contracts, both parties make significant investments of resources that constitute *sunk costs* in that particular cooperative relationship. These sunk costs can include the investment of capital, training, expertise, or time; they can also involve opportunities foregone by not entering into other, alternative cooperative relationships. Before incurring such sunk costs, a firm will want to insure as far as possible that its trading partner will not engage in exploitative behavior against the firm, using the leverage of the sunk costs to prevent the firm from abandoning the relationship. In short, a firm will wish to know that a potential partner in a relational contract will behave equitably in those many situations where the rights and duties of cooperation are not spelled out *ex ante*. The reputation of the potential partner for behaving equitably in the past can help to provide such knowledge.[48]

Reputation plays such an informational role even in cooperative relationships that are hierarchical. Take, for example, the case of a non-union employee seeking a job with a large corporation. Once the employee takes that job and holds it for a certain period of time, he has gained seniority and foregone the opportunity to gain seniority at another corporation. These are his sunk costs, of which an exploitative corporation could take advantage. Since the contractual relationship in most such situations is a relational one in which future increases in salary and benefits are not spelled out, what is to keep the corporation from using the leverage of the employee's sunk costs in order to pay the employee less than market rates? A large part of the answer is reputation: "When the hierarchically superior party has a reputation to protect or enhance, a reputation that turns on how hierarchical authority is exercised, then the inferior party need not presume the worst. He can count on the superior party to live up to an implicit contract in her own interests."[49] The reason that the corporation will act equitably in the absence of a specified contractual obligation to do so is that the corporation needs to hire employees in the future. If it does not consistently act equitably toward its workers, the corporation will lose potential employees to rival firms that *have* developed reputations for equitable treatment. Thus reputations for equity are important not only to cooperative relationships among roughly equal eco-

---

[48] Williamson, *Economic Instituions of Capitalism*, chap. 7; and David Kreps, "Corporate Culture and Economic Theory" (Paper prepared for the Second Mitsubishi Bank Foundation Conference on Technology and Business Strategy, August 1984), pp. 19–25.

[49] Kreps and Wilson, "Reputation and Imperfect Information," p. 28.

nomic entities, but also to hierarchically structured relationships. Even immense power advantages do not destroy the importance of reputation in signaling equitable intentions to potential cooperative partners.

Relational contracts and equitable trust operate in a similar manner in the international system. Nations find it advantageous to enter into a host of continuing cooperative relationships with one another in which the exact rights and duties of each participant cannot be specified in advance. (The European Economic Community would be an obvious and critically important example of such a relationship.) While it is true that a nation will usually have the ability to withdraw from such cooperative relationships, there are generally significant sunk costs involved in the building of a cooperative partnership. Thus a state will wish to insure insofar as possible that its potential cooperative partners are likely to behave equitably in those situations not covered by the initial cooperative agreement. As a consequence, a reputation for equitable conduct will greatly enhance a nation's capacity to enter into cooperative relationships and profit from them. The value of such a reputation is not confined to relationships between states with roughly equal power capabilities. For just as a large corporation in a market system has an incentive to maintain a reputation for equity so that it can attract future employees and suppliers, so, too, a hegemon will have an interest in developing a reputation for behaving equitably in its cooperative relationships so that it can form such relationships with minimal compliance costs.[50]

Recent work in sociology has proposed that certain social norms function as shared "identity-indicators" that signal to the members of the society what type of person one is.[51] Robert Keohane has proposed that moral norms play such a role in the international system: "Adhering to a moral code may identify an actor as a political cooperator, part of a cluster of players with whom mutually beneficial agreements can be made, as in Robert Axelrod's model. That is, publicly accepting a set of principles as morally binding may perform a labeling function."[52]

---

[50] Robert Keohane and Joseph Nye argue that even in hegemonic regimes there must be a certain level of cooperation on the part of middle-level states for the regime to succeed at acceptable costs to the hegemon. For such cooperation to occur, these middle-level states must believe that the regime is legitimate, that it genuinely serves the interests of all involved. Equitable conduct by the hegemon can help to attain that legitimacy. (Robert Keohane and Joseph Nye, *Power and Interdependence* [Boston: Little, Brown and Company, 1977], p. 271.)

[51] Francesca Cancian, *What Are Norms?* (Cambridge: Cambridge University Press, 1975), p. 148.

[52] Keohane, *After Hegemony*, p. 127.

Because cooperative relationships in the international system share the general characteristics of relational contracts, states have an incentive to wish to be labeled "equitably trustworthy." Following moral norms can help to establish such a reputation. Moreover, not following a moral norm can have the potent effect of labeling a nation "nonequitable," which can seriously undermine an actor's ability to enter into future cooperative relationships or a hegemon's capacity to gain compliance cost-effectively. It is not really surprising that moral norms should serve this function. For relational contracts require the very qualities which moral norms touch upon. As one of the progenitors of relational-contract theory has pointed out, "In ongoing contractual relations we find such broad norms as distributive justice, human dignity, social equality and inequality, and procedural justice."[53] The fact that a nation follows an international moral norm can signal that that nation respects these values in its international dealings; conversely, the fact that a nation violates an international moral norm can lead other states to label it noncooperative and exploitative.

Political action by victims of moral-norm violations can dramatically enhance this reputational role for moral norms and can make a norm structurally salient for state decision makers. This is because a state actor can draw attention to a violation of a moral norm, make it a focus of international discussion and action, and in this way inflict significant reputational damage upon the nation violating the norm. The key to accomplishing this is for the nation that is mobilizing against the norm violation to force third parties to take a stand on the dispute. If the mobilizing state can successfully frame the issue as a violation of a moral norm, then third-party states will have significant incentives to side against the violating nation. This is because third parties will themselves benefit from building a reputation as states that respect international moral norms.[54] An effective mobilizing actor can generate a strong coalition against the violating nation, and in this way can dramatically increase the reputational costs of breaking the moral norm in question.[55]

[53] Macneil, "Contracts," p. 898.

[54] Robert Axelrod has used the term *metanorm* to describe the mechanism for punishing of those who do not punish a norm defection (*The Evolution of Cooperation* [New York: Basic Books, 1984]). Since the punishment for not punishing a violation of a moral norm is itself reputational and therefore relatively cost-free to administer, the hypotheses of this work escape one of the central problems with Axelrod's treatment (Axelrod generally conceives of metanorms as invoking punishments that are costly to administer, and this raises the question of why a person would bear the cost of punishing a nonpunisher).

[55] Actually, there are several reasons why a nation might join such a coalition against a norm-violating nation. First of all, a nation might dislike the violator in general and thus wish to increase the reputational damage. Second, a nation might have a special

The formation of such a coalition can affect the foreign-policy decision-making process of the violating nation in two distinct ways. First of all, such a coalition can lead the state decision makers of the violating nation to give increased attention to the issue in dispute and to raise it to a higher level on their policy agenda. At the very least, these decision makers will have to devise a strategy to try to counter the "moral" case against them. The second impact of the effort to mobilize around the moral norm will be felt when the violating nation recalculates the configuration of its national interests involved in the dispute. For the violating nation's decision makers will have to include in these new calculations the reputational damage that their country is suffering. At times, this reputational damage will be significant enough to counterbalance the national interests that originally argued in favor of violating the moral norm, and in such a case the violating nation will reverse its original decision to violate the norm.

Thus the structural pathway from moral norms to state behavior arises from nations' desires to avoid gaining a reputation for inequitable conduct in the international system. By drawing attention to the violation of an international moral norm, a state actor can mobilize other actors against the violation and thus significantly increase the reputational damage that accrues to the violator. This damage or threat of damage can lead the violating nation to give greater attention to the policy that is violating the norm and can even lead the violating nation to conclude that the national interest calls for a reversal of the policy in dispute.[56]

THE QUESTION OF MORAL CONFLICT

The liberal internationalists proposed that international moral norms could help moralize foreign policy through the pathways of conscience, domestic politics, and international reputational pressures. But they were well aware of the fact that international moral norms, like all moral norms, are merely generalized ethical formulations that attempt to point toward the moral course of action. Most moral norms

interest in maintaining the strength of the moral norm because it would be likely to benefit from the norm in the future. Third, a nation's leaders or people might have conscience-related reasons for objecting to violations of the norm. While the first reason is largely unrelated to the existence of the moral norm in question, the other two reasons are quite clearly dependent upon the existence of the norm, as is the reputational incentive to side with the norm and against the violator.

[56] It is interesting to note that in the nineteenth century, the notion of reputation was quite important in international diplomacy. It may be no coincidence that Morgenthau saw in this period of diplomacy a much greater adherence to international morality than in the twentieth century. (Hans Morgenthau, *Politics among Nations* [New York: Alfred A. Knopf, 1948], pp. 187ff.)

have exceptions. Even more importantly, state decision makers will at times find themselves in situations in which they are torn between a moral duty to follow an international moral norm and a countervailing duty to realize another and equally important moral value that conflicts with the international moral norm.

This does not mean, as the early realists were inclined to argue, that all state actions are morally ambiguous. What it does mean is that at times there are genuinely moral motivations that can lead state decision makers to refuse to follow an international moral norm. Marshall Cohen has cited the British and French refusal to live up to their commitments to sanction Italy after its invasion of Abyssinia as an example of moral conflict in operation:

> Britain and France refused to fulfill their duties under the League Covenant, but they did so because they feared that honoring them would seriously impair their ability to defend either themselves or the fundamental values of a liberal civilization in what they could see was the coming struggle against fascism. In acting on these weightier obligations, Britain and France acted not simply with political realism, but in what was, from a moral point of view, the better way.[57]

This phenomenon of moral conflict has two implications for this work. The first is that in historical cases of key foreign-policy decisions touching upon international moral norms, there will likely be situations where genuinely moral claims are cited to support policy options that contravene the international moral norm. While such moral claims *may* be utilized in particular cases for rhetorical purposes only, it is quite possible that these moral claims are being advanced for genuinely ethical reasons.

The second implication of the phenomenon of moral conflict for this work is that one cannot automatically assume that the policy option indicated by an international moral norm is the morally correct policy option. There may be instances where countervailing moral claims are of such magnitude that they outweigh the moral claim underlying the international moral norm. For the purposes of this work, it is not necessary to demonstrate conclusively that in each historical case the international moral norm pointed to the ethically correct course of action. For this work is empirically, rather than normatively, oriented. It merely seeks to show that the existence of international moral norms creates pathways of conscience, domestic politics, and international

---

[57] Marshall Cohen, "Moral Skepticism and International Relations," *Philosophy and Public Affairs* 13 (Fall 1984): 306. Cohen's discussion of moral conflict has greatly informed the discussion presented here. See also Bernard Williams, "Ethical Consistency," in *Problems of the Self* (Cambridge: Cambridge University Press, 1973), pp. 166–186.

reputational pressures that lead state decision makers at times to make policy decisions reflective of an international moral norm.

Conclusions

The fact that the period following World War I did not witness the abolition of war or the comprehensive moralization of foreign policy should not obscure the fact that the case made by the liberal internationalists for the ability of international moral norms to influence foreign-policy decision making has strong theoretical support. This century has witnessed the emergence of certain elements of an international society and the formation of a substantial number of international moral prescriptions that have transcultural roots and that have been formally endorsed by the major governments of the world. Moreover, the pathways of conscience, domestic politics, and international reputational pressures to which the internationalists pointed as the channels for the moralization of foreign policy all seem more understandable and more realistic in light of recent findings in social psychology, political science, and the "new institutional economics."

These theoretical supports lend credibility to the internationalist case and help to specify how the three channels might operate in the state system. But in the final analysis, the most effective way of evaluating the liberal argument that morality can affect foreign policy is to put the internationalist claims to the empirical test. Are there cases of significant foreign-policy decision making in which the channels of individual conscience, domestic politics, and international reputational pressures have operated so as to bring international moral norms to bear on foreign policy in the way that the internationalists had predicted?

The following chapters seek to show that there are. All of them are drawn from American foreign-policy decision making in the twentieth century, for four reasons: (1) a desire to show that it is possible to find significant instances of all three channels operating within a single country's decision-making process during a limited time period; (2) the need for exhaustive and open primary sources in several of the cases in order to rule out counterarguments that other, interest-based factors rather than international moral norms lay behind the decisions in question; (3) the fact that the constitutional structure of the United States approximates the type of liberal republican society envisioned by Kant and the internationalists; and (4) the fact that the realist critique of liberal internationalism has been largely based upon analysis of American foreign policy making.

The first case study investigates the role that the international moral norm on famine relief played in the 1921 U.S. decision to send massive food aid to the Soviet Union; this is an example of the pathway of individual conscience in operation. The second case study concerns Richard Nixon's 1969 decision to radically alter U.S. policies on chemical and biological warfare as a result of domestic pressures to observe the international moral norm on chemical and biological weapons. And the third case study discusses the U.S. decision to negotiate a treaty conveying the Panama Canal and Canal Zone to the Republic of Panama; this decision is largely attributable to international reputational pressures that converged around the international moral norm against territorial colonialism. A final case study discusses the bombing of Dresden during World War II and indicates why the moral norm of noncombatant immunity was violated; this is a "failed case" that can help to explain why moral norms will at times be violated in the international system.

The use of historical cases to illustrate the role of morality in foreign-policy decision making has been undertaken in several important previous works. J. E. Hare and Carey Joynt use historical cases "to form a reflective moral judgment about the past conduct of international policy" in *Ethics and International Affairs*.[58] Stanley Hoffmann cites from historical situations in order to guide his two commentaries on the proper role of ethics in international affairs.[59] And Joseph Nye has effectively used historical cases to bolster his effort to promote a dialogue between the empirical study of international relations and the field of applied ethics.[60] But there is no existing study that utilizes in-depth case-study analysis to evaluate the claim that international moral norms can affect the formulation of foreign policy through the channels of individual conscience, domestic politics, and international reputation. The following chapters seek to address this need.[61]

[58] J. E. Hare and Carey Joynt, *Ethics and International Affairs* (London: Macmillan Press, 1982), p. v.

[59] *Duties beyond Borders*; and *The Political Ethics of International Relations* (New York: Carnegie Council on Ethics and International Affairs, 1988).

[60] Joseph Nye, *Nuclear Ethics* (New York: The Free Press, 1986).

[61] This use of case studies in order to explore, clarify, and validate the internationalists' hypotheses about international moral norms draws heavily upon the methodological insights contained in Alexander George, "Case Studies and Theory Development" (Paper presented to the Second Annual Symposium on Information Processing in Organizations, Carnegie-Mellon University, October 15–16, 1982); Arend Lipjhart, "Comparative Politics and the Comparative Method," *American Political Science Review* 65 (September 1971): 682–693; idem, "The Comparable-Case Strategy in Comparative Research," *Comparative Political Studies* 8 (July 1975): 158–177; and Harry Eckstein, "Case Study and Theory in Political Science," in *Handbook of Political Science*, ed. by F. I. Greenstein and Nelson Polsby (Reading, Mass.: Addison-Wesley Publishing Company, 1975), 8:79–138.

Chapter Three

UNITED STATES FAMINE RELIEF TO
SOVIET RUSSIA, 1921

IN 1921 United States foreign policy was dedicated to isolating the Soviet government in world affairs, with the hope and expectation that the Bolshevik regime would soon be overthrown. The United States refused to recognize the Soviet government, to allow the establishment of the credits necessary for private trade between American firms and the Soviet Union, or even to accept Soviet gold into the United States so as to allow the Russian government to pay outright for the American goods that it desired to purchase for its postwar economic recovery. The Harding administration viewed the Soviet government as a major threat to American interests because of Soviet propaganda efforts to destabilize capitalist regimes in Europe; in addition, the U.S. government believed that the Soviet repudiation of prewar Russian debts and confiscation of foreign holdings in Russia constituted a precedent that, if unpunished, could threaten the integrity of the international trading system. American foreign policy toward the Soviet Union was clear: the United States would not intervene to topple the Bolshevik regime, but would cut off the Soviets from American trade with the hope that an isolated Soviet government would be unable to meet Russia's pressing economic needs and thus would eventually topple.

In the spring of 1921 the Soviet government faced the very type of threat to its existence and legitimacy that the American government had been hoping for: the outbreak of a massive famine in the Volga region that left tens of millions starving. Hundreds of thousands of refugees had already begun leaving their villages and drifting into the major cities of the Soviet Union, and famine-related epidemics were sweeping through many of the provinces of western Russia. Lenin, assessing the extent of the famine and the danger it posed to the young Bolshevik government, predicted that if no way could be found to feed the peasants suffering from the famine, the Soviet regime would perish. Desperate for some way of meeting the crisis, the Soviet government authorized an appeal to the West to send immediate food relief so that millions of Russians would not starve.

Within days of the Soviet appeal, Secretary of Commerce Herbert

Hoover began to mobilize a massive American relief effort to avert the starvation in Russia and to help produce an abundant Russian harvest for 1922. President Warren G. Harding asked for and received a congressional authorization to spend $24 million on the Russian relief effort, an amount equal to almost 1 percent of the 1921 federal budget. And the War Department provided massive amounts of medical supplies from its military stocks to assist in fighting disease in the famine-affected districts of the Soviet Union. This U.S. government assistance helped to feed ten million Russians for a period of eleven months and dramatically reduced the prevalence of typhus and smallpox in the Soviet Union. In the process, it allowed the Soviet regime to solidify its hold on the Russian nation and to launch Russian economic recovery through the New Economic Plan.

Why did the United States, when faced with a famine that promised to destabilize the Soviet regime, give massive amounts of relief to the Russian people? Why did the Harding administration, which considered the policy of isolating the Soviet Union and weakening its government to be one of the centerpieces of American foreign policy, sacrifice that policy in order to feed citizens of a foreign state? It will be argued here that a large part of the answer to these questions lies in the existence of an international moral norm that obliges nations with food surpluses to aid famine-stricken countries regardless of their political regime. Leading U.S. decision makers had internalized the tenets of that moral norm, and thus in conscience they could not sit by and watch millions of Russians starve to death, even if providing famine relief meant helping to stabilize the detested Soviet regime. The case of famine relief to the Soviet Union is thus an instance of the first pathway from moral norms to foreign policy: the internalization of moral norms by leading state decision makers.

THE FAMINE-RELIEF NORM

Ever since the 1874 drought in India, famine has been defined as existing when the food production in a given area has fallen to 25 percent of normal annual production.[1] In general, famines arise from a lack of water, crop disease, pests, wars, floods, or earthquakes. Up until the 1860s, famines were common even in Great Britain, France, and Germany, but advances in agriculture and the development of sophisticated international commodity networks in the latter half of the

---

[1] Gunnar Blix, Yngve Hofvander, and Bo Vahlquist, ed., *Famine: A Symposium Dealing with Nutrition and Relief Operations in Times of Disaster* (Uppsala: Almquist and Wiksells, 1971), p. 22.

nineteenth century virtually eliminated famine in the industrialized world.[2] As a result, famines came to be seen not as part of the cyclical nature of agriculture, but as rare disasters that could be alleviated through outside aid.

The international famine-relief norm is part of a larger set of moral norms that arose in the early twentieth century concerning international aid for major natural disasters. Until World War I, disaster relief was considered largely a national problem. The European colonial powers did send relief to their colonies during intense crises, such as the Indian famine of the 1890s, and the U.S. Congress had appropriated aid for occasional disasters such as the Venezuelan earthquake of 1812 and the Sicilian earthquake of 1908; but in general there was no international mobilization by governments when famine or earthquake or flood devastated a nation.[3] World War I radically altered the nature of disaster relief by creating reconstruction needs in Central Europe so great that they were beyond the ability of any nation to meet single-handedly. The immediate postwar period showed the need for what Jovica Patrnogic has called "solidarity in international relief": the principle that national governments have a moral obligation to help other countries that have been devastated by disaster.[4]

This principle of solidarity was first displayed in the efforts by the victorious Allies to feed Europe's hungry after World War I. For the Armistice of 1918 signaled the end of one war on the European continent and the intensification of another: the war to avert mass starvation in the Central European nations devastated by four years of bloodshed. The campaigns of 1914–18 had crippled the economies of Poland, Germany, Austria, and Hungary, and agricultural production had fallen by as much as 90 percent in many areas of the Continent. The Allies found themselves faced with two hundred million starving men, women, and children, and a potential human disaster greater than any Europe had faced since the Thirty Years' War. The governments of Germany and Austria-Hungary were in ruins, without legitimacy or the capability of meeting the desperate need of their peoples

[2] B. M. Nicol, "Causes of Famine in the Past and in the Future," in Blix, Hofvander, and Vahlquist, *Famine*, pp. 10–11.

[3] Hans Singer, *Food Aid* (Oxford: Clarendon Press, 1987), pp. 17–18. The U.S. efforts to mobilize in order to aid international disaster victims were hampered during the late nineteenth and early twentieth centuries by a strict construction of the general-welfare clause of the U.S. Constitution, a construction that held that Congress had no power to assist citizens of countries other than the United States.

[4] Jovica Patrnogic, "Some Reflections on Humanitarian Principles Applicable in Relief Actions," in *Studies and Essays on International Humanitarian Law*, ed. Christopher Swinarski (Geneva: Martinus Nijhoff Publishers, 1984), pp. 925–936.

for food. If the Allies did not take dramatic steps immediately, mass starvation would be inevitable.[5]

As soon as the Armistice was signed, the United States, the British Empire, France, and Italy undertook a massive relief effort to supply food to the people of Central Europe. The United States, which alone had the capacity to contribute immense amounts of foodstuffs, provided a congressional appropriation of $100 million for relief in the liberated nations.[6] Great Britain provided $59 million worth of aid, which was used to transport food and to purchase American, Canadian, and Australian grain for those who were most in need.[7] France and Italy gave much lesser amounts, but were particularly helpful in transporting food to Austria, which no longer had the economic capacity to pay for food and was not eligible for aid under the American congressional appropriation.[8] Together, the Allies fed Poland, Czechoslovakia, Yugoslavia, Rumania, Austria, Hungary, Armenia, Turkey, and Bulgaria during the critical period from 1918 to 1919 and thus averted mass starvation on the European continent.[9]

This monumental international relief effort by the Allied nations constituted an important precedent for future government-supported famine-relief programs. It also caused the international community to reconsider the approach that had been taken to the whole question of disaster relief in the past. The International Red Cross, which had emerged from the war as the world's preeminent humanitarian organization, convened a series of meetings in 1919 and 1920 to radically restructure the international disaster-relief regime. Out of these meetings emerged two principles that were to shape disaster relief in the twentieth century. The first of these principles was the belief that in

[5] See Frank M. Surface and Raymond Bland, *American Food Aid in the World War and Reconstruction Period* (Stanford: Stanford University Press, 1931), pp. 23–36.

[6] Herbert Hoover, *Memoirs*, vol. 2 (New York: Macmillan Company, 1951), pp. 18–19. Hoover headed the American relief effort for the Wilson administration during the early postwar period.

[7] Surface and Bland, *American Food Aid*, p. 54.

[8] Ibid., p. 60. Since Austria was not a "liberated nation," it was not eligible for outright gifts under the congressional appropriation. Still, the Wilson administration found a way of providing credits to Austria that helped to bring tens of thousands of tons of American wheat and corn to the Austrian people.

[9] The question of aid to Germany was much murkier than the issue of aid to the other nations of Central Europe. During the period after the Armistice, the Allied nations enforced the blockade against Germany in order to pressure the Germans to sign the Treaty of Versailles. While the victorious powers did allow enough food into Germany to avoid mass starvation, the continuation of the blockade was an example of the very different attitude toward postwar reconstruction that the Allies took in the case of the German people. See Suda Bane and Ralph Lutz, ed., *The Blockade of Germany after the Armistice, 1918–1919* (Stanford: Stanford University Press, 1942).

the future truly effective disaster relief would require the financial and material assistance of the governments of the world; no longer could purely private institutions hope to supply the food and medicines needed to assist devastated countries. The second principle that emerged from the Red Cross meetings of 1919–20 held that international institutions would have to be developed that would systematically elicit governmental assistance for disaster relief and apply it to areas of greatest need, regardless of political considerations.[10]

The first step toward institutionalizing the moral obligation of nations to contribute to disaster relief in all countries of the globe was realized by the formation of a centralized International Red Cross organization in March 1921. The formerly disparate Red Cross national societies pledged to work together as a truly international network for relief assistance, and to solicit funds from their governments for continuing disaster relief.[11] Since the national Red Cross societies typically included in their ranks many of their countries' most influential leaders, this assertion of every nation's moral obligation to assist in disaster relief would be brought to the highest levels of government.[12]

In addition, the principle of international solidarity in disaster relief was incorporated into the Covenant of the League of Nations; Article 25 explicitly encouraged member governments both to form national Red Cross societies and to contribute materially to the relief of international disasters. When a typhus outbreak and food shortage hit Poland during the Russo-Polish War in 1920, the League solicited sufficient funds from its member governments to meet the crisis. In March 1921 the League established a Bureau of Relief to encourage governments to provide international assistance in times of emergency.[13] In June of that same year the League Council wrote to all members of the League informing them of their obligation to render all possible assistance to international relief efforts, including credits and the free transportation of supplies.[14] And in July 1921 the League began work on a comprehensive international disaster-relief network that would be funded by the League member governments based on their ability to pay; the principle behind this disaster-relief fund was

[10] Andre Durand, *History of the International Committee of the Red Cross*, vol. 2 (Geneva: Henry Dunant Institute, 1978), pp. 140–178.

[11] Ibid.

[12] In 1919 the American Red Cross had more than twenty million members. Its honorary president was Woodrow Wilson, and its president was Harry Davison, director of J. P. Morgan and Company.

[13] Charles Levermore, ed., *The Second Year Book of the League of Nations* (New York: Brooklyn Daily Eagle, 1922), p. 98.

[14] League of Nations, *Official Journal of the League of Nations* (Geneva, 1921), p. 607.

the assertion that there is "a human right of nations stricken by calamities which could not be foreseen, to be assisted by the [international governmental] solidarity, if the mobilization of their own powers is found insufficient to succor the suffering within their territory."[15] Thus by 1921 a radical shift had occurred in the international approach to disaster relief. The principle that disaster relief was purely a national affair had been replaced by an international moral norm that obliged nations with an abundance of food and medical supplies to contribute toward the relief of devastated areas.

As the twentieth century progressed, this principle was increasingly institutionalized in the international system. The League of Nations erected ever more formalized structures for mobilizing its member governments for famine relief throughout the interwar period, and after World War II the United Nations undertook a series of steps to organize governmentally supported famine relief.[16] In 1952 the UN approved formal criteria for the certification of famine conditions and declared that famine relief was an international responsibility that was to be carried out by the United Nations Disaster Relief Organization. In 1954 the Food and Agriculture Organization drew up guidelines for the distribution of world food surpluses, which underscored the obligation of nations with an abundance of food to provide immediate assistance in famine situations. And in 1967 most of the world's nations became signatories of the Food Aid Convention, pledging to pay an annual tax in foodstuffs based upon their agricultural production and population; this tax was to be deposited in a food reserve that could be immediately drawn upon in time of famine anywhere in the world.[17] The fact that all of the major food producers of the world were willing to assume this tax points to the strength that the famine-relief norm has taken on in its seventy years of existence.

AMERICAN FOREIGN POLICY TOWARD THE SOVIET UNION: 1921

The Bolshevik Revolution radically transformed the United States' attitude toward Russia: what had before been seen as a democratic ally assisting in the fight against Germany now became a dangerous enemy seeking world revolution. In part, this transformation resulted

---

[15] League of Nations, *Official Journal of the League of Nations* (Geneva, 1922), pp. 1216ff.; and Randolph Kent, *Anatomy of Disaster Relief* (London: Pinter Publishers, 1987), p. 32.

[16] See League of Nations, *Official Journal* (1922), 1216ff.; Charles Levermore, ed., *The Third Year Book of the League of Nations* (New York: Brooklyn Daily Eagle, 1923), p. 98; and Singer, *Food Aid*, pp. 27ff.

[17] Singer, *Food Aid*, pp. 27–28, 54–78.

from the Bolshevik desire to conclude a quick peace with Germany in order to begin the reconstruction and communization of Russia; the Treaty of Brest-Litovsk was seen as a betrayal of the Allied cause and a serious blow to the Allied war plans. But in a much more profound way, the attitude that the United States took toward the Soviet government sprang from a belief that bolshevism represented something new and dangerous in world affairs, something that was a threat to the United States.[18]

This perception of the Soviet regime as a threat to U.S. interests arose from three Bolshevik policies that were to prove an insuperable obstacle to pacific U.S.-Soviet relations in the 1920s: the Soviet effort to destabilize Western governments through the use of propaganda; the Soviet repudiation of Russia's prerevolutionary debts to other nations; and the confiscation of foreign holdings within the Soviet Union.[19] U.S. fears of these aspects of Soviet policy were not groundless. Soviet propaganda had proven critically important in the Communist takeover of Hungary and in the near-takeovers of some of the German principalities after the fall of the Kaiser, and the United States was greatly concerned that the Bolshevik propaganda apparatus would be used effectively against the shaky fledgling governments of Central Europe.[20] The repudiation of Russia's state debts did not damage the United States substantially, since America held less than 3 percent of Russia's prerevolutionary debt; but the U.S. government viewed debt repudiation as a dangerous precedent that could undermine the international financial system and lead other debtor nations to refuse to pay their obligations.[21] Finally, the United States viewed with alarm the Soviet confiscation of all foreign holdings within the old Russian empire. Once again, the American share of these holdings was dwarfed by the lost investments of Britain, France, Germany, and Belgium, but the United States believed that the precedent of confis-

[18] From the very first day of the Soviet government, the American ambassador to Russia had refused to deal with the Bolsheviks, and he pressed for strong anti-Soviet measures by the U.S. government. (Louis Fischer, *The Soviets in World Affairs* [New York: Vintage Books, 1960], p. 6)

[19] Frederick Schuman, *American Policy toward Russia since 1917* (New York: International Publishers, 1928), p. 277. Woodrow Wilson made the repudiation of these three policies the *sine qua non* of relations with the Soviets, as did the Harding, Coolidge, and Hoover administrations.

[20] Rudolf Tokes, *Bela Kun and the Hungarian Soviet Republic* (New York: Frederick Praeger Publishing Company, 1967), pp. 72–81, 123–146; Gerhard Schulz, *Revolutions and Peace Treaties, 1917–1920* (London: Methuen and Company, 1972); and John Thompson, *Russia, Bolshevism, and the Versailles Peace* (Princeton: Princeton University Press, 1966), pp. 14–16, 391–393.

[21] Thompson, *Russia*, pp. 298–299.

cation posed a significant threat to the integrity of the international trading system. These factors, combined with a continuing belief by the American government that the Soviet regime was constantly on the verge of toppling, led U.S. policymakers to bring significant pressure to bear on the Bolshevik government.

The focus of this pressure was economic, and it was designed to keep the Soviet government from gaining the Western equipment that it needed for postwar reconstruction. After the Armistice of 1918, France and Britain had maintained a blockade against the Soviet Union in an effort to destabilize the Russian government.[22] The United States had refused to participate in the blockade because of its traditionally held position that blockades are illegal; but the American government had done its part to weaken the Bolshevik regime by outlawing all trade with the Soviet Union. The collapse of the White armies led to a lifting of the Allied blockade, but France, Great Britain, and the United States pledged that this action would not in any way diminish the Allies' opposition to the Soviet government nor their resolve to isolate the Bolsheviks from normal trade and intercourse with the West.[23] On August 10, 1920, U.S. Secretary of State Bainbridge Colby made clear the continuing American opposition to the Bolshevik government in a major declaration that was to form the basis for U.S. policy toward the Soviet Union for over a decade:

> Without any desire to interfere in the internal affairs of the Russian people or to suggest what kind of government they should have, the Government of the United States does express the hope that they will soon find a way to setting up a government representing their free will and purpose. When that time comes, the United States will consider the measures of practical assistance which can be taken to promote the restoration of Russia. . . . The existing regime is based upon the negation of every principle of honor and good faith and every usage and convention underlying the whole structure of international law—the negation, in short, of every principle upon which it is possible to base harmonious and trustful relations, whether of nations or individuals. . . . the Bolshevist government is itself subject to the control of a political faction with extensive international ramifications through the Third International, and this body, which is heavily subsidized by the Bolshevist government from the

[22] The Allies also sent troops into Russia in 1919 in an effort to rescue Czech soldiers, guard Allied military stores, prevent German encroachment, and harass the Soviet government. For a discussion of the very mixed American motives for participation in this project, see Linda Killen, *The Russian Bureau* (Lexington: University of Kentucky Press, 1983), pp. 13–14.

[23] Schuman, *American Policy toward Russia*, p. 173.

public revenues of Russia, has for its openly avowed aim the promotion of Bolshevist revolutions throughout the world. . . . In the view of this Government, there cannot be any common ground upon which it can stand with a power whose conceptions of international relations are so entirely alien to its own, so utterly repugnant to its moral sense.[24]

Public opinion strongly supported the administration's opposition to diplomatic or commercial relations with the Soviet Union. The American Federation of Labor, the American Legion, the League of Women Voters, and the Chamber of Commerce all came out against opening trade with the Bolshevik government. And the great majority of Americans, bolstered by stories of massacres of White Russian women and children by the Soviet government, did not want America to support a Communist government by sending its products to the Soviet Union.[25]

In formulating its trade policies, the Wilson administration decided to remove the legal proscription on Soviet trade because it had been a fertile source of Bolshevik propaganda in Europe.[26] Instead, the U.S. government erected a set of barriers to trade that effectively eliminated the possibility of American commerce with Russia, while stopping short of a legal prohibition. The first of these barriers was a campaign by the State Department to dissuade leading American lending institutions from granting credits to the Soviet government; without such credits, the Soviets would be forced to pay for their purchases in gold.[27] The second barrier to trade was the U.S. mint's refusal to accept Soviet gold. The Wilson administration estimated that the Soviets had approximately $300 million in gold.[28] Some of it had belonged to the imperial treasury, but the vast bulk of the Soviet gold supply had been confiscated from private Russian holdings. The U.S. government argued that both the imperial gold and the private gold were "stolen" and thus their title could not be assured. As a result, the mint was ordered to make all sellers of gold file a sworn affidavit that the gold they were selling did not come from the Soviet Union.[29] With no

[24] Benson Grayson, *The American Image of Russia: 1917–1977* (New York: Frederick Praeger Publishing Company, 1978), pp. 57–59.

[25] Peter G. Filene, *Americans and the Soviet Experiment, 1917–1933* (Cambridge: Harvard University Press, 1967), pp. 69–70.

[26] Schuman, *American Policy toward Russia,* p. 196.

[27] Killen, *The Russian Bureau,* pp. 132–133, 141–142.

[28] U.S. Congress, House, Committee on Foreign Affairs, *Hearings on Conditions in Russia,* 66th Cong., 3d sess., 1921 (Washington: U.S. Government Printing Office, 1921), p. 85.

[29] Robert Paul Browder, *The Origins of Soviet-American Diplomacy* (Princeton: Princeton University Press, 1953), pp. 26–27.

source of bank credits and no possibility of paying for purchases in cash, the Soviets were totally unable to buy the American equipment that they needed for the reconstruction of Russia. And the Wilson administration was able to rest secure knowing that America was doing everything realistically possible to shorten the time until the Soviet regime would be overthrown because of internal turmoil in Russia.[30]

On March 21, 1921, the Soviet government sent newly inaugurated President Warren G. Harding a message requesting that the Wilson policy of diplomatically and commercially isolating Russia be reversed:

> President Wilson, who without cause and without any declaration of war, had attacked the Russian Republic, showed during his whole administration a growing hostility toward the Russian Republic. Soviet Russia hopes that the American Republic will not persist in obdurately following this path and that the new American government will clearly see the great advantage for the two republics of the reestablishment of business relations and will consider the interests of both peoples which imperatively demand that the wall existing between them should be removed.[31]

The American response was not long in coming. On March 25, Secretary of State Charles Evans Hughes sent a message to the Soviet leadership that ended any hopes of a significant change in U.S. policy:

> It is only in the productivity of Russia that there is any hope for the Russian people, and it is idle to expect resumption of trade until the economic bases of production are securely established. Production is conditioned upon the safety of life, the recognition of firm guarantees of private property, the safety of contracts and the rights of free labor. If fundamental changes are contemplated, involving due regard for the protection of persons and property and the establishment of conditions essential to the maintenance of commerce, this Government will be glad to have convincing evidence of the consummation of such changes, and until this evidence is supplied this Government is unable to perceive that there is any proper basis for considering trade relations.[32]

[30] House Committee on Foreign Affairs, *Hearings on Conditions in Russia*, pp. 220–226. Under Secretary of State Norman Davis told the House Foreign Affairs committee in early 1921 that the United States would not recognize the valid title of Soviet gold because it wanted to avoid any commercial relations with Russia that could bolster the Soviet regime and because it wanted to preserve the Russian gold stock intact for the capital needs of the democratic government that would soon replace the Bolshevik junta.

[31] Schuman, *American Policy toward Russia*, p. 200.

[32] Ibid., p. 201.

That same week, Secretary of Commerce Herbert Hoover stressed the same theme, that a productive Russian economy and commercial relations with the U.S. were impossible under a Soviet regime: "The question of trade with Russia is far more a political question than an economic one as long as Russia is in control of the Bolsheveki."[33]

Hoover had long been a bitter foe of the Soviet government. Writing to President Wilson in 1919, he proposed that the United States could not think of entering into diplomatic or commercial relations with the new Communist government:

> The Bolsheviks have resorted to terror, bloodshed and murder to a degree long since abandoned even among reactionary tyrannies. . . . We cannot even remotely recognize this murderous tyranny without stimulating activist radicalism in every country in Europe and without transgressing . . . every national ideal of our own.[34]

Hoover recognized that the Bolshevik government had been able to seize power because of the misery and poverty wrought by three centuries of Romanov rule, but he regarded the Communist regime as a cure worse than the disease it was meant to remedy. Hoover's continuing opposition to any commercial or diplomatic relations between the United States and Russia subjected him to severe criticism from the far left in the United States and caused him to be labeled as "the most obstinate anti-Bolshevik" in the Harding administration.[35] In the late spring of 1921, the leading officials of the Harding administration, including Herbert Hoover, believed that the Soviet regime was on the verge of collapse.[36] Although the White armies had been defeated, the massive destruction from World War I remained, and the Russian Civil War and the Russo-Polish War continued: industries were crippled, the transportation network was in ruins, and the central government had little control over affairs in the outlying provinces. On top of all these challenges, it was becoming increasingly obvious that a severe famine was going to devastate the harvest of 1921, leaving the Russian peasants without food for themselves or crops to ship to the cities. In June, Herbert Hoover alerted the Amer-

[33] Benjamin Weissman, *Herbert Hoover and Famine Relief to Soviet Russia: 1921–1923* (Stanford: Hoover Institution Press, 1974), p. 42.

[34] Grayson, *American Image of Russia*, p. 47.

[35] *The New Statesman*, May 20, 1921, p. 3.

[36] *New York Times*, April 24, 1921, sec. 2, p. 3; Memorandum from Edgar Rickard to Walter Lyman Brown, June 21, 1921, box 20, Papers of the American Relief Association (Russian Operations), Archives of the Hoover Institution on War, Peace, and Revolution, Stanford, Calif. (hereinafter called ARA Papers).

ican Relief Association to prepare for a major feeding operation in
Russia to commence if the Bolshevik government should fall.[37]

FAMINE AND THE CALL OF CONSCIENCE

The famine that hit the Soviet Union in 1921 decimated an agricultural harvest that had already been much reduced by seven years of
warfare (see Table 3.1), and it left twenty million people starving in
seventeen provinces of Russia. In the province of Samara, 90 percent
of the population was totally without food, and the peasants had begun eating bark and roots in order to survive. Typhus and smallpox,
the constant companions of famine, were sweeping through the
black-earth regions of the Volga valley, and a flood of refugees moving
from country to town threatened to overwhelm the cities of the Soviet
Union with plague and death. The abandonment by the farmers of
their fields robbed the country of a new planting, and shipments of
food from eastern Russia were totally incapable of meeting the crisis.[38]

The Soviet government recognized clearly the magnitude of the

TABLE 3.1
Agricultural Production, Schilling Commune (Russia), 1919–21

	1919	1920	1921
Crop (in puds[a])			
Rye	4,930	3,552	150
Oats	256	245	8
Wheat	22,820	4,640	55
Potatoes	7,000	19,800	1,450
Livestock			
Horses	1,223	891	451
Cows	582	461	313
Sheep	1,332	1,156	424
Pigs	781	246	58

[a] A pud is a Russian unit of measurement equal to about 36.11 pounds.
Source: U.S. Congress, House, Committee on Foreign Affairs, *Hearings on Relief of
the Distressed and Starving People of Russia*, 67th Cong., 2d sess., 1921 (Washington:
U.S. Government Printing Office, 1921), pp. 8–9.

[37] Rickard to Brown, June 3, 1921, box 20, ARA Papers.
[38] Hugh Fisher, *The Famine in Soviet Russia* (New York: Macmillan Company,
1927), pp. 138–139, 255–261, 278–280; U.S. Congress, House, Committee on Foreign
Affairs, *Hearings on Relief of the Distressed and Starving People of Russia*, 67th Cong.,
2d sess., 1921 (Washington: U.S. Government Printing Office, 1921), pp. 3–13.

threat, not only to the survival of millions of Russians, but also to the survival of the Soviet system itself. At the Tenth Party Congress in March, Lenin had predicted that crop failure in 1921 would mean the downfall of the Bolshevik government and the end of the Communist experiment:

If there is a crop failure, it will be impossible to appropriate any surplus because there will be no surplus. Food would have to be taken out of the mouths of the peasants. If there is a harvest, then everybody will hunger a little, and the government will be saved; otherwise, since we cannot take anything from people who do not have the means of satisfying their own hunger, the government will perish.[39]

By summer it was apparent that the crop failure of 1921 was worse than anything Lenin could have imagined three months earlier, and the disenchantment with the Soviet government that Lenin had predicted was becoming apparent. *Izvestia* reported that "there is increased discontent on the part of the workers, who were starving even when there was actually bread in the villages. As a result there is a decline in manufactured goods; factories are standing idle; there is poor work; we can see the failure of our economic plans and a deterioration in the international situation."[40] Among the Russian émigrés in the West who longed for the downfall of the Bolshevik regime, celebrations began, and the Soviet government was faced with desperate choices if it was to survive.[41]

Maxim Gorky, the famous Russian author, approached the Soviet government with a proposal that he make a public appeal to the West to try to secure assistance for alleviating the famine. Lenin was skeptical that the West would actually provide substantial assistance, but believing that the famine was "a disaster that threatened to nullify the whole of the Bolsheviks' organizational and revolutionary work," he approved Gorky's proposal despite the embarrassment it would cause to the Soviet regime.[42] On July 13, 1921, Gorky published a dramatic appeal to the West:

The corn-growing staples are smitten by crop failure, caused by drought. The calamity threatens starvation to millions of Russian people. Think of the Russian people's exhaustion by war and Revolution, which considerably reduced its resistance to disease and its physical endurance. Gloomy days have come to the land of Tolstoy, Dostoyevsky, Mendeleyev, and

[39] Weissman, *Famine Relief*, p. 2.
[40] Ibid., p. 7.
[41] *New York Times*, November 4, 1921, p. 8.
[42] Weissman, *Famine Relief*, pp. 8, 13–14.

Pavlov, and I venture to trust that the cultured European and American people, understanding the tragedy of the Russian people, will immediately succor with bread and medicines.[43]

Gorky's appeal to the West had activated the famine-relief norm by making public the grave conditions in the Soviet Union and by signaling a willingness on the part of the Soviet government to accept famine aid. The key question was whether the West would breach the wall of isolation that it had erected around the Soviet Union in order to let in food and medical assistance.

Herbert Hoover was the linchpin for any American response to the Russian famine. Hoover had directed the famine-relief effort in Belgium in World War I and had overseen American food aid to Europe after the Armistice. In addition, he still functioned as the chairman of the American Relief Association, the U.S. relief agency that had distributed the $100 million congressional appropriation for European reconstruction.[44] Because of these activities, Herbert Hoover had become the personification of American idealism and humanitarianism by 1921; he was looked upon not only as a national leader who had been successful in the many pursuits that he had undertaken in life, but also as one who was concerned for the well-being of those who were less fortunate.

This humanitarian bent in Hoover's character may well be traceable to the staunchly Quaker home in which he was raised. As one biographer has noted, Hoover was reared in a religious and moral setting that taught that "every man was entitled to the bounty of his work, but that the possession of property carried with it an obligation of service to one's neighbors."[45] Hoover himself was uncommonly generous with his personal wealth. A mining engineer who had accumulated an immense fortune by the age of forty, he gave away the great bulk of that fortune relatively early on in his life and insisted on anonymity in many of the largest of his donations.[46] Hoover believed that the business skills that had made him wealthy did not find their ultimate utilization in the mere creation of more riches, but in projects that would

[43] Box 20, ARA Papers.

[44] Technically, the American Relief Association that existed in 1921 was a private organization that Hoover had created as the successor to a governmental entity of the same name. Hoover transferred the ARA name to the successor agency so that it would retain the prestige generated by the American relief effort in Europe, and he also transferred some $7.5 million of the congressional appropriation.

[45] Richard Norton Smith, *An Uncommon Man: The Triumph of Herbert Hoover* (New York: Simon and Schuster, 1984), p. 61.

[46] George Nash, *The Life of Herbert Hoover: The Engineer (1874–1914)* (New York: W. W. Norton and Company, 1983), pp. 525–526, 571–572.

be of benefit to others.[47] Thus when Hoover undertook the relief effort in Belgium that was to consume his energies for five years and lead to ever-widening commitments to the assistance of Europeans devastated by war, the future president told his associates that theirs "was probably the greatest work that will ever come within the scope of our life time," and he led the way in refusing any monetary compensation for his relief work on the grounds that the saving of lives "is of more use than money."[48]

Immediately upon receiving word of Maxim Gorky's plea for aid to the starving people of Russia, Hoover notified the staff of the American Relief Association (ARA) to prepare for a massive relief effort. Then he sent a memorandum to Secretary of State Hughes seeking his approval for a positive response to Gorky: "I would like to suggest that as head of the American Relief Association I send an offer to Gorky by cable of which I enclose a draft. I believe it is a humane obligation upon us to go in if they comply with the requirements set out; if they do not accede we are released from responsibility."[49] The requirements that Hoover spoke of were the same that the ARA had demanded in every one of the twenty-three countries in which it had operated during the period of European reconstruction: a declaration by the Soviet government that aid was needed and that the government approved of the provision of American aid; full freedom of movement for the ARA workers inside Russia; and ARA control of the distribution of food to insure impartiality. In addition, the Soviets were asked to release American citizens held on political charges within Russia; Hoover considered this gesture to be "the most primary evidence of the willingness of the Soviet government to assure the life and liberty of the ARA staff."[50] In return for the Soviets meeting these conditions, the American Relief Association was prepared to undertake a wide-ranging relief effort aimed primarily at children. The Association would also guarantee that no ARA personnel would engage in any political activity in Russia whatsoever.

On July 23, Hoover sent his proposal to Gorky with Hughes's approval. Two days later, Gorky notified Hoover that the Soviet govern-

[47] George Nash, *The Life of Herbert Hoover: The Humanitarian (1914–1917)* (New York: W. W. Norton and Company, 1988), pp. 93–94.

[48] Ibid., p. 95.

[49] Hoover to Hughes, July 22, 1921, box 19, ARA Papers.

[50] Hoover to Walter Lyman Brown, director of European operations of the ARA, August 21, 1921, box 19, ARA Papers. At the time, the State Department believed that there were only seven Americans held on political charges. Thus the U.S. government was surprised when the Soviets released twenty "political prisoners" as a sign of their good faith to Hoover.

ment had accepted the program that Hoover had proposed. On August 10, representatives of the ARA and the Soviet government met in Riga, Latvia in order to conclude a more comprehensive agreement for the provision, transportation, and distribution of American aid. The negotiations dragged on for ten days, bogging down over the American insistence on guarantees that the aid would not be diverted to the Red Army and over Soviet reluctance to grant true freedom of action to the ARA representatives in Russia. At a particularly difficult point in the discussions, a discouraged Hoover cabled from Washington that the ARA team should make every effort to reach an accommodation, but should not depart from the fundamental principles that had proven so valuable in the European relief effort: "Our interest is solely humanitarian. Public feeling as to assistance to Russian famine is one of Christian resignation to duty, but undoubtedly there would be a great sense of relief in the public mind if the Soviets refuse our terms."[51] Fortunately, with compromises on both sides, a formal agreement was concluded on August 20, 1921, and Hoover immediately began to organize the Russian relief effort. Writing to Walter Lyman Brown, the ARA's director of European operations, and to George Haskell, the newly appointed director of Russian operations, Hoover stressed the two principles that were to be fundamental in the outreach to the Soviet Union:

> I wish to impose upon each one of [the ARA representatives in Russia] the supreme importance of their keeping entirely aloof not only from action, but even from any discussion of political and social questions. Our own people are not Bolsheviks, but our mission is solely to save lives and any participation even in discussion will only lead to suspicion of our objectives. . . .
>
> . . . The service which we are able to perform must be given in a true spirit of charity. There must be no discrimination as to politics, race, or creed. Charity can take no interest in international politics, and any individual who does not so conceive his work should immediately be withdrawn upon your initiative.[52]

Political considerations were to be eradicated from all facets of the American relief effort, and effectiveness in feeding the hungry was to be the only criterion of success.

Meanwhile, in Europe, the International Red Cross and the League of Nations had taken up debate on the Russian relief question. The

---

[51] Hoover to Brown, August 17, 1921, box 263, ARA Papers.

[52] Hoover to Brown, August 9, 1921, box 19, ARA Papers; Hoover to Haskell, September 2, 1921, box 20, ARA Papers.

Red Cross called a conference in Geneva on August 10, 1921 to discuss famine aid for the Soviet Union, and this conference formed an International Committee for Russian Relief and appointed Fridtjof Nansen of Norway as high commissioner.[53] In addition, the conference called upon the League of Nations to arrange comprehensive financing for the Russian relief effort.[54] At the League debate on the question in September, the Belgian ambassador demanded swift action, stressing the themes of solidarity and cooperation in time of natural disaster: "Hamlet in princely irony cried 'Words, words, words'. Gentlemen—no brothers—other brothers of ours, human beings, are about to die of hunger at the ends of Europe. I refuse, and you will refuse with me, to feed our brothers who ask for bread, with nothing but words and theories."[55] But the Yugoslav ambassador spoke for many in the Assembly when he objected that aid for the Russian famine would only perpetuate the Soviet regime that threatened the governments of Europe and oppressed the Russian people:

> The problem before us is as follows: We have to save Russia without saving Bolshevism. Indeed, if the Bolshevists still remain in power after the catastrophe of this year, any efforts we may put forth to save Russia will have been made in vain, because the maintenance of Bolshevism in Russia is equivalent to the sure and progressive extermination of the Russian people. I do not think that it will be to the interest of Europe to bring this about.[56]

In the ensuing debate, all participants acknowledged the general obligation of the member governments to help a devastated country in times of famine, but the nagging question of aid to bolshevism remained. In the end, pressure from France prevented the League from enacting any corporate financing scheme for Russian relief, and the Assembly merely exhorted its members to aid the relief effort on their own.[57] Commissioner Nansen was bitter about the lack of more direct

[53] The conference had originally intended to appoint Nansen and Hoover co-commissioners, but Hoover felt that as secretary of commerce he could not accept such a position. Hoover also had been disillusioned about cooperative relief efforts because of French actions that interfered with genuine relief during his work on European reconstruction.

[54] Fisher, *Famine*, pp. 62–65.

[55] League of Nations, *Records of the Second Assembly* (Geneva, 1922), p. 566.

[56] Ibid., pp. 551–552.

[57] The French press had unleashed a barrage of criticism against Nansen and any effort to bring relief to Russia on the grounds that such aid would play right into Soviet hands by stabilizing the Bolshevik government. See "Chronology of Events," p. 5, box 7, ARA Papers; and "Press Reactions," box 260, ARA Papers.

action by the League, and he blamed it on a deliberate campaign by several countries to block relief credits:

> I think that I know what is the underlying thought in this campaign. It is this—that the action we propose will, if it succeeds, strengthen the Soviet government. . . . Suppose that it does help the Russian government. Is there any member of this Assembly who is prepared to say that rather than help the Soviet government, he will allow twenty million people to starve to death? I challenge the Assembly to answer that question.[58]

In the end, despite the lack of a coordinated European financing package for Russian relief, the British, Swedish, German, Swiss, Norwegian, and Belgian governments did provide significant material support for Nansen's international relief committee, allowing the committee to ship tens of thousands of tons of food to the starving in Russia. But if starvation was to be avoided, massive American intervention would still be needed.

ORGANIZING AND FINANCING AMERICAN RELIEF TO RUSSIA

On September 1, 1921, the SS *Phoenix* sailed into Petrograd harbor with the first ARA shipment of wheat, and in the ensuing weeks Hoover's relief workers organized a network of feeding stations that would eventually number some sixteen thousand. ARA personnel oversaw the unloading and transportation of the relief supplies and organized local village committees to assist in preparing and distributing food. In addition, the Americans initiated massive inoculation and sanitation campaigns throughout the famine regions in order to combat the typhus, cholera, and smallpox that had become epidemic.[59] The skills that the ARA personnel had built up through three years of relief work in Europe served them in good stead as they faced the challenges of a dilapidated transportation system, a central government that had little effective control in many of the famine regions, and a degree of widespread starvation that Europe had not known in the darkest days of postwar reconstruction.

Initially, Hoover paid for the Russian operations with $10 million that remained in the ARA treasury as the residual from its European relief efforts. In addition, he drew upon a $3 million contribution that the American Red Cross had made for the purchase of medical supplies. But Hoover knew from the beginning that these sums could not begin to address the monumental needs of the Russian famine. He

[58] League of Nations, *Records of the Second Assembly*, p. 568.
[59] Fisher, *Famine*, pp. 427–444.

also recognized that the immediacy of the crisis in the Soviet Union and anti-Bolshevik feeling in the United States made it impossible to raise sufficient funds through a national voluntary campaign. Therefore, he convinced President Harding to request two appropriations from Congress: a $10 million expenditure to buy grain that could be shipped to the Soviet Union, and an authorization for the War Department to transfer $4 million worth of medical supplies to the ARA.

Hoover feared serious opposition to the relief bills in Congress because of hostility to the Bolsheviks, an economic downturn that had hit the United States in 1921, and the fact that the Harding administration had refused to raise veterans' health benefits as part of its drive to trim the federal budget.[60] So he arranged for the Soviet government to let U.S. press representatives into the famine districts so that they would send home reports on the desperation of the Russian people.[61] Soon the newspapers of the United States were filled with accounts of the famine; an article from the *New York Times* of November 4, 1921 was typical:

> Children are living in the woods and fields like young animals in some parts of the famine district of Saratov, says an official wireless dispatch from Moscow. They are little waifs who have fled from the famine-stricken cities and villages, and they subsist on roots and grass. When adults approach they flee, showing every sign of fear.[62]

Raymond Hopkins has pointed out that famines are a particularly poignant form of human disaster that tend to receive wide-ranging and in-depth coverage and are capable of mobilizing elite sentiment in favor of direct relief.[63] Hoover was certainly aware of this reality, and throughout the Russian relief operation he encouraged the greatest possible press coverage to educate Americans about the depth of the needs in the Soviet Union.

Hoover also sent James Goodrich, the former governor of Indiana, as his personal representative to survey the famine conditions. Upon his return, Goodrich was the leadoff witness in the congressional hearings on the relief appropriation bill. Goodrich reported that the crop in the famine regions was only 7 percent of the already-low 1920 crop; as a result, two-thirds of the children would starve in many prov-

[60] Letter from Vernon Kellog to George Baker, August 9, 1921, box 18, ARA Papers; and Fisher, *Famine*, pp. 140–151.

[61] Cablegram from Hoover to Brown, August 9, 1921, box 19, ARA Papers.

[62] *New York Times*, November 4, 1921, p. 8.

[63] Raymond Hopkins, "Food Aid and Development: The Evolution of the Food Aid Regime," in *Report: Seminar on Food Aid* (Rome: World Food Program, 1983), p. 77.

inces if no outside aid was forthcoming.[64] The former governor spoke glowingly of the relief operations already launched by the ARA, but stressed the immensity of the needs in Russia and urged the Foreign Affairs committee to raise the food appropriation to $20 million.[65] "You would not want, and I would regret to see, this country start in and not do the job right because of the lack of a few million dollars."[66] Hoover, in his own testimony, stressed the traditional generosity of the American people and the relative smallness of the appropriation compared to America's resources: "This country is spending something like one billion dollars a year on tobacco, cosmetics, ice cream, and other non-essentials of that character. It does not look to be a very great strain on the population to take twenty million dollars for a purpose of this kind."[67]

When the bill got to the floor of the House and Senate, supporters pointed to the urgency of the need and the relative prosperity of the United States: "No dollar spent for relief by the U.S. as a government and no dollar ever spent by our people as contributors to the relief of any suffering in any part of the world has ever been a mistake or ever will be. As long as food is here we must help. If there is not time to organize great relief through private sources, we must do it through public sources."[68] There were references to the beneficial effects that grain purchases could have on domestic prices, but most agreed with the sentiments of Senator William Edgar Borah of Idaho, who pointed out that the purchase of fifteen million bushels of grain for Russia would make little dent in a 1921 U.S. market of 2.3 billion bushels: "I do not think that the bill will help the farmers in this country. I vote for it precisely as I would give food to a hungry man at my door in a starving condition—because I haven't the heart to refuse it."[69] The case that supporters made for the appropriation bill was that there was

[64] House Committe on Foreign Affairs, *Hearings on Relief*, p. 5.

[65] Hoover and Goodrich had discussed this matter before the hearings and jointly decided to urge an increase in the appropriation. This did not reflect any reluctance on Harding's part to give aid to Russia, since the original $10 million figure had come from Hoover. Rather, it showed that the famine needs were turning out to be even greater than originally estimated.

[66] House Committee on Foreign Affairs, *Hearings on Relief*, p. 12.

[67] Ibid., p. 39.

[68] *Congressional Record*, 67th Cong., 2d sess., 1921, 62, pt. 1:470.

[69] Ibid., p. 1123. It is interesting to note how tentative supporters were in arguing that the farmers might benefit from the bill. The sponsor, Congressman Joseph Fordney of Michigan, ventured only to say, "If this has any effect on the market in the country, it will have the effect of increasing values. . . . If it benefits anybody it will benefit the farmers of the country." (House Committee on Foreign Affairs, *Hearings on Relief*, p. 3)

a genuine human need in Russia, and that no matter how despicable the Soviet government was, the United States had a moral obligation to help feed the Russian people.

The opposition focused on three major objections to the bill. The first was that it violated a strict construction of the Constitution: "Congress cannot go beyond [maintaining the common defense or promoting the general welfare] and make appropriations for purposes extraneous to this country."[70] The second objection raised to the bill was that the money would be used to stabilize and support a Communist government: "We are placing at the disposal of the Red Armies of Bolshevik Russia twenty million dollars worth of grain for food and seed purposes, with which they are enabled to continue to scatter the destructive seeds of socialism even in fair America."[71] And the final rallying point for the opposition was the needs of unemployed Americans for government assistance, especially veterans and farmers: "There are in this country the unemployed, thrown out of work, with nothing on which to live. The people of this country who have something must first take care of the people who have not."[72]

When the vote came in the House, 181 representatives voted yes, while 71 voted no.[73] Of the 71 no votes, 60 were from Southern states; in fact, almost every Southerner opposed the bill both on constitutional grounds and because of a fear that the relief would aid bolshevism. In the Senate, the bill passed on a voice vote, and a conference-approved bill was passed on a voice vote by both houses on December 22; it was signed immediately by the president. The bill authorizing the War Department to transfer $4 million worth of medical supplies to the ARA for Russian relief was passed and signed into law on January 12, 1922.[74]

Armed with the congressional appropriation, Hoover purchased 660,000 tons of grain during the next ten months.[75] Because of the

[70] *Congressional Record*, 67th Cong., 2d sess., 1921, 62, pt. 1:472.

[71] Ibid., p. 481.

[72] Ibid., p. 468. Several farm-state representatives tried to turn the $20 million appropriation toward a revolving-credit fund for farmers, while veterans' supporters attempted to include an appropriation for veterans' health care. Both efforts were defeated.

[73] The large number of abstentions (175) occurred because the vote came on December 17, when many of the members had already left Washington for the Christmas recess.

[74] Although the bill stipulated a ceiling of $4 million, this was a ceiling on the original cost to the government of the medicines that were to be transferred. In 1921 the market value of the transferred materials was approximately $8 million.

[75] Fisher, *Famine*, p. 448. Technically, the purchases were made by the U.S. Grain

difficulty of transferring these foods within Russia, the grain purchases had to be made gradually over the entire period of Russian
relief. In organizing this vast transfer of foodstuffs, Hoover clearly
thought of himself as an arm of the U.S. government. He told the ARA
board in early 1922 that "the A.R.A. is working under funds derived
from a Congressional appropriation and we are acting as distributors
for the American government. When the appropriation is expended
and distributed, then the A.R.A. quits."[76]

THE SOVIET GOLD CONTRIBUTION

Shortly after the Riga agreement between the ARA and the Soviet
government was signed in August, Herbert Hoover took steps to insure that the Soviet government was doing its full share to alleviate
the famine in Russia. Invoking a principle that had guided the American relief efforts to Central Europe after World War I, Hoover told the
ARA board that external assistance should be seen as a supplement to
internal disaster relief, not as a substitute.[77] Accordingly, he requested
the Soviet government to use the $10 million in gold that it still had
from the imperial treasury to buy grain to feed the hungry in Russia.[78]
Said Hoover to his European chief, "We wish to force their hand to do
their share of the adult feeding."[79]

In attempting to force the Soviet government to do its share for the
famine-relief effort, Hoover was not seeking a new market for American grain. In fact, the Commerce secretary encouraged the Russians
to buy grain in the Balkans, which had a surplus of some ten million

---

Purchasing Commission, headed by President Harding, but in fact Hoover ran the entire operation.

[76] Minutes of the ARA Board meeting, March 11, 1922, p. 7, box 113, ARA Papers.

[77] Minutes of the ARA board meeting, August 14, 1921, p. 4, box 16, ARA Papers.

[78] As previously noted, the U.S. government believed that the Soviets actually held
some $300 million worth of gold. Most of this had been confiscated from private Rus-
sian citizens at the time of the Revolution, but some $10 million of it had been taken
from the old imperial treasury. The United States did not recognize the Soviet title even
to the imperial gold, since the United States still recognized the democratic Russian
government of March 1917; but at least the $10 million did belong to the government
of Russia, and so Hoover believed that it should be expended for relief of the Russian
people.

[79] Hoover to Brown, August 26, 1921, box 110, ARA Papers. The ARA had always had
a special devotion to the feeding of children. In fact, the Riga agreement spoke of the
ARA's commitment only in terms of feeding children, since the funds that the ARA had
on hand in August 1921 had been donated only for the feeding of children. Fortunately,
the congressional appropriation of December had no such restriction, and thus Hoover
was able to expand the ARA effort in Russia to include adults as well.

bushels.[80] The Soviets responded that they were more than willing to make the suggested purchases of grain, but that they preferred to buy in the American market, since they had no purchasing or transportation network in the Balkans.[81] Hoover agreed to supply American grain at cost, but he wanted the Soviets to understand that there was absolutely no need for them to spend the $10 million in the United States: "We do not wish to be put in the position of having any commercial color to the American gift."[82]

Actually, the Soviet preference to buy grain in the United States created a serious problem for the Harding administration. For three years the United States government had declared that the Soviets had no legitimate title to any of the gold in their control, including that contained in the former imperial treasury. Now Hoover was proposing that the United States accept Soviet title to that gold in order to pay for grain for famine relief. The State Department was at first reluctant to make the exception to the gold ban, but finally relented on the grounds that "the tender of this gold constitutes a special case in view of the fact that the gold is being expended for humanitarian purposes."[83] So great was the sensitivity of the State and Treasury departments on this subject that Hoover asked the ARA leadership to keep secret the facts of the Soviet grain purchase as long as possible: "These two Departments have, as you know, strenuously opposed the entrance of any Soviet gold to the U.S. in the past, which will probably cause them tremendous trouble in answering questions as to why a distinction was made in our case."[84]

In collaboration with the Soviet government, it was decided that the U.S. congressional appropriation should be used predominantly for the purchase of grain to feed the Russian people, while the $10 million Soviet gold purchase should be devoted to buying seed grains for the new harvest. Hoover requested ARA agricultural experts working in the Soviet Union to determine which seed grains would be most productive in the Russian climate, and he made seed purchases strictly according to the recommendations he received from the field. When the varieties that had been suggested were completely depleted on the U.S. market, Hoover began to buy seed on the Canadian mar-

[80] Hoover to Brown, August 26, 1921, box 110, ARA Papers; and Phillip Carroll, acting ARA Chief in Russia, to Maxim Litvinov, Soviet Assistant Commissar for Foreign Affairs, August 30, 1921, box 20, ARA Papers.

[81] "Chronology of Events," September 16, 1921.

[82] Cablegram from Hoover to Brown, December 27, 1921, box 110, ARA Papers.

[83] Letter from Secretary of State Charles Evans Hughes to Secretary of the Treasury Andrew Mellon, January 10, 1922, box 290, ARA Papers.

[84] Hoover to Perrin Galpin, January 27, 1922, box 250, ARA Papers.

ket in order to meet the Russian need.[85] Similarly, when the ARA
could not secure American ships at reasonable prices to transport
foodstuffs and grain to Russia, Hoover authorized the use of non-
American vessels for transport.[86]

Eventually, news of the Soviet gold purchase did become public,
and when it did Hoover went to great lengths to emphasize that the
Bolshevik government was doing all in its power to alleviate the famine. ARA literature in 1922 very prominently listed the $10 million
Soviet contribution as part of the relief effort, and it even calculated
the dollar value of the "in-kind" contributions which the Soviet government had made to the ARA's work for such items as the provision
of offices in Russia, the transportation of ARA food on the Russian rail
system, and the provision of personnel in the local food kitchens.[87] In
every possible way, Hoover hoped to sustain American support for the
Russian relief effort by pointing to a vigorous campaign by the Soviet
government to do its own share for famine relief, even at the cost of
sacrificing a potentially valuable basis for future anti-Bolshevik propaganda.

EXPANSION AND TERMINATION OF THE RELIEF CAMPAIGN

The congressional appropriation allowed the ARA to expand its operations sufficiently to meet the full needs of the Russian people in the
famine-affected provinces, and no child or adult was turned away during the harsh winter of 1922 because of a lack of available food.[88] By
February of that year, there were 35,000 ARA distribution centers in
the Soviet Union, and 10.5 million people were eating daily in ARA
kitchens. More than 7 million Russians were inoculated for typhus
and smallpox during 1922, and the incidence of typhus fell from 19
per thousand to .3 per thousand in one year. With the seed grain that
had been provided through ARA channels, some 8 million acres were
planted in the worst of the famine regions, and the fear that a lack of
seed grain would bring continuing famine was alleviated. Just as important as the material resources that the ARA provided were the skill
and expertise of the American relief personnel; both the inoculation
campaign and the agricultural rejuvenation effort in the famine dis-

[85] Hoover to Harding, January 19, 1922, box 278, ARA Papers.

[86] Hoover to Clarence Stetson, January 10, 1922, box 263, ARA Papers.

[87] "American Relief Association: 1922 Report," p. 16, box 14, ARA Papers. Eventually,
the gold purchases came to total $12 million because the Ukrainian Republic purchased
$2 million dollars worth of food with its own gold.

[88] The European relief Committee was, of course, contributing substantially, but the
bulk of the work was carried out by the ARA.

tricts drew heavily upon the experience that the U.S. relief workers had gained in postwar European reconstruction.

By late 1922, crop reports submitted by ARA staff representatives in Russia pointed to a good harvest. The charitable doctrine of the American Relief Association had always held that food assistance should be an emergency endeavor rather than a long-term social-welfare program, and that "American charity should be withdrawn instantly whenever the economic recovery either of the nation or of a given locality enabled it to produce or purchase supplies sufficient to carry the population."[89] Accordingly, Hoover ordered a gradual phaseout of U.S. aid to take effect whenever given regions achieved food self-sufficiency. This decision was reinforced in December 1922 when the British government notified the United States that the Soviet government had begun exporting large amounts of wheat from the Ukraine to other parts of Europe.[90]

The actual liquidation of ARA operations in the Soviet Union took six months, as the staff disengaged from the feeding projects that still remained and turned over the sizeable remaining stockpiles of food to the provincial food representatives. In almost every province during the spring of 1923, there was an elaborate farewell ceremony to thank the Americans for their service to the Russian people; and on July 10, the Soviet government issued a formal commendation of the American relief effort:

> In the trying hour of a great and overwhelming disaster, the people of the United States, represented by the A.R.A., responded to the needs of the population, already exhausted by intervention and blockade, in the famine stricken parts of Russia and Federated Republics. Unselfishly, the A.R.A. came to the aid of the people and organized on a broad scale the supply and distribution of food products and other articles of prime necessity. Due to the enormous and entirely disinterested efforts of the A.R.A., millions of people of all ages were saved from the horrible catastrophe which threatened them.[91]

The Soviet government, which had been at odds with the United States ever since the Bolshevik Revolution, was thanking America for saving it from a crisis that even Lenin had thought would doom the Communist movement. And the United States, which had intervened in Russia only to bring food to starving men, women, and children,

[89] "American Relief Association: 1922 Report," p. 2.

[90] Hoover had requested the British to watch closely European ports for signs of Soviet grain-export activity. It was the confirmation of large Russian exports that led Hoover to decide that the time had come to terminate the ARA program in the Soviet Union.

[91] Fisher, *Famine*, p. 398.

was now about to resume its policy of total isolation with the somewhat diminished hope that the Soviet government would still fall in some future crisis.

In March 1923, Secretary of State Hughes made clear that the basic requirements for U.S. recognition of and establishment of trade relations with the Soviet Union had not changed, nor had the U.S. conviction that the Soviet government continued to refuse to meet these requirements:

> Not only would it be a mistaken policy to give encouragement to repudiation and confiscation, but it is also important to remember that there should be no encouragement to those efforts of the Soviet authorities to visit upon other peoples the disasters that have overwhelmed the Russian people. . . .
>
> Now I desire to see evidence of the abandonment of that policy. I desire to see a basis for helpfulness. We want to help, . . . but the world we desire is a world not threatened with the destructive propaganda of the Soviet authorities, and one in which there will be good faith and the recognition of obligations and a sound basis of international intercourse.[92]

The speech that President Harding was to deliver on the day he died reiterated the anti-Bolshevik policies to which the United States had hewed since 1920, and the newly inaugurated President Calvin Coolidge quickly confirmed the foreign policy that sought to isolate the Soviet regime: "Whenever there appears any disposition to compensate our citizens who were despoiled, and to recognize the debt contracted with our government, . . . whenever the active spirit of enmity to our institutions is abated, our country ought then to be the first to go to the economic and moral rescue of Russia."[93]

Herbert Hoover, despite the efforts that he had made during the relief campaign to assure the American people that the Soviet government was doing its part to feed the hungry in Russia, had not changed his opinions about bolshevism or about American foreign policy toward the Soviet Union. Writing to the American-Russian Chamber of Commerce in June 1923, Hoover stated that the United States should not in any way support a government pledged to the destruction of private property and to world revolution, and he reiterated his contention that no encouragement regarding future trade with Russia should be given to American businessmen.[94] For Hoover, as for the U.S. gov-

[92] Xenia Eudin and Harold Fisher, *Soviet Russia and the West, 1920–1927* (Stanford: Stanford University Press, 1957), pp. 193–194.

[93] Ibid., p. 194.

[94] Hoover to S. R. Bertron, June 11, 1923, box 250, ARA Papers. The American-Russian Chamber of Commerce had been founded to promote commerce during the tsarist

ernment as a whole, the famine-relief episode had not changed American-Soviet relations or altered the course of policy that should be taken toward the first Communist government in the world. Bolshevism still remained something threatening to U.S. interests, and it was to be isolated in the hope that it would either perish or radically change.

EXPLAINING THE DECISION ON FAMINE RELIEF

The foreign policy of the United States in 1921 was hostile to the Soviet Union and sought the downfall of the Bolshevik regime. Yet when a historic challenge to Bolshevik rule surfaced in the Russian famine of 1921, the United States government provided the food and medical supplies necessary to avert social disintegration in the Soviet empire. As a result, the Bolshevik regime survived a crisis that even Lenin had believed would doom the Communist movement.[95] How can this intervention by the United States government be explained?

Four possible explanations have been suggested for the American decision to send food aid to the Soviet Union: (1) the United States was seeking to subvert the Bolshevik government; (2) the United States undertook the famine-relief effort as a way of opening trade with the Soviet Union; (3) the ARA was a convenient way to dispose of the American grain surplus of 1921; and (4) leading U.S. decision makers, especially Hoover, believed that America had a moral obligation to feed starving Russians despite the hostility of the Soviet government to American interests. Of these hypothetical explanations, only the last is consistent with the facts of the American Relief Association campaign of 1921.

The idea that the ARA aid to the Soviet Union was a subterfuge for destabilization was first proposed by official Soviet historical tracts in the 1950s. In the edition of the *Great Soviet Encyclopedia* printed in 1950, it was argued that "the A.R.A. used this opportunity to create an apparatus in Soviet Russia for spying and wrecking activities and for supporting counterrevolutionary elements. The counterrevolutionary activities of the A.R.A. provoked firm protests from the wide masses of toilers in Soviet Russia."[96]

---

regime; it had supported the democratic revolution of March 1917, but remained staunchly anti-Bolshevik.

[95] For assessments of the stabilizing effects that American famine relief had on the Soviet government, see George Kennan, *Russia and the West under Lenin and Stalin* (Boston: Little, Brown and Company, 1961), pp. 180–181; and Weissman, *Famine Relief*, pp. 135, 281.

[96] Weissman, *Famine Relief*, p. 185.

There are several problems with such an explanation. In the first place, the original *Great Soviet Encyclopedia* of 1926 presented the ARA assistance to the Soviet Union as a purely philanthropic endeavor that fed ten million Russians at the height of the famine.[97] Second, during the entire two years that the ARA functioned in Russia, the Soviet government never complained about any anti-Bolshevik efforts by the ARA; moreover, upon the termination of the relief effort, the Soviet government glowingly praised the Association and the U.S. government for all that they had done to help the Soviet people. Finally, the papers and internal memorandums of the American Relief Association consistently point to a rigid prohibition of any political activity by ARA personnel. Hoover and his lieutenants even went so far as to make sure that no American personnel sent to Russia had had any contact with pre-Bolshevik Russia, a stringent requirement that made the early operations of the ARA much more arduous. The assertion that the United States government provided famine relief to Russia as part of an effort to undermine the Bolshevik government should be seen for what it is, propaganda from the 1950s that has no historical basis in fact.

The idea that the United States was willing to provide famine relief as a prelude to opening trade relations with the Soviet Union does not date from the 1950s; in fact, many members of the Soviet government believed from the beginning that this was the factor motivating U.S. aid. In an interview given shortly after the start of the American relief program, Trotsky told the Russian people that the ARA workers were not philanthropists, but missionaries of capitalism who sought to open Russian markets to the U.S. in order to relieve "the great and unprecedented trade-industrial crisis all over the world, especially in America and England."[98] The main problem with this interpretation is that the very U.S. government officials who organized the American relief effort were among those in the United States most opposed to resuming trade with the Soviet Union. When Governor Goodrich met with the Soviet leadership in 1922 to discuss the issue of U.S.-Soviet trade, Secretary of State Hughes and Hoover ordered him to maintain the demands that had long been made by the U.S. as a condition for resumption of commerce: the acknowledgment of private property, the recognition of past debts, and an end to Soviet propaganda campaigns in Europe.[99] And at every juncture when there was a possibility of reopening trade or extending recognition to the Soviet Union, Hughes

[97] Ibid., p. 184.
[98] *Sputnik Kommunista* (Moscow), September 4, 1921, p. 15; text and translation contained in box 216, ARA Papers.
[99] Goodrich Notes, box 276, ARA Papers.

and Hoover reiterated their unbending opposition, both publicly and privately. If the famine-relief aid was conceived as an opening to Russia, it is hard to understand why U.S.-Soviet trade figures remained flat and negligible during the period from 1921 to 1923 and why there does not exist any positive evidence whatsoever to suggest that during this period the U.S. initiated steps toward normalization of trade and diplomatic relations with the Soviet Union (see Table 3.2).

The argument that the food aid to Russia was motivated by a desire to reduce the American grain surplus and raise crop prices at least has some evidence to support it. During the congressional debate, several senators and representatives pointed to the fact that the appropriation *might* help farmers in the United States; and in speaking of the ARA relief work in later years, Hoover argued that there was some beneficial effect upon farm prices because of the grain purchases for Russian relief. But once again, the evidence conflicts at critical points with the hypothesis that U.S. famine-relief policy toward Russia was significantly motivated by a desire to boost domestic farm prices. If domestic farm prices had been determining U.S. aid policies, Hoover would never have suggested that the Soviets purchase $10 million worth of grain in the Balkans. Nor would Hoover have gone to Canada to purchase large amounts of a seed grain that had been completely sold out in the U.S. market. If the Harding administration had wanted

TABLE 3.2
U.S. Trade with the Soviet Union, 1913–23

	Imports from the Soviet Union	*Exports to the Soviet Union*
1913	$24,377,070	$ 26,909,707
1914	14,569,397	27,956,337
1915	3,086,595	169,993,904
1916	8,618,695	470,508,254
1917	14,514,431	424,510,509
1918	10,760,007	17,335,518
1919	9,663,088	82,436,185
1920	12,480,516	28,717,518
1921	1,073,381	3,073,556
1922	591,564	2,818,920
1923	1,515,779	3,563,148

Source: Frederick Schuman, *American Policy toward Russia since 1917* (New York: International Publishers, 1928), pp. 58–61.

Note: The statistics for 1918–20 represent trade with those sections of the Soviet Union under the White armies while the Allies were blockading trade with other parts of the Soviet Union. The statistics for 1921–23 do not include the food and medicine sent from the United States to the Soviet Union as part of the famine-relief effort.

to use the famine-relief appropriation to raise agricultural prices, it would have expended the federal monies all at once in order to give a boost to the sagging market, rather than making purchases over a six-month period. And if the U.S. government had wanted to send food to Russia in order to justify spending federal monies on commodity purchases, it would have selected the crops it was going to purchase according to market conditions; instead, the internal memorandums of the ARA indicate quite clearly that grain purchases were based on the climatic and nutritional needs of Russia, and timed accordingly.

The only convincing explanation for U.S. aid to Russia during the famine of 1921 is that leading American decision makers believed that the U.S. had a moral obligation to come to the assistance of the Russian people. Hoover moved immediately to answer Gorky's plea, Harding asked Congress for a governmental appropriation, and Hughes approved the famine-relief program because they were convinced that America's abundance of food imposed upon it special obligations to help those in desperate need. Internal administration memorandums and the papers of the ARA speak time and again of "the humanitarian responsibility" and the "Christian duty" of the U.S. to come to the aid of the Russian people. Never is there any mention of subordinating that humanitarian responsibility to interest-based motives of American foreign policy or of using the famine-relief program as a subterfuge for other objectives. Neither is there any mention of domestic political pressure to provide famine relief; in fact, the leadership of the Harding administration was apprehensive that the proposed congressional appropriation might meet stiff opposition and thus sought to disseminate information about the depth of the Russian famine. The moral norm of famine relief was operative and dominant at every vital stage of U.S. decision making about disaster assistance to the Soviet Union because leading members of the Harding administration had internalized that norm and felt compelled to follow it.

Herbert Hoover was the prime mover behind the Russian relief effort, and his actions from 1921 to 1923 point in a particularly powerful way to the fact that the U.S. response to the Soviet famine was shaped by the famine-relief norm. During his work in Europe, Hoover had become wholeheartedly committed to the central tenets of that norm: that the governments of the world, particularly those with food surpluses, have an obligation to help countries facing famine; that such aid should be for emergency purposes only and should be distributed without regard to political, religious, or ethnic considerations; and that considerations of international politics should not be allowed to interfere in the international response to famine conditions. At every step in the organization and implementation of the ARA relief operations in Russia, Hoover was guided by these tenets. Upon receiving Gorky's plea, he did not hesitate even for a day, but immediately began to mobilize the U.S. government in support of food aid even though he recognized that such aid might well stabilize the Soviet regime. In recruiting and instructing the ARA personnel for Russia, Hoover endeavored strenuously to incorporate in the U.S. relief operation an apolitical ethic that sought only to distribute food effectively and impartially. And when the actual food emergency was over, Hoover withdrew American food aid in keeping with the famine-relief norm's delimited obligation to provide only temporary food assistance, rather than continuing agricultural support. At every stage in the Russian aid operation, Hoover betrayed a deeply felt commitment to the principles of the famine-relief norm and a resentment of those who did not share that commitment. Hoover was not unaware of the importance of international politics and American economic and strategic interests, but in the case of famine relief to Russia he allowed the moral obligation of aiding those who were starving to override considerations of economic, political, and strategic interest.

Thus the case of famine relief to the Soviet Union is an instance in which the first theoretical pathway from moral norms to state conduct was operative: a consensually held international moral norm was internalized by leading members of the U.S. government and helped to shape a critical foreign-policy decision. Without consistent reference to the power of international moral norms, it is impossible to understand why the United States responded to Gorky's plaintive call for help, why the Harding administration was willing to appropriate almost 1 percent of the federal budget for aid to the Soviet Union, or why the United States did not let the food crisis in Russia grow so great that the pressure on the Soviet government would have been overwhelming. But by recognizing the power of moral norms to affect the consciences of state leaders, the answers to all of these questions become quite clear.

Chapter Four

AMERICA'S RENUNCIATION OF CHEMICAL
AND BIOLOGICAL WARFARE

ON NOVEMBER 25, 1969, President Richard Nixon held a news conference to announce a series of decisions that were to shape U.S. policy on chemical and biological warfare for at least twenty years. The president stated that the United States would unilaterally destroy its stockpiles of biological weapons, formally pledge not to initiate the use of lethal chemical weapons in warfare, and begin ratification proceedings on the Geneva Protocol of 1925, which forbade first use of either chemical or biological weapons in combat. Nixon's announcement was not an unexpected one, since the topic of chemical and biological weapons had been hotly debated during the preceding months, both in Congress and in the public at large. But from the viewpoint of the study of international relations, the American decision to abandon the field of offensive chemical and biological warfare is an intriguing one: it included the first no-first-use pledge in American history (a precedent the Pentagon was loath to accept); it constituted the first elimination of an entire class of U.S. weapons for reasons other than obsolescence; and it committed the United States to unilaterally abandoning a form of warfare without any formal assurances that other nations would follow suit. Why did the United States take this step, especially since it clashed in fundamental ways with the philosophical stance that underlay America's other efforts at arms control during the 1960s?

There were several factors that contributed to the Nixon decisions on chemical and biological warfare. But the most important of these in the president's mind was the domestic political pressure that arose from the public perception that United States policies were violating the international moral norm against chemical and biological warfare. Throughout 1969, leading segments of the scientific community, the media, and Congress had acted in concert to press for a reversal of America's policies, and they used the moral norm proscribing chemical and biological warfare in order to mobilize significant segments of American society in favor of a change in U.S. policy.

As a result of this mobilization, President Nixon was faced with two choices: he could reaffirm existing U.S. policies on chemical and biological weapons and thus subject his administration to significant political and reputational damage; or he could reverse America's policies and lend a patina of moral respectability to the administration's foreign policy. Not surprisingly, he chose the latter option. Thus the 1969 decisions on chemical and biological warfare are an example of the operation of the second pathway for international moral norms that was described in chapter 2: opponents of a particular policy sought to change that policy by mobilizing around the violation of a moral norm in order to build domestic political pressure for change.

"CONDEMNED BY THE GENERAL OPINION OF THE CIVILIZED WORLD"

In a 1969 report on the status of chemical and biological weaponry in the world, a United Nations team of experts defined chemical weapons as "chemical substances, whether gaseous, liquid, or solid, which might be employed because of their direct toxic effects on man, animals, and plants." The same report defined biological (also known as bacteriological) weapons as "living organisms, whatever their nature, or infective material derived from them, which are intended to cause disease or death in man, animals, or plants, and which depend for their effects on the ability to multiply in the person, animal or plant attacked."[1] Ever since chemical and biological warfare (CBW) became a potential method of waging major wars in the late nineteenth century, the peoples of the world have regarded these weapons with a unique degree of horror and condemnation, and the international moral norm proscribing CBW arose in order to insure that these weapons of mass destruction would not be incorporated into the arsenals of the world's armies and used in combat.

The origins of this effort to prevent the use of chemical and biological weapons can be traced to the major international conferences that dealt with warfare in the period just before World War I. At the Brussels Convention of 1874, the major nations of the world prohibited both the use of poison weapons in war and the employment of arms designed to cause unnecessary suffering. At the first International Peace Conference at The Hague in 1899, the European powers agreed to "abstain from the use of projectiles, the objective of which is the diffusion of asphyxiating or deleterious gases."[2] And at the Hague

[1] United Nations, *Chemical and Bacteriological (Biological) Weapons and the Effects of Their Possible Use: A Report to the Secretary General* (New York: United Nations, 1969), p. 5.

[2] Stockholm International Peace Research Institute (SIPRI), *The Problem of Chemical and Biological Warfare*, vol. 4: *Chemical and Biological Disarmament Negotiations, 1920–1970* (New York: Humanities Press, 1971), p. 17.

Conference of 1907, the signatories reiterated their commitments to refrain from the use of gas and chemicals in any type of combat.

But it was the experience of massive chemical warfare in World War I that gave the moral norm against CBW the strength, clarity, and comprehensiveness that it enjoys today. Some seventeen thousand chemical troops were deployed, over one hundred tons of chemical weapons were utilized, and more than 1.3 million casualties were attributable to gas warfare, including ninety-one thousand deaths (see Tables 4.1 and 4.2). Just as important as the number of casualties were the uniquely traumatizing effects that the use of chemical weapons had upon the units that saw chemical warfare firsthand; there

TABLE 4.1
Casualties from Chemical-Warfare Agents in World War I
(Fatal and Nonfatal)

Germany	200,000
France	190,000
British Empire	189,000
Austria-Hungary	100,000
Italy	60,000
Russia	475,000
U.S.	73,000
Total	1,287,000

Source: Stockholm International Peace Research Institute, *The Problem of Chemical and Biological Warfare*, vol. 4, *Chemical and Biological Disarmament Negotiations, 1920–1970* (New York: Humanities Press, 1971), pp. 128–129.

TABLE 4.2
Tons of Chemical-Warfare Agents Used in World War I

	1915	*1916*	*1917*	*1918*	*Total*
Germany	2.9	7.0	15.0	28.0	52.9
France	0.3	3.5	7.5	15.0	26.3
British Empire	0.2	1.6	4.9	7.7	14.4
Austria-Hungary	0.0	0.8	2.7	4.4	7.9
Italy	0.0	0.4	2.5	3.4	6.3
Russia	0.2	1.8	2.7	0.0	4.7
U.S.	0.0	0.0	0.0	1.0	1.0
Total	3.6	15.1	35.3	59.5	113.5

Source: Stockholm International Peace Research Institute, *The Problem of Chemical and Biological Warfare*, vol. 4, *Chemical and Biological Disarmament Negotiations, 1920–1970* (New York: Humanities Press, 1971), pp. 128–129.

seemed to be a particularly insidious dimension to this invisible killer, and the men who returned home to tell of their war experiences impressed upon the societies of Europe the sheer terror and ghastly form of death that accompanied CBW. As a result, the immediate postwar period witnessed a dramatic series of international conferences designed to highlight the immorality of chemical and biological warfare and to insure that these weapons were never again used in combat.

This idea that certain types of weapons and tactics should be inadmissible in warfare did not begin with the effort to proscribe CBW after World War I. For the "just-war" tradition, the primary ethical consensus about the conduct of war in Western culture, had held for some fifteen centuries before 1914 that there were rules of warfare that rendered some tactics and weapons unacceptable because of the pain that they inflicted or because of their inability to discriminate between civilians and soldiers.[3] Those who were seeking to ban CBW after World War I appealed to this tradition and argued that of all the immoral tactics proscribed by the just-war tradition, none was so menacing or dehumanizing as chemical and biological warfare. Antigas proponents in America, France, and Great Britain waged successful grass roots campaigns to generate enthusiasm for the renunciation of all chemical weapons, and they enlisted veterans and widows and orphans from the war in order to make their case poignantly.[4]

As a consequence of these efforts, the leading governments of the world began to press for international agreements barring the use of chemical and biological weapons in war. In 1920 the British delegation to the League of Nations proposed that the League should take concrete steps to reinforce the conviction of the world community that the use of poison gas was "fundamentally cruel."[5] In the 1922 Washington Treaty for the Limitation of Naval Armaments, the signatories pledged never to resort to the use of gas in warfare. And in 1925 the League convened a conference at Geneva in an effort to control the spread of arms in the world, setting the stage for what was to become the primary codification of the international ban on chemical and biological weapons. During the course of the Geneva Conference, the

[3] For a discussion of the historical development of the just-war tradition, see Frederick Russell, *The Just War in the Middle Ages* (Cambridge: Cambridge University Press, 1975); and Roland Bainton, *Christian Attitudes toward War and Peace* (New York: Abingdon Press, 1960).

[4] In 1922 the American Advisory Committee on Disarmament, appointed by President Harding, held a national poll that found 366,975 respondents opposed to any use of gas in warfare, and 19 in favor of allowing gas warfare. See Frederic Brown, *Chemical Warfare: A Study in Restraints* (Princeton: Princeton University Press, 1968), p. 69.

[5] SIPRI, *Disarmament Negotiations*, p. 19.

United States suggested that the participants draw up a protocol banning the export of all poisonous gases. The French delegation suggested that the protocol should be broader, so as to proscribe any use of gas in warfare. The Polish representatives expanded the protocol still further to include a ban on bacteriological weapons, which were then at a rudimentary, though ominous, state of development. After several weeks of debate, on June 17, 1925, the parties to the convention signed the Geneva Protocol on the Prohibition of Poison Gases and Bacteriological Weapons. The Geneva Protocol clearly rooted the prohibition of gas and bacteriological warfare in the fact that it had been "justly condemned by the general opinion of the civilized world." The protocol provided that all signatories would renounce the combat use of asphyxiating and poisonous gases, as well as all bacteriological agents. It further provided that the parties would "exert every effort to induce other States to accede to the present agreement."[6] In 1925 more than thirty countries ratified the protocol. By 1969 eighty-seven countries had ratified it.[7] The United States was not among them.

Two points of clarification regarding the Geneva Protocol should be mentioned, since they bear directly upon the 1969 U.S. decision on CBW. First, many of the countries that ratified the protocol between 1926 and 1969 reserved the right to retaliate with gas or bacteriological weapons against nations that initiated their use in combat. Thus the Geneva Protocol generally came to constitute a prohibition against the first use of chemical or biological weapons rather than a blanket prohibition of all uses. Second, in 1930 Great Britain submitted to the International Disarmament Commission a brief arguing that tear gas should be interpreted as prohibited under the protocol. Since there was some discrepancy in translation between the original French and the English versions of the protocol, the British wanted to insure that there was general agreement that tear gas and indeed all incapacitating gases were banned in warfare. The French, Soviet, Chinese, and Italian delegations affirmed the British interpretation, and it came to be accepted as the authoritative reading of the agreement. Only the U.S. delegation objected, but since the United States was not a signatory, this did not affect the ruling of the International Disarmament Commission.[8]

[6] U.S. Congress, House, Committee on Foreign Affairs, Subcommittee on National Security Policy and Scientific Developments, *Hearings on Chemical-Biological Warfare: U.S. Policies and International Effects*, 91st Cong., 2d sess., 1969 (Washington: U.S. Government Printing Office, 1970), p. 269.

[7] Ibid., p. 270.

[8] SIPRI, *Disarmament Negotiations*, pp. 102–103. For a more extensive treatment of the tear gas question, see R. R. Baxter and Thomas Buergenthal, "Legal Aspects of the

The ban on chemical and biological weapons was surprisingly well observed during the period from 1919 to 1969. Mustard gas was used by Italy against Ethiopia during the 1930s, and sanctions by the League of Nations did little to end the killing of Haile Selassie's troops by poison gas. But no chemical or biological weapons were used during World War II, despite the fact that all major participants had significant stockpiles of chemical weapons. In his investigation of why chemical agents were not utilized in the period from 1939 to 1945, Frederic Brown argues that each of the major participants did consider employing chemical weapons during the war. But Brown points to four major constraints that operated upon American, British, and German state decision makers to hinder the deployment of chemical weapons: (1) during the early years, mass public opinion in Britain and Germany would not countenance the introduction of chemical weapons; (2) even when mass public opinion ceased to be an effective restraint, elite opinion continued to oppose breaking the barrier against chemical weapons; (3) there was a significant belief that the introduction of chemical weapons by one side would provide only a temporary military advantage; and (4) moral opposition to chemical weapons existed, as well as questions about the military value of chemical warfare.[9] Thus while one cannot say that the international ban on CBW precluded the use of chemical weapons in World War II, the international moral norm against the use of chemical weapons did have significant direct and indirect effects that greatly hindered recourse to chemical warfare.[10]

In 1946 the UN General Assembly established a commission to deal with the growth of "weapons of mass destruction" in the world's arsenal. Originally designed to deal primarily with nuclear issues, the commission was instructed in 1948 to consider also issues related to lethal chemical and biological weapons, since these were also to be classified as weapons of mass destruction. But it was not until the 1960s that pressure for chemical and biological disarmament began to intensify significantly. In part, this pressure arose from debate

---

Geneva Protocol of 1925," in *The Control of Chemical and Biological Weapons* (New York: Carnegie Endowment for International Peace, 1971), pp. 1–23.

[9] Brown, *Chemical Warfare*, pp. 150–154, 176–182, 212–213, 217–218, 244–245.

[10] George Bunn, former legal counsel to the U.S. Arms Control and Disarmament Agency, carried out a historical investigation of the scope and force of the Geneva Protocol. He concluded that it was the protocol, institutionalizing an international norm, that largely prevented nations from having recourse to CBW in World War II. "The threat of retaliation, of course, constituted a deterrent. But it was the Protocol that placed poison gas and germs in a special class and provided a standard for belligerents to follow." (House Subcommittee on National Security Policy, *Hearings on Chemical-Biological Warfare*, p. 50.)

about the use of tear gas by the United States in Vietnam and the use of mustard gas by Egypt in 1967. In part, it arose from advances in microbiology that made biological warfare more threatening and more alluring in the minds of many scientists and military experts. And, in part, the thrust for advances in chemical and biological disarmament arose as part of the general movement toward arms control that developed during the 1960s. In 1964 the Pugwash Conference, an international body of scholars interested in arms control, began to study the issue of CBW in depth, and for the next decade the conference provided significant technical data, policy analysis, and moral reflections designed to stimulate progress toward the elimination of chemical and biological weapons.[11] In 1966 an influential documentary by the BBC stirred widespread public debate in the English-speaking world on the future of chemical and biological weapons. And in 1966 and 1968, the United Nations declared the principles of the Geneva Protocol to be customary international law and thus binding on all nations.

In the 1969 UN report on the dangers that CBW posed to the world, leading scientists from throughout the world emphasized the need for maintaining the international norm against the use of chemical or biological weapons: "All weapons of war are destructive of human life, but chemical and biological weapons are in a class of their own as armaments which exercise their effects solely on living matter. . . . Were these weapons ever to be used on a large scale in war, no one could predict how enduring the effects would be, and how they would affect the structure of society and the environment in which we live."[12] It was this special horror with which the peoples of the world regarded chemical and biological warfare that had spurred the erection of a moral norm proscribing CBW; and it was this same horror that gave the norm great strength in the international system.

UNITED STATES POLICY ON CHEMICAL AND BIOLOGICAL WARFARE

On June 28, 1918, President Woodrow Wilson established the Chemical Warfare Service under his wartime powers in order to allow the United States to "develop, produce and test materials and apparatus for gas warfare, and to organize and train officers and troops in meth-

[11] The Pugwash Conference in 1967 merged with the Stockholm International Peace Research Institute, and its membership contained much of the international scientific elite in issues related to arms control.

[12] United Nations, *Chemical and Bacteriological Weapons*, pp. 87–88.

ods of defense against gas."[13] In 1920 the Chemical Warfare Service became a permanent part of the military, responsible to the army. By 1946 it had become the Army Chemical Corps, and its primary missions were to conduct research into offensive and defensive chemical and biological warfare and to procure weapons for the prosecution of and defense against CBW.

After World War I, the United States became a leader in the international effort to ban all future use of chemical and biological weapons. It was the United States, buoyed by public opinion hostile to gas, that led the effort to proscribe poison gas at the Washington Conference of 1922.[14] And it was the United States that first introduced the topic of chemical warfare during the Geneva Conference of 1925. Thus it was a great surprise both to opponents of CBW and to the Coolidge administration when intense lobbying by the chemical industry and the American Legion swayed enough senators against the Geneva Protocol to cause its sponsor, Senator William Edgar Borah, to withdraw the protocol from the floor. Even though public opinion in the United States remained strongly against the deployment of chemical weapons, U.S. policy in the period from 1926 to 1939 oscillated between strong support for international prohibitions on CBW and an isolationist unwillingness to be drawn into peace pacts with other nations. And the Geneva Protocol of 1925 was never ratified.

In June 1943, President Franklin D. Roosevelt received reports indicating that Japan might be contemplating the use of chemical weapons in combat. He responded on June 8 with a declaration that "use of such weapons has been outlawed by the general opinion of civilized mankind. This country has not used them, and I hope that it will never be compelled to use them. I state categorically that we shall under no circumstances resort to the use of such weapons unless they are first used by our enemies."[15] The Roosevelt declaration came to be seen as the official U.S. policy statement on the deployment of chemical and biological weapons both during World War II and in the postwar era. It signaled a willingness to abide by the international norm

[13] John Cookson and Judith Nottingham, *A Survey of Chemical and Biological Warfare* (New York: Monthly Review Press, 1969), p. 68.

[14] Although the United States did ratify the Washington Treaty of 1922, which contained a provision banning all use of poison gas, the treaty had to be ratified by France to take effect. French ratification was never forthcoming; hence, the United States had not legally (or morally, in any official way) bound itself not to use gas in combat.

[15] U.S. Congress, Senate, Committee on Foreign Relations, Subcommittee on Disarmament, *Chemical-Biological-Radiological Warfare and Its Disarmament Aspects*, 86th Cong., 2d sess., 1960 (Washington: U.S. Government Printing Office, 1960), p. 43.

of no first use of chemical and biological weapons, and it labeled such weapons "barbarous," "inhuman," and "inhumane."

Presidents Truman and Eisenhower publicly affirmed the principle of no first use of chemical or biological weapons, but during the early 1960s, U.S. real spending on chemical and biological weapons grew— from $37 million in 1958 to $129 million in 1964. In large part, this growth reflected the Kennedy administration's desire to achieve maximum flexibility in its capability to respond to aggression. Addressing Congress in 1963, Pentagon Director of Research and Development Harold Brown stated that

> to a degree chemical and biological munitions may be considered to provide an intermediate level of capability between conventional high explosives on the one hand, and nuclear weapons on the other. Though some of these materials, if used, might escalate the intensity and cause the conflict to spread, they seem to be subject to certain inherent limitations in this regard, especially when compared with nuclear weapons; that is to say, they cannot raise the intensity of conflict as high as nuclear weapons can.[16]

While there was no public repudiation of the no-first-use doctrine in the Kennedy administration, there was constant pressure from the Pentagon to maintain the fullest possible range of options for the United States in the sphere of chemical and biological warfare.

The most controversial element of American CBW policy in the 1960s concerned the use of tear gas and herbicides in Vietnam. In 1964, with the consent of American military advisors, South Vietnamese troops began to use American-supplied tear gas in combat operations. By 1966 U.S. troops were using the riot-control agents CN and CS routinely in their own combat operations, in order to attack occupied positions, defend American positions, clear the enemy out of tunnels, rescue downed airmen, and break off contact with the enemy.[17] Annual use of CS in Vietnam rose from 126 tons in 1965 to 798 tons in 1966 to 3,029 tons in 1969.[18] In its defoliation and crop-destruction campaigns in Vietnam, the United States sprayed enough Agent Orange, Blue, and White to cover 1.5 million acres in 1968 alone.[19] Both the Department of State and the Department of Defense maintained

---

[16] Seymour Hersh, *Chemical and Biological Warfare: America's Hidden Arsenal* (Indianapolis: Bobbs-Merrill Company, 1968), p. 52.

[17] Subcommittee on National Security Policy, *Hearings on Chemical-Biological Warfare*, pp. 224–228.

[18] Carnegie Endowment, *Control of Chemical and Biological Weapons*, p. 68.

[19] Subcommittee on National Security Policy, *Hearings on Chemical-Biological Warfare*, p. 242.

throughout the Vietnam period that the use of all such weapons was exempt from the Geneva Protocol and did not constitute a violation of the moral prohibition on the use of chemical and biological weapons because CS, CN, and Agents Orange, Blue, and White were not lethal.

In 1969 the U.S. had seven standardized chemical-warfare agents in its arsenal. They included sarin, a highly lethal nerve gas originally developed by the Germans during World War II; VX, a British invention that enters the body through the skin and requires only a tiny droplet for almost instantaneous death; the blister agent HD, a type of mustard gas that causes incapacitation rather than death and acts by burning the eyes, skin, and respiratory tract; and BZ, a temporary incapacitant that distorts normal mental and bodily processes and is capable of causing violent and bizarre behavior for a period of several days. In addition to these fatal or severely incapacitating chemical agents, the U.S. arsenal contained three riot-control agents: CS and CN, the tear gases that were used in Vietnam; and DM, which causes violent sneezing, nausea, and vomiting. The most dangerous chemicals in the U.S. arsenal, sarin and VX, were available in a host of delivery systems in 1969: 105-millimeter howitzer shells, five-inch cannons, 155-millimeter howitzers, 762-millimeter rockets, and thousand-pound bombs.[20]

The biological-weapons arsenal of the United States was also formidable in 1969. One informed estimate stated that the stockpile of bacteriological weapons in that year contained in excess of 3.8 billion doses.[21] America's leading biological agents of war in the late 1960s included tularemia, an often-fatal disease that produces pneumonia-like symptoms and is highly contagious; Venezuelan encephalomyelitis, an incapacitating disease that is extremely debilitating but seldom fatal; undulant fever, which has a long incubation period and is thus useful for covert action; psittacosis, which causes delirium and has a high mortality rate; anthrax, which causes high fever and is almost 100 percent fatal; and plague, the scourge of medieval Europe, which the U.S. harnessed as a means to render isolated enemy positions completely unusable for an indefinite period of time.[22]

[20] U.S. Congress, Senate, Committee on Foreign Relations, *Hearings on Chemical and Biological Warfare*, 91st Cong., 1st sess., 1969 (Washington: U.S. Government Printing Office, 1969), pp. 4–8.

[21] U.S. Congress, House, Committee on Armed Services, *Hearings on H.R. 9745, H.R. 9749, H.R. 10011, H.R. 10012*, 93d Cong., 1st sess., 1973 (Washington: U.S. Government Printing Office, 1973), pp. 7, 13–14.

[22] Hersh, *Chemical and Biological Warfare*, pp. 82–96.

It was these weapons and their potential use that were to become
the focus of a vigorous public debate within the United States
throughout 1969. The first year of the Nixon presidency was to see
the scientific community coalesce in strong support of reversing
America's CBW policies. It was also to see two network documentaries
on chemical and biological weapons, and increasing grass-roots pressure for the United States to formally observe the Geneva Protocol.
During the year, Congress took an ever more confrontational stance
toward the administration on CBW; and criticism of America's policies
on chemical and biological weapons came from many quarters, not
only from among those critical of U.S. involvement in Vietnam. This
substantial growth of opposition to America's CBW policies placed increasing pressure upon the Nixon administration to alter U.S. policy
on chemical and biological warfare; it also offered the administration
an opportunity to significantly enhance its moral image by changing
the U.S. position. The story behind the 1969 decisions on CBW is the
story of how these various pressures came into being and how they
led Richard Nixon to conclude that U.S. policies should be radically
altered.

THE VOICE OF THE SCIENTIFIC COMMUNITY

The initial thrust for change in U.S. policy in 1969 came from the
scientific community. American scientists stood in a unique relation
to the problem of CBW. On the one hand, they were the primary con-
sultants whom the Pentagon utilized in designing new chemical and
biological weapons and in carrying on basic research in the field of
chemical and biological warfare. On the other hand, they best understood the destructive capacity of chemical and biological weapons,
both to human beings and to the ecosystem of the planet. During
1969 the scientific community increasingly took on the role of pointing to the need to maintain a clear international norm against the use
of any chemical or biological weapons; and, surprisingly, it was the
very scientists who had long consulted on U.S. CBW policies who
were most prominent in urging a change in American policy.

Professor Matthew Meselson, a Harvard biologist who had increasingly become active in public protests against U.S. use of chemical
weapons in Vietnam, was the leader of the scientists' movement
against all forms of CBW. Meselson had been a consultant to the Arms
Control and Disarmament Agency (ACDA) since 1963; he was also a
close friend of Henry Kissinger. Meselson's concern about the direction of American CBW policy, and about the tendency of the Pentagon's experts to minimize the dangers of CBW, dated from work that

he had conducted in 1964. In an article written in that year criticizing the Chemical Corps's pleas for greater flexibility and funding for chemical and biological warfare, Meselson observed that

> behind most discussions of the brutality of toxic warfare lies a very wide-spread concern with its moral implications. What consideration can be given to moral factors in the conduct of war—society's least moral activity? Widespread restraints against certain forms of human combat may be partly based on instinct and accordingly may be wiser than we know. . . . In the course of the development of increasingly more powerful weapons, governments and people have come to countenance ever increasing levels of destruction in the pursuit of national objectives. At some point this process must be arrested and then reversed if civilization is to overcome the threat to its existence posed by the application of science to warfare. . . . It would be a backwards step to extend the varieties of violence which we now tolerate to include such hitherto reviled means as chemical and biological warfare.[23]

This was the fundamental message that Meselson was to preach for the next five years as he pressed for American CBW policies that erected a clear barrier to the combat use of chemical and biological agents. Meselson argued that biological agents were difficult to control and to deliver effectively, while any use of chemical agents would certainly lead to a general introduction of chemical weapons that would leave both sides in a conflict worse off. These military limitations of chemical and biological weapons, combined with their redundancy in a nuclear age, meant that offensive chemical and biological weapons offered relatively few military benefits to the United States. Together with Paul Doty, a Harvard colleague who was a former member of the president's Science Advisory Committee, Meselson organized a major American conference on these issues sponsored by the American Academy of Arts and Sciences.[24] Just as importantly, he functioned as the primary representative of the scientific community in a series of hearings that were held in 1969 by the House and Senate on chemical and biological weapons.

Complementing Meselson's efforts was the work of Dr. Joshua Lederberg, a Stanford Nobel laureate in genetics who in 1968 undertook a major campaign to educate the nation on the dangers of chemical

[23] Matthew Meselson, review of *Tomorrow's Weapons, Chemical and Biological*, by Jacquard Rothschild, *Bulletin of the Atomic Scientists* 20 (October 1964): 35–36.

[24] Joel Primack and Frank von Hippel, "Matthew Meselson and the United States Policy on Chemical and Biological Warfare," in *Advice and Dissent: Scientists in the Political Arena*, ed. Joel Primack (New York: Basic Books, 1974), p. 151.

and biological weapons.[25] Lederberg saw three major threats inherent in America's CBW policy. The first threat was posed by the development of new toxic biological agents that could bring previously unknown diseases to humankind. The second was the danger posed to the American people by accidents involving CBW tests. The third and most important threat that Lederberg pointed to was the weakening of the moral and psychological barrier against biological weapons that had grown up in the international system:

> Why ratify the Geneva Protocol? Very simply, our ratifying the protocol would give it increased attention and effectiveness as a barrier to chemical and biological warfare. The concept of barriers is important. The barriers which exist today to chemical and biological warfare are political and psychological ones. Conventions, the rules of war, and historical precedent all have played important roles in keeping mankind from using chemical and biological weapons. These weapons are popularly viewed as repugnant instruments of war. Political leaders seem to believe using such weapons is wrong. Scientists everywhere seem strongly to dislike working on chemical and biological weapons. Curiously, this morality is very much less pronounced in the case of nuclear weapons. . . . A mystique seems to have developed around this mode of warfare which, rationally or not, has caused nations not to build capacities actively. The world has erected political and psychological barriers to chemical and biological warfare.[26]

Lederberg believed that the United States should respect and build up these barriers, not weaken them by failing to ratify the Geneva Protocol and by using chemical weapons in Vietnam.

The scientific community's critique of America's CBW policies extended far beyond the work of Matthew Meselson and Joshua Lederberg. It was reflected in the symposiums of the National Academy of Sciences and the Federation of American Scientists. Criticism was leveled by those who were generally critical of the Nixon administration, such as George Wald and Paul Doty, as well as by such administration stalwarts as Lee Dubridge, presidential science advisor, and

[25] See Joshua Lederberg, "Congress Should Examine Biological Warfare Tests," *Washington Post*, March 30, 1968; idem, "Mankind Had a Near Miss from Mystery Pandemic" and "The Infamous Black Death May Return to Haunt Us," *Washington Post*, September 7, 1968; and idem, "Swift Biological Advance Can Be Bent to Genocide," *Washington Post*, August 17, 1968. See also *New York Times*, June 20, 1969, p. 32, for Lederberg's comments at a meeting of interested members of Congress on June 19, 1969.

[26] Testimony of Joshua Lederberg to House Subcommittee on National Security Policy, *Hearings on Chemical-Biological Warfare*, p. 93.

Ivan Bennett, the administration's representative to the 1969 UN study on CBW.[27] By the end of 1969, the scientific community, although not monolithically opposed to further development of offensive chemical and biological weapons, had come out strongly against existing U.S. policies on CBW and was pressing strongly for ratification of the Geneva Protocol. And through the channels of communication and influence open to leading critics in the scientific community—channels that included national symposiums, the major media, and consultancies to Congress, the Pentagon, the State Department, and the White House—a corps of distinguished and politically well connected scientists generated the knowledge and the impetus for the anti-CBW movement of 1969.

THE CONGRESSIONAL DEBATE

United States chemical-weapons policies in Vietnam had sparked significant congressional debate ever since 1965. But in March 1969, this debate reached a much greater intensity and could no longer be ignored by the White House. The stimulus to this intensified debate lay in three media events: the publication of reporter Seymour Hersh's *Chemical and Biological Warfare: America's Hidden Arsenal* in 1968, and the airing of documentaries by NBC and CBS on CBW in February 1969. Hersh's book, which relied heavily upon unclassified materials provided by Matthew Meselson, constituted a thorough review of America's CBW capabilities, stockpiles, and policies. It focused upon the United States' use of tear gas and herbicides in Vietnam, and it argued that American CBW policy was severely at odds with international public opinion and the rules of war. The NBC and CBS documentaries provided chilling footage of the effects of chemical and biological weapons. They reported that a nerve-gas accident in Dugway, Utah had killed some six hundred sheep in 1968, and they sharply contrasted U.S. CBW policies with those of other Western nations.[28]

[27] Members of the administration, such as DuBridge and Bennett, generally did not make their criticisms public, although Bennett did join in the formal UN report that called upon all nations to immediately ratify the Geneva Protocol and stop chemical and biological weapons development. These critics may have played as important a role in the eventual Nixon decision as did the public critics in the scientific community, for it was a presidential Science Advisory Committee study that was a critical element in Nixon's eventual decision to reverse U.S. policy. For discussions of the scientific community's public and private efforts to change American CBW policy, see Primack and von Hippel, "Matthew Meselson"; Richard McCarthy, *The Ultimate Folly* (New York: Alfred A. Knopf, 1969); and Senate Committee on Foreign Relations, *Hearings on Chemical and Biological Warfare*.

[28] The NBC and CBS documentaries may have been inspired by a 1966 BBC docu-

One of the viewers of the NBC documentary was Congressman Richard McCarthy, a New York Democrat who happened to be watching "First Tuesday" with his wife, Gail. McCarthy remembers both the program and the response it occasioned in him:

> Shocked by what she saw about U.S. germ and gas warfare projects, Gail peered at me and pointedly asked: "You're a congressman. What do you know about this?" "Nothing," I answered. But my interest and indignation climbed as I continued to watch the story unfold; indignation because I realized that I had undoubtedly voted funds for this kind of activity which, apparently, were buried in other appropriation bills. . . . The morning after the NBC show, I found myself still deeply concerned about what I had seen. After discussing the matter with Wendell Pirgman of my staff, I telephoned the two Democrats from my state on the House Armed Services Committee, Otis Pike and Samuel Stratton. Each told me he knew little about CBW but suggested I request a briefing from the Army on the various aspects of the program. I followed this advice (and) took to the floor at noon to announce the plan.[29]

McCarthy's chance viewing of "First Tuesday" turned out to be a highly significant event for the CBW debate in 1969, for the congressman from New York was to prove dogged in his pursuit of the facts on American CBW policy and in his drive for major changes in the U.S. position. In McCarthy's view, the United States' refusal to ratify the Geneva Protocol was wrong because it damaged America's reputation in the world and because it had led to the development of a weapons capacity that was intrinsically immoral:

> Although all warfare is inhumane, as civilized human beings we must do everything in our power to assert our humanity. By agreement, either written or tacit, all nations have generally avoided the use of chemical weapons since World War I. And biological weapons have not been used in the twentieth century. In my opinion, the United States should do everything it can to strengthen the ban on use of these forms of warfare. It would run directly contrary to all our principles of honor and humanity to be the nation to encourage a breakdown of this arms limitation.[30]

McCarthy did persuade the Army to provide a briefing on CBW for interested House members on March 4, 1969. But it was a most unsatisfactory session from McCarthy's view, since the Army representatives refused to answer many of the congressional questions and in-

mentary on chemical and biological weapons entitled "A Plague on Your Children." See Primack and von Hippel, "Matthew Meselson," p. 149 n. 18.

[29] McCarthy, *The Ultimate Folly*, p. 126.

[30] Ibid., p. 146.

stead used the meeting as an opportunity to push for more funds. An angry Congressman McCarthy decided to do his own investigating, and he convinced other colleagues in the House that U.S. policies should be thoroughly reviewed. As a start, McCarthy sent a series of detailed and probing questions about the American position on chemical and biological weapons to the secretary of defense, the secretary of state, the ACDA, and the director of the National Security Council (NSC).

The campaign to alter American CBW policies was given a boost in the spring of 1969 when it was learned that the Army had formulated a plan to transport massive amounts of aging chemical weapons from its Rocky Mountain Arsenal near Denver to the New Jersey coast, where the chemical agents would be transferred to ships and dumped in the Atlantic. Code-named Operation Chase, the Army plan called for some 27,000 tons of poison-gas weaponry, 12,000 tons of lethal nerve-gas bombs, and 2,600 tons of leaking nerve-gas rockets to be shipped across six states. Not surprisingly, the publication of the plan caused a tremendous public uproar, and the Army was forced to substantially modify, and ultimately cancel, the planned shipments.

As a result of the NBC and CBS documentaries, the initiatives of Congressman McCarthy, and the revelation of Operation Chase, the spring and summer of 1969 were filled with congressional hearings on American CBW policies. On April 30, the Senate Foreign Relations committee began secret hearings on the diplomatic, military, and political implications of America's policies; Matthew Meselson was the principal witness.[31] On May 8, the Subcommittee on International Organizations of the House Foreign Affairs committee began hearings on the international implications of dumping chemical weapons and of U.S. CBW policies in general.[32] On May 20, the House Government Operations Subcommittee on Conservation and Natural Resources opened hearings on the environmental dangers of the Pentagon's chemical and biological weapons testing and disposal plans.[33] And in the fall, the Subcommittee on National Security Policy of the House Foreign Affairs committee opened wide-ranging hearings on American CBW policies in response to a petition signed by 108 House members calling for the president to (1) submit the Geneva Protocol to the Senate for ratification; (2) conduct an extensive review of U.S. CBW

[31] Senate Committee on Foreign Relations, *Hearings on Chemical and Biological Warfare.*
[32] *Congressional Quarterly Weekly Report* 27, no. 31 (August 1, 1969): 1402.
[33] Ibid.

policies; and (3) reassert the traditional no-first-use doctrine that had been enunciated by Franklin Roosevelt.[34]

Meanwhile, major newspapers began a series of searing editorials calling for a full-scale investigation of American CBW policies and demanding the resubmission of the Geneva Protocol to the Senate. On April 7, the *New York Times* excoriated Congress for allowing Pentagon claims of national security to severely limit its oversight of U.S. CBW policies in the past, and the *Times* called upon both the administration and Congress to review the American position on chemical and biological weapons from the ground up:

> This policy of silence and deliberate mystification is inexcusable in a free nation. As Senator Gaylord Nelson of Wisconsin has observed, there is no reason why the public cannot know the facts and debate the issues of chemical and biological warfare just as it has come to know and debate those of nuclear warfare. . . . Last August the British government moved at the United Nations for a new international agreement to clarify and update the Geneva convention with regard to chemical and biological warfare. A U.N. staff study on this proposal is due by July first. But it is not necessary for the U.S. to wait before discharging its own responsibilities. The Nixon Administration can offer a straightforward exposition of its policies in this field. Congress can take down the "Please Do Not Disturb" sign from this program and begin to discharge its normal functions of review and debate.[35]

On April 23, the *Times* reiterated its call for major changes in American CBW policies and emphasized that U.S. efforts should aim to strengthen international barriers to the development and use of CBW, rather than weaken them:

> Experience in Vietnam has already demonstrated the dangerous temptation to erode the difference between this country's official policy of never using such weapons first and its actual employment of chemical weapons in marginal ways. It is imperative that the U.S. strongly support the banning of these weapons in all forthcoming arms control negotiations.[36]

And on May 23, the *Times* ran an editorial that cited the Pentagon's approach to CBW as a major source for the distrust of the military that was pervasive in American society.[37]

The Nixon administration was increasingly feeling the pressure to

---

[34] House Subcommittee on National Security Policy, *Hearings on Chemical-Biological Warfare.*

[35] *New York Times*, April 7, 1969, p. 42.

[36] *New York Times*, April 23, 1969, p. 46.

[37] *New York Times*, May 23, 1969, p. 46.

review the U.S. position on chemical and biological weapons. Foreign criticism of the use of tear gas and herbicides in Vietnam combined with new initiatives on chemical and biological arms control from the UN and the Soviet-bloc countries to cause American diplomats to seek a review, if only for the purposes of policy rationalization. The questions that Congressman McCarthy had submitted to the State Department, the Pentagon, and the ACDA required answers, and increasing congressional and media scrutiny meant that those answers had to be substantial and consistent.[38] Matthew Meselson had spoken at length with his friend Henry Kissinger, Nixon's advisor for national security affairs, about the need for a complete review of the American CBW position.[39] And the increasing attention that the subject of CBW was getting on television and in print had created a general uneasiness about U.S. policies in the public mind. For all these reasons, on May 28, 1969, the president authorized a full-scale review of all U.S. CBW policies under the auspices of the NSC, and he ordered that the review be completed by summer.

In looking at the steps that led to Richard Nixon's decision to place the issue of chemical and biological weapons on the U.S. foreign-policy agenda, it is important to note how well they bear out the hypotheses about the second pathway from international moral norms to state behavior. A series of prominent opinion leaders who opposed the American stance on CBW used influential social institutions such as scientific federations, the media, and Congress in order to mobilize public opinion around the moral norm proscribing chemical and biological warfare. These opinion leaders pointed out that existing U.S. policies did not accept the binding nature of the norm against CBW, and that the escalating buildup of U.S. chemical and bacteriological stocks threatened to lead the United States down the path of resort to chemical and biological warfare. In addition, these opinion leaders used the American violation of the norm in Vietnam to rally public support for wholesale changes in the U.S. approach to CBW. By May 1969, Richard Nixon faced what he knew was going to become a "live" issue in American political debate, and he initiated a study to

[38] On April 21, 1969, McCarthy placed into the *Congressional Record* the answers he had received, as well as an analysis of the contradictions between those answers and statements that Pentagon and administration officials had made in other public forums. The responses to McCarthy indicate an attempt at coordination among at least some of the queried departments, but the analysis of contradictions points to the lack of policy rationalization on chemical and biological weapons. See House Subcommittee on National Security Policy, *Hearings on Chemical-Biological Warfare*, pp. 347–367.

[39] Primack and von Hippel, "Matthew Meselson," p. 149; and David Rosenbaum, "Matthew Stanley Meselson: Activist Germ War Foe," *New York Times*, November 26, 1969.

determine how he should respond in that debate. As a result of the mobilization effort, the question of CBW could no longer be ignored, and the whole constellation of CBW issues had become part of the nation's foreign policy agenda.

DEBATE AND CONFRONTATION

The announcement of the NSC review was greeted with enthusiasm in the media and in Congress, but it did not stem the pressure to change existing U.S. policy. In fact, the decision to take a fresh look at the issue of chemical and biological weapons prompted a flurry of articles in major publications on the nature and scope of the U.S. capacity to engage in CBW.[40] These articles uniformly noted the lethal nature of U.S. chemical and bacteriological stocks, the American use of chemical weapons in Vietnam, the U.S. failure to ratify the Geneva Protocol, the Dugway nerve-gas leak of 1968, and Operation Chase. Taken together, the articles represented an enormous educational effort directed toward the American people on the topic of CBW. Such reporting was complemented by continuing editorial calls for substantial modifications of American CWB policy, and even conservative commentators joined the fray. James Kilpatrick, in an article entitled "Time to Lift the Veil on Grisly CB Weapons," demanded that the U.S. ratify the Geneva Protocol and do all in its power to stop the spread of these weapons of mass destruction. "Chemical-biological warfare," wrote Kilpatrick, "is a crazed monster, capable of poisoning whole populations. . . . It is an unseen hell."[41]

The movement to reverse America's commitment to offensive chemical and biological weapons was not well received at the Pentagon. In response to Congressman McCarthy's questions on the need for an offensive CBW capacity, John Foster, the deputy director of defense, research, and engineering for the Pentagon, wrote:

> It is the policy of the U.S. . . . to develop and maintain a limited offensive capability in order to deter all use of CB weapons by the threat of retaliation in kind. This policy on CB weapons is part of a broader strategy designed to provide the U.S. with several options for response against various forms of attack. . . . Chemical weapons, in many tactical situations, are more effective than conventional (high explosive and projectile)

[40] See, for example, "The Dilemma of Chemical Warfare," *Time*, June 27, 1969; "Gas and Germ Warfare: A Look inside the Arsenal," *U.S. News and World Report*, August 8, 1969; and "Silent Arsenal," *Saturday Review*, September 27, 1969.

[41] James Kilpatrick, "Time to Lift the Veil on Grisly CB Weapons," *Washington Evening Star*, July 1, 1969.

weapons. Accordingly, it is believed wise to deter their use. If two approximately equally effective military forces were engaged in combat, and one side initiated a CB operation, it could gain a significant advantage even if the opposing side has protective equipment. Neutralization of this advantage could not be achieved with conventional arms. . . . The U.S. policy and its rationale with regard to biological warfare is generally the same as that for chemical.[42]

The Pentagon presented much the same argument in testimony before the House Appropriations Committee in July 1969.

On July 3, 1969, the Senate Armed Services Committee dealt a stunning blow to the Pentagon by deleting the entire authorization for fiscal year 1970 for research on and deployment of offensive chemical and biological weapons. Because of complaints about the U.S. CBW program, the committee had set up a special subcommittee in June to study the Department of Defense research and development program. That subcommittee, headed by Senator Thomas McIntyre of New Hampshire, argued in its report that a failure to delete the funds for offensive CBW capacities might endanger passage of the entire Pentagon research and development program; moreover, it would be a denial of the nation's moral attitude toward chemical and biological weapons. "The subcommittee felt that we must do all that we can to protect our people and our troops against biological and chemical agents," McIntyre noted, "but measured against the nation's traditional opposition to the offensive use of such agents we could not justify research and development expenditures for that purpose."[43] The Senate Armed Services Committee action stimulated a move for similar restrictions in the House authorization bill, and a working alliance began to form between House and Senate opponents of CBW. As August began, *Congressional Quarterly Weekly Report* concluded that "the subject [of chemical and biological weapons] may become one of the most significant issues to appear before the American public this year and may become a key Congressional and Administration issue following the present debate over the deployment of the anti-ballistic missile system."[44]

During the first week of August, seven amendments to oversee or cut back the American chemical and biological weapons programs were introduced into the Senate. Some of these amendments dealt

[42] House Subcommittee on National Security Policy, *Hearings on Chemical-Biological Warfare*, p. 353.

[43] *New York Times*, July 4, 1969, p. 4; and *Congressional Quarterly Weekly Report* 27, no. 31 (August 1, 1969): 1402.

[44] *Congressional Quarterly Weekly Report* 27, no. 31 (August 1, 1969): 1398.

with the testing of chemical weapons and reflected public anger over the revelations of the Dugway nerve-gas accident and a leak of gas that had occurred in American chemical stocks stored on Okinawa in July. Some of the amendments restricted the Pentagon's ability to transport and dispose of biological and chemical agents; these were motivated largely by the furor over Operation Chase. But the remaining amendments sought to provide continuing general restrictions to the development of offensive chemical and biological weapons. In the debate that followed, opponents of CBW focused repeatedly on the moral questions involved in CBW and on the implications of the American CBW position for U.S. foreign policy. Gaylord Nelson argued that the American people would never approve of the use of chemical or biological weapons, and that therefore they should not be deployed.[45] Claiborne Pell repeatedly pointed to the damaging effect that U.S. chemical-weapons policies were having on America's reputation, and he called for the resubmission of the Geneva Protocol, the prohibition of all future CBW development, and an end to the use of chemical weapons in Vietnam.[46] And Charles Goodell followed the lead of many other speakers in framing the issue in explicitly moral terms: "What we need to consider are the grave moral issues which arise when we stockpile munitions filled with lethal gas and disease-producing bacteria. What is needed is an in-depth examination of the Pentagon's retaliation-in-kind concept used to justify the program."[47] On August 7, the Senate voted 91-0 to accept a compromise amendment worked out by Senator McIntyre, Senator John Stennis, and Defense Secretary Melvin Laird. The compromise required semiannual reports on the research, testing, transportation, and procurement of chemical and biological weapons; it prohibited the procurement of missiles or delivery systems specifically used for chemical and biological warfare; and it eliminated most outdoor testing of chemical and biological agents.[48]

The House took up debate on the defense authorization bill in October. Congressman Richard Nedzi offered an amendment on October 3 that paralleled the restrictions passed in the Senate. In offering his amendment, Nedzi said, "We regard ourselves, justifiably, as a humane nation. We want to survive as a nation without doing damage to our ideals, traditions, and well-being. This amendment is framed with these ideas in mind."[49] In the ensuing debate, opponents of CBW

---

[45] *Congressional Record*, 91st Cong., 1st sess., 1969, 115, pt. 17:22283.

[46] Ibid., p. 22290.

[47] Ibid., p. 22284.

[48] *Congressional Quarterly Weekly Report* 27, no. 33 (August 15, 1969): 1535.

[49] *Congressional Record*, 91st Cong., 1st sess., 1969, 115, pt. 21:28427.

stressed the degree to which future development of chemical and biological weapons clashed with American principles, as well as the effect that American actions were having on the international barriers to CBW. Richard McCarthy's argument was typical:

> We have changed from a nation that introduced and signed the ban on chemical weapons at the Geneva Convention of 1925, from the nation whose Presidents spoke out in the name of humanity against the use of these weapons, to a nation that uses gas—even though it is tear gas—as an aid to killing the enemy. We are breaking down the traditional barriers against the use of chemical warfare rather than upholding one of the few international agreements that have limited man's inhumanity to man.[50]

Opponents of the Nedzi resolution stressed that the United States needed the flexibility to respond in kind to enemy aggression and that the use of chemicals in Vietnam did not violate the Geneva Protocol. They also made the point repeatedly that the White House was reviewing the entire spectrum of American CBW policy and that any congressional efforts to change U.S. policy should await the outcome of that review.[51] On October 3, the House passed a less restrictive amendment introduced by Congressman Philip Philbin, and the matter went to conference. The final conference report required semiannual reports concerning research, development, testing, and procurement of all lethal and nonlethal chemical and biological agents. It prohibited the procurement of delivery systems specifically designed to disseminate lethal chemical or biological agents. And it required states to be notified when plans were being made to transport chemical or biological agents through them.[52] Congress had made clear that if the administration did not soon substantially alter U.S. policies on CBW, the House and Senate would begin to do it for them. Congress had also made it clear that the debate over chemical and biological weapons would not go away.

THE ADMINISTRATION DEBATE

When he ordered a full-scale review of American CBW policies in May 1969, President Nixon took steps to include every major body in the executive branch that had a potential interest in the subject of chem-

---

[50] *Congressional Record*, 91st Cong., 1st sess., 1969, 115, pt. 17:22292.

[51] *Congressional Record*, 91st Cong., 1st sess., 1969, 115, pt. 21:28431ff.

[52] U.S. Congress, *1969 Conference Report on Defense Appropriations*, 91st Cong., 1st sess., 1969 (Washington: U.S. Government Printing Office, 1969), p. 23. The conference report on the authorization bill had deleted the restrictions on delivery-system procurement, but the appropriations bill reinserted them.

ical and biological weapons: the NSC, the Departments of State and Defense, the Central Intelligence Agency, the ACDA, and the president's Office of Science and Technology. Three interdepartmental task forces were formed, each taking the lead in a different area of investigation: the CIA in identifying the CBW capabilities of other nations, the Joint Chiefs of Staff in assessing the military utility of chemical and biological weapons for the United States, and the NSC and Department of State in weighing the diplomatic implications of various policy options open to the president. The mandate given to these task forces was extremely broad, as the ACDA report for 1969 illustrates:

> The study covered every aspect of the question. The participants were instructed to delineate the nature of the threat to the United States and its Allies and possible alternative approaches to meeting the threat; to discuss the utility of and circumstances for possible employment of chemical and biological weapons; to define research and development objectives; to review current applications of U.S. policy relating to chemical riot control agents and chemical defoliants; and to assess the implications of chemical warfare and biological research programs for U.S. foreign relations.[53]

The original target date for the completion of the study was September 1, but conflicts within the various task forces delayed the project until mid-November.

The NSC met to discuss the future of America's CBW policies on November 18, the same day that the House Foreign Affairs committee opened a new series of wide-ranging hearings on CBW. As the NSC meeting began, General Earl Wheeler presented the military's position clearly: the United States should preserve all options except for the first use of chemical and biological weapons; the Geneva Protocol should not be resubmitted; America should press ahead with its development of chemical weapons and should preserve its biological-weapons stockpile; and no restrictions should be placed on the use of tear gas and herbicides in Vietnam or in future conflicts.[54] Representatives of the State Department, the ACDA, the U.S. Information Agency, and the NSC staff recommended a far different plan: the resubmission of the Geneva Protocol to the Senate, the destruction of the American biological-weapons arsenal, a formal renunciation of the first use of all chemical weapons, and a halt in the production of new

[53] Arms Control and Disarmament Agency, *Ninth Annual Report to Congress* (Washington: U.S. Government Printing Office, 1970), p. 10.

[54] Robert Homans, "Military Rebuffed on CBW," *Washington Post*, November 27, 1969, p. 1.

chemical weapons.[55] In explaining the differences between the Joint Chiefs' position and that of the others participating in the meeting, Defense Secretary Melvin Laird later said, "The military was asked to look at the problem from a military perspective. There are certain differences that exist when you look at anything from a military position, without looking at the political considerations. They understand that. So do I."[56]

In part, these "political considerations" reflected the need for the United States to respond to diplomatic initiatives at the UN designed to strengthen the ban on chemical and biological warfare. The United States was being portrayed as a reluctant participant in the effort to proscribe CBW, and the foreign-policy experts present at the NSC meeting were anxious to stem this reputational damage. But far more important for the decisions that ultimately emerged from the meeting were domestic "political considerations." The administration was already on the moral defensive because of its Vietnam policies, and a decision to endorse the Joint Chiefs' agenda on CBW would have subjected the president to sustained attacks accusing him of violating international morality. Conversely, if the president decided to radically alter U.S. CBW policies in order to bring them into accord with the spirit and the letter of the norm against chemical and biological warfare, the administration could expect to enhance substantially its moral reputation in the foreign-policy sphere. This was the key consideration in the ultimate decision. As Phillip Farley, who was acting director of the ACDA in 1969, remembers, "President Nixon made the changes in [CBW] policies because he wanted to make clear to the American people that the administration's foreign policy had an ethical side to it."[57]

As a result, the president adopted almost the entire agenda advanced by the State Department, the ACDA, and the NSC. It was decided that the Geneva Protocol would be resubmitted to the Senate, the United States would renounce the first use of all *lethal* chemical weapons and all biological weapons, and the American stockpile of biological agents would be destroyed. In addition, the United States would go on record in favor of the United Kingdom's draft resolution banning the production and use of biological weapons. The Joint Chiefs did achieve victory on the issue of incapacitating chemical agents, that is, tear gas and herbicides; it was decided that the United

[55] Ibid.

[56] *New York Times*, December 2, 1969, p. 24.

[57] Author's interview with Phillip Farley, May 16, 1989. A 1970 study by the Congressional Research Service also supported this interpretation of the decision-making process (see the *New York Times*, May 16, 1970, p. 6).

States would continue to authorize their use in Vietnam and would argue that such a use was not proscribed by the Geneva Protocol.[58]

In announcing these decisions on November 25, 1969, Nixon said, "Mankind already carries in its own hands too many seeds of its own destruction. By the examples that we set today, we hope to contribute to an atmosphere of peace and understanding between all nations."[59] The international reaction to the U.S. decision was immediate and quite positive: allies such as the United Kingdom and West Germany were especially effusive in their support; the nonaligned world was extremely laudatory; and even the Soviet Union complimented the American initiative.[60] In Congress, those who had been most critical of the administration in recent months because of its CBW stand were now most vocal in their praise of the president. The liberal Republican members of the Senate drafted a letter signed by thirty-five GOP senators describing the Nixon decision as "the reassertion of the moral and humanitarian leadership of the U.S. on pressing world issues."[61] The *New York Times* ran an editorial extensively praising Nixon and predicting that the new policy on chemical and biological weapons would raise the president's personal prestige and that of the nation as a whole.[62]

MORAL NORMS AND FOREIGN POLICY: THE CASE OF CHEMICAL AND BIOLOGICAL WEAPONS

The decisions made by President Nixon in 1969 on the subject of chemical and biological warfare vividly illustrate the influence that a strong international moral norm can have upon the formulation of foreign policy. The existence of a clear and widely accepted prohibition on the use of chemical and biological weapons created a series of pres-

[58] Arms Control and Disarmament Agency, *Documents on Disarmament: 1969* (Washington: Government Printing Office, 1969), pp. 590–591.

[59] Ibid., p. 592. It is interesting to note that the announcement of the NSC decisions on CBW was made quite hurriedly after the meeting of November 18. White House spokesman Ronald Ziegler admitted that "he could not recall any other N.S.C. decision that was brought so promptly to public attention." (*Washington Post*, November 26, 1969, p. A6.) One can only speculate that the reason for this haste was a desire to defuse the growing debate in Congress.

[60] *New York Times*, November 26, 1969, p. 16. The USSR did ascribe the American decision to the international pressure that had been placed upon the United States to reverse its CBW position.

[61] *New York Times*, December 7, 1969, p. 1.

[62] *New York Times*, November 26, 1969, p. 44. Similar editorial support was forthcoming from the *Los Angeles Times*, November 26, 1969, p. 16; the *Washington Post*, November 26, 1969, p. A12; the *Chicago Tribune*, November 26, 1969, p. 18; and a host of other major newspapers.

sures upon the Nixon administration that led the president to make substantive changes in American military doctrine and force structure, despite the fact that the military leaders of the United States continued to raise powerful objections to these changes. Some of these pressures flowed from the international reputational damage that the United States was suffering in the United Nations because of its perceived reluctance to accept the Geneva Protocol. But a much more salient set of pressures, from President Nixon's perspective, was the domestic opposition that was coalescing around the moral norm proscribing CBW. The president recognized that a failure to alter American CBW policies would stimulate a much more vigorous debate on chemical and biological weapons in the next session of Congress, and Nixon did not need another searing debate on his foreign-policy objectives. Moreover, Nixon recognized that dramatically altering America's CBW policies would enhance the moral reputation of his administration and thus garner him political support. For these reasons, the president was willing to sacrifice the modest, though not insignificant, security interests that argued against reversing America's CBW stand. He was willing to accept a no-first-use precedent and to jettison the U.S. commitment to retaliation in kind because domestic political incentives outweighed these considerations.

It is important to underscore the role of the scientific community, the media, and Congressman McCarthy in the decision-making process that led to the change in America's CBW policies. Matthew Meselson and Joshua Lederberg spearheaded an effort to focus public attention upon the nature of chemical and biological weapons and the dangers that CBW posed to humanity; they brought to the public debate on CBW their scientific expertise, access to key decision makers, and a commitment to the principle that the moral norm proscribing biological and chemical warfare was a barrier that humankind could violate only at its peril. Meselson and Lederberg were aided by Seymour Hersh, who popularized the issue of CBW by making America's policies public and understandable to a broad audience; it was Hersh's work that stimulated the CBS and NBC documentaries that brought the horrors of CBW into the living rooms of America. And the work begun by Meselson, Lederberg, and Hersh was brought into the center of the domestic political process by Congressman Richard McCarthy, who was horrified by American CBW policies and made it his personal agenda to press for U.S. adherence to the letter and the spirit of the moral norm against CBW. Working together, these individuals publicized existing U.S. policies, showed how they undermined the moral norm against CBW, and organized an effective coalition in Congress to press for change. And in the end it was the pressures created by this coalition that proved decisive in the president's mind.

Thus the 1969 decisions on CBW constitute an instance where the second pathway from international moral norms to foreign-policy decisions was at work. A group of individuals utilized an existing international moral norm to mobilize domestic political support in favor of norm observance. The president, recognizing that this was a decision that would reflect in either a morally favorable or a morally unfavorable way upon him and his administration, chose to reap the political rewards that would accrue from embracing the moral norm. And he was willing to sacrifice substantive security interests to do so.

Chapter Five

COLONIALISM AND THE PANAMA CANAL

WHEN THE Panama Canal treaties were signed in 1977, twenty-two Latin American heads of state traveled to Washington and acclaimed the new agreements as a historical turning point in America's relationship with the other nations of the hemisphere.[1] The twin treaties, which were ratified by the Senate in 1978, provided for a gradual transfer of ownership and control over the canal to Panama by 1999, and they ended the de facto sovereignty that the United States had exercised over the ten-mile-wide Canal Zone since 1903. In looking at the process that led to the negotiation, signing, and ratification of these treaties, three significant issues emerge:

(1) As the 1970s began, the Panama Canal was not a significant foreign-policy issue for the United States. As one top policymaker put it, "Panama is always sixteenth on any list of the fifteen top issues."[2] But by 1976 the canal had emerged as one of the most provocative issues in American electoral politics, and it had come to be seen by the nations of the Third World as a litmus test of America's willingness to treat them as full-fledged members of the international community. When President Jimmy Carter entered the White House, he selected the Panama Canal treaties as the first major foreign-policy initiative of his administration, and he eventually staked almost his entire political capital on the ratification of the new pacts. How had this radical shift in the importance of Panama for America's foreign-policy agenda come about, and how can the study of international relations help to explain this sudden importance that the canal took on in American domestic and international politics?

(2) By the beginning of the 1970s, the military and economic importance of the Panama Canal to the United States had declined somewhat. The new generation of aircraft carriers in the American fleet was too large to transit the canal, and the increasing relative economic advantages of rail transport and supertankers made the United States less dependent upon the canal for the maintenance of its trading relationships. Nevertheless, the Panama Canal still offered sub-

---

[1] *New York Times*, March 8, 1977, p. 1.

[2] Thomas Franck and Edward Weisbad, "Panama Paralysis," *Foreign Policy* 2 (Winter 1975–76): 171.

stantial military and commercial advantages to the United States. As
four retired chiefs of naval operations were to point out during the
national debate on the canal treaties, the canal remained capable of
providing transit between the Atlantic and the Pacific for almost every
ship of the U.S. navy, and there was no existing major war plan for
the United States that did not demand that the Panama Canal be
available for full-time, priority use.[3] The Panama Canal was also a major choke point for routine military transit; having the canal in hostile
hands could immensely complicate continuing logistical support for
U.S. forces around the globe and dramatically increase the costs for
routine naval military supply.[4] Finally, the Canal Zone served as the
headquarters for the Southern Command of the United States, which
coordinated American military operations throughout Latin America
and was especially well placed to monitor the increasingly volatile situation in Central America. In addition to these military considerations, the economic value of the canal to the United States remained
quite high throughout the 1970s. Some fourteen thousand ships
passed through the canal annually, with approximately 60 percent of
them either originating or terminating their voyages in U.S. ports. The
canal was the focal point for fifteen major trade routes critical to
American economic growth (including the newly important route
from the oil fields of Alaska to the eastern coast of the United States),
and fully 10 percent of U.S. oceangoing trade traveled through
Panama[5] (see Table 5.1). In short, as both proponents and opponents
of the Panama Canal treaties of 1978 were to argue, the Panama Canal remained a significant military and economic asset of the United
States. Why, then, did the United States agree to transfer ownership
and control of this critically important asset to the government of Panama?

[3] Congressional Research Service, *Senate Debate on the Panama Canal Treaty*
(Washington: U.S. Government Printing Office, 1979), p. 181.

[4] Paul Ryan, *The Panama Canal Controversy* (Stanford: Hoover Institution Press,
1977), p. 143. Ryan, a former naval officer, discusses at length the continuing military
importance of the canal to the operations of the U.S. Navy in times of emergency and
increased alert.

[5] Hanson Baldwin, "Con: The Panama Canal: Sovereignty and Security," *AEI Defense
Review* 4 (August 1977): 15–18; and testimony of Howard Casey, deputy assistant sec-
retary for maritime affairs, Department of Commerce, to Senate Committee on Foreign
Relations, in *Hearings on the Panama Canal Treaties*, 95th Cong., 1st sess., 1978
(Washington: U.S. Government Printing Office, 1978), 1:443–448. Casey noted that by
using the canal a ship could decrease its voyage by 28 percent in a trip from Gulf of
Mexico ports to Asia and by 57 percent in a trip from Valdez, Alaska to the gulf. Casey
also noted that costs would increase substantially if the 10 percent of U.S. foreign trade
that passed through the canal had to go around Cape Horn.

TABLE 5.1
Long-Term Trends in Panama Canal Traffic

U.S. Cargo Passing through the Canal (millions of tons)	
1958	27.2
1959	28.9
1960	34.8
1961	37.5
1962	40.5
1963	35.5
1964	40.7
1965	44.1
1966	48.6
1967	53.1
1968	57.8
1969	63.9
1970	74.8
1971	77.9
1975	85.6
Panama Canal Traffic (transits)	
1915	1,108
1921	3,371
1936	6,435
1951	7,751
1966	11,925
1967	12,412
1968	13,199
1969	13,146
1970	13,658
1971	14,020
1972	13,766
1973	13,841
1974	14,033
1975	13,609
1976	13,201
1980 (projected)	15,400
1990 (projected)	17,600
2000 (projected)	21,300

Source: U.S. Congress, Senate, Committee on the Judiciary, Subcommittee on the Separation of Powers, *The Panama Canal Treaties*, 95th Cong., 2d sess., 1978, pp. 297–298.

(3) At the beginning of 1973, there seemed little hope that Panama would soon negotiate a treaty giving it control and ownership of the canal and the Canal Zone. The negotiating position of the United States was becoming increasingly hard-line, and although there was support for Panama among the nations of Latin America on the canal issue, this support was unfocused and sporadic. Moreover, Panama faced the hurdle of getting U.S. Senate ratification for any treaty it could negotiate with the American executive branch. As declarations by blocs of House and Senate members made clear throughout the 1960s and early 1970s, the idea of transferring the canal to Panamanian hands had many enemies and few friends in Congress. Yet by 1978, the Panama Canal treaties had generated a broad, focused, and effective coalition of support that ranged from the nations of Latin America to America's European allies to the U.S. media and foreign-policy establishment. How had this wide-ranging coalition been organized, and what were the forces that held it together long enough to attain ratification of the 1978 treaties?

It will be argued here that the role of international moral norms is critical to answering these three questions. For the moral norm against colonialism, which had emerged after World War II and had become firmly entrenched in the international system by 1970, played a critical role in elevating the canal issue to prominence, in building a coalition of support for the new treaties, and in changing the configuration of domestic and international interests that American decision makers faced in confronting the canal question.

THE NORM OF DECOLONIZATION

It is quite appropriate that the term *decolonization* first appeared in the 1930s, a decade that witnessed dramatic growth in the national independence movements of Asia and Africa.[6] For these independence movements resulted not only in the decolonization of some sixty-three nations between 1945 and 1975, but also in the construction of an international moral norm that proscribes nations from holding dominion over non-self-governing territories without their consent. The origins of this decolonization norm lay in the Western principles of freedom and self-determination that the European democracies had accepted for themselves in the nineteenth century, and more immediately in the inherent inconsistency between those same principles and European imperial practices.

The primary thrust for the establishment of an international prin-

---

[6] M. E. Chamberlain, *Decolonization* (London: Basil Blackwell, 1985), p. 1.

ciple of decolonization came from the colonized peoples themselves. As Sir Samuel Hoare, the British minister for India in the 1930s, noted in his arguments for the decolonization of the Indian empire, the very practices that Britain had undertaken to satisfy the elites of colonial societies had merely made them more conscious of the contrast between British theories of democracy and British domination in India: "I do maintain that the old system of paternal government, great as has been its achievements, is no longer sufficient. Good as it has been, it cannot survive a century of Western education, a long period of free speech and free press, and our deliberate policy of developing local Parliamentary government."[7] The leaders of the nationalist movements in British, French, German, and Belgian colonies during the period from 1930 to 1960 were almost all educated in the universities of the imperial countries, and they returned to their homelands all too keenly conscious of the inherent contradictions between the tenets of Western political thought and the reality of imperial domination.

These same leaders formed an international network during the period from 1930 to 1960, and they pressed repeatedly in international educational, religious, cultural, and political forums for an end to all territorial domination of one country by another. Jawaharlal Nehru, the unofficial spokesman for this movement, outlined in his pathbreaking "Colonialism Must Go" speech the argument that would guide the development of the decolonization norm:

> Behind [the colonial problem] today lies the passion and hunger for freedom, equality and better living conditions which consume hundreds of millions of people in Asia and Africa. That hunger cannot be ignored, for anything that drives vast numbers of human beings is a powerful factor in the dynamics of today. . . . [There must be] a clear renunciation of colonialism and imperialism and a recognition of the national independence of all dependent countries.[8]

In 1955 the representatives of twenty-four African and Asian nations met in Bandung, Indonesia and formulated a strategy to convince world opinion that colonialism was an evil that should be ended immediately.[9] Following up on the momentum provided by Bandung, the political, trade-union, and educational leadership of the free African states met in Ghana in 1958 to formulate a domestic and foreign

[7] Rudolph von Albertini, *Decolonization*, trans. Francesca Garvie (Garden City: Doubleday and Company, 1971), p. 69.

[8] Dorothy Norman, *Nehru: The First Sixty Years* (New York: John Day Company, 1965), p. 209.

[9] Thomas Hovet, *Africa in the United Nations* (Chicago: Northwestern University Press, 1963), p. 25.

policy for Africa that stressed as its foundation the right of all dependent nations to be set free in the immediate future.[10] The peoples of Africa and Asia were pressing for decolonization to be an international moral norm, accepted even by the societies that had themselves practiced imperialism.

The demands of the colonized nations were not falling on totally deaf ears in the capitals of the leading imperial nations, for many Europeans in the 1930s also began to see the contradiction between democratic values and colonization. In 1933 the British Labour party issued a report entitled *The Colonial Empire* that proposed that Britain begin moving immediately to a process of independence for its colonies, with the hope of achieving a commonwealth of self-governing units within a generation.[11] Even outside the more liberal wing of British politics, there was an uneasy feeling that the philosophical foundations of colonialism were shamefully contradictory to the English political tradition. As a consequence, by 1935 there were few who did not base any argument for continuing colonial rule on the need to nurture self-government among the colonized peoples before granting them independence, and the rationale for empire became not the good of the metropolitan state, but the obligation of the metropole to decolonize gradually in order to prevent chaos in the colonies.

By the 1950s, support for colonialism was rapidly eroding. The United States had an anticolonial tradition that dated from its birth as a nation, and America's political, cultural, and social influence in the postwar years helped to solidify and legitimate anticolonial sentiment in the international system.[12] In England, the independence of India had shown that decolonization could produce a democratic self-governing state, and the Labour party served as the core of a wide-ranging coalition that pressed ardently for full decolonization on the grounds that it was unjust to subjugate another people, even under the pretext of tutoring them in democracy.[13] In France the right of self-determination was asserted by a strange but effective coalition that included the Communist party, the Catholic church, the Social-

[10] Ibid., pp. 26–34.

[11] von Albertini, *Decolonization*, p. 120.

[12] It is important to recognize that the United States itself was not wholly consistent in its foreign-policy approaches to colonialism in the postwar world. But even so, the net impact of American cultural, political, and social dominance in the 1940s and 1950s was to help extend and legitimate the decolonization norm in the international system.

[13] For a philosophical discussion of the complexities of the problem of decolonization as they appeared to England at the end of the 1950s, see John Plamenatz, *On Alien Rule and Self-Government* (London: Longmans, 1960).

ists, labor, and even Charles de Gaulle.[14] French imperial policy had always been different from its British counterpart because the French empire was based upon an assimilationist philosophy that regarded all members of the empire as French citizens.[15] But even this assimilationist approach was under attack by proponents of self-determination, since it did not give the colonies the right to choose whether or not they wished to be part of France. In 1958 de Gaulle ended the debate by including the principle of self-determination in the constitution of the Fifth Republic and holding plebiscites throughout the French empire.[16]

The turning point for decolonization as an international moral norm came in 1960, when forty-three African and Asian nations introduced the Declaration on the Granting of Independence to Colonial Countries and Peoples to the United Nations General Assembly. The declaration proclaimed that

(1) the subjection of peoples to alien subjugation, domination and exploitation is a denial of fundamental human rights;

(2) all peoples have the right to self-determination by virtue of which they freely determine their political status and freely pursue their economic, social and cultural development;

(3) the "inadequacy of political, economic, social and educational preparedness" should never serve as a pretext for delaying independence;

(4) immediate steps should be taken, in trust and non–self-governing territories, to transfer all powers to the peoples of those territories, without any conditions or reservations, in accordance with their freely expressed will and desire;

(5) any attempt aimed at the partial or total disruption of the national unity and territorial integrity of a country is incompatible with the purposes and principles of the United Nations Charter.[17]

When the vote came on the declaration, ninety-three nations voted in favor and not one abstained or voted in opposition.

Perhaps the most vivid way of charting this growth of the decolonization norm in the twentieth century is to contrast the 1960 declara-

[14] In 1958 de Gaulle made the right of self-determination a part of his official policy. And the constitution that he designed in that year gave all overseas territories except Algeria the right to acquire independence. (Paul Clay Sorum, *Intellectuals and Decolonization in France* [Chapel Hill: University of North Carolina Press, 1977], pp. 97–103.)

[15] Rupert Emerson, *From Empire to Nation* (Boston: Beacon Press, 1960), pp. 68–72.

[16] Sorum, *Intellectuals and Decolonization*, pp. 97–103.

[17] United Nations, Department of Political Affairs, *Decolonization* 2, no. 6 (December 1975): 10.

tion with the arguments supporting the League of Nations mandate system and the original United Nations trusteeship system. At the Versailles peace conference of 1918, the victorious countries wished to divide the German colonies and Arab territories among themselves; the mandate system was designed as a way to give the great powers maximum discretion in their control of these territories, while providing a thin veneer of international supervision. The territories did have the possibility of achieving independence, but only "if the people are capable of governing themselves in the difficult conditions of the modern world."[18] The United Nations trusteeship system, in contrast, took as its starting point the assertion that all peoples had the right to self-determination and that the trustee nations should help to prepare non–self-governing lands for independence. The trusteeship system also demanded that trustee nations provide annual data to the United Nations on the steps taken to prepare territories for self-governance, thus recognizing that self-determination was an international issue.[19] Finally, the declaration of 1960 took the process a step further by asserting that non-self-governance was an evil that should not be continued even for the stated purpose of helping train less-developed nations. The progression of decolonization as an international moral norm is clear: in the 1920s colonization was considered legitimate in the international system; by the end of World War II it could be justified only as a step on the road to self-governance; and by 1960 territorial colonization was consensually seen by the peoples of the world to be an evil that should be eradicated.

THE UNITED STATES AND PANAMA: 1900–73

Panama's geography has been both its historical blessing and its historical curse. The Spanish conquerors were the first to recognize that the narrow isthmus at Panama provided the best crossing in the Western Hemisphere from the Atlantic to the Pacific, but they had to settle for a footpath rather than a canal. In 1850 American entrepreneurs built a railroad linking the two oceans in order to transport passengers and cargo. By 1876 Panama had become part of the nation of Colom-

---

[18] von Albertini, *Decolonization*, p. 7.

[19] The UN trusteeship system was the result of a compromise between the United States, which pushed for much fuller self-determination, and Great Britain, which wanted to preserve its empire in some form after the war. But even though the system was a compromise, it constituted a significant step toward international support for decolonization. See William Roger Louis, *Imperialism at Bay* (New York: Oxford University Press, 1978).

bia, and Ferdinand de Lesseps won a concession from the Colombian government to build a canal across Panama using French capital. But the task turned out to be monumentally difficult, and in 1889 de Lesseps's company went bankrupt, having completed only one-third of its task.

In the wake of the French failure, the United States began to consider seriously taking up the canal project. At first the American government leaned toward building the channel in Nicaragua, but the shorter crossing at Panama and fears about the seismic stability of the Nicaraguan route led Congress and President Theodore Roosevelt to focus upon the Panamanian route that the French had begun. Colombia, however, proved unwilling to accede to American demands for reduced Colombian sovereignty in a ten-mile-wide strip across the isthmus, and negotiations stalled.

Roosevelt was infuriated by the Colombian refusal to give the United States the desired concessions, and so when a group of Panamanian nationalists declared their independence from Colombia in 1903, the United States quickly recognized the new nation and declared its intention of protecting Panama from Colombian efforts to reclaim it. The leaders of the Panamanian revolution had relied for some months on the advice of Philippe Bunau-Varilla, a Frenchman living in Washington who had become interested in Panamanian affairs because he represented the successor company to de Lesseps's bankrupt enterprise. After the successful revolt, Bunau-Varilla was designated the temporary representative of the Panamanian government in Washington, and he was informed that Panama would send a delegation to Washington immediately in order to negotiate a treaty on the canal concession. In instructing Bunau-Varilla, the Panamanians clearly ordered him not to enter into any negotiations that might injure Panamanian sovereignty. But Bunau-Varilla, more interested in gaining money for the company he represented than in serving the Panamanian government, approached the U.S. State Department in an effort to conclude a canal treaty before the new Panamanian delegation arrived. Thus was born the Hay-Bunau-Varilla Treaty of 1903. It gave the United States the right to build a canal and also granted in perpetuity the use, occupation, and control of a ten-mile strip of land across the middle of Panama. In return, the United States agreed to guarantee the independence of Panama, to pay the new government $10 million for the canal and Canal Zone rights, and to pay an annual fee of $250,000. In its most important clause, the treaty ceded in perpetuity to the United States "all the rights, power, and authority within the Zone which the United States would possess and exercise if it were the sovereign of the territory, . . . to the entire exclusion of the exercise by the Republic of Panama of any such sovereign rights, power or authority."[20]

The Panamanian delegation, when it arrived in Washington, was devastated by the terms of the treaty, especially since Bunau-Varilla had managed to obtain for his own company a $40 million payment from the United States for residual rights to the canal concession. But when the Panamanians sought to renounce the treaty, they were told by Bunau-Varilla that the United States would withdraw its protection of Panamanian independence if the new treaty were not ratified by Panama. Thus on December 2, 1903, the Panamanian junta, citing the "indispensable need" to guarantee U.S. support for the independence of Panama, consented to the Hay-Bunau-Varilla Treaty and surrendered its powers of sovereignty over the centerpiece of its national territory.[21]

Thus began one of the great chapters of American history: the building of a canal that skeptics had labeled an impossible feat. Thus began also a continuing source of friction between the United States and Panama: the existence of a colonial enclave in the heart of Panama that was entirely under U.S. control. The Canal Zone had its own American police, American court system, and American jails; thus Panamanians who committed crimes within the Zone were prosecuted by American authorities. In addition, there were overtly discriminatory aspects to the administration of the Zone: Panamanians were excluded from the Zonian school system, hiring practices insured that all high-paying jobs at the canal and within the Zone went to Americans, and until the late 1940s there were even separate drinking fountains for Americans and Panamanians.

The Panamanian approach to these issues was to press for restrictions on the American exercise of sovereignty within the Canal Zone and to seek a greater share of the canal revenues. The American response was to show a willingness to negotiate increases in the pay-

[20] Congressional Research Service, *Background Documents Relating to the Panama Canal* (Washington: U.S. Government Printing Office, 1977), p. 280. This volume of background documents prepared for the canal-treaty hearings contains the records of all official transactions that the United States entered into regarding the building of an isthmian canal, beginning with the negotiations with Colombia and extending until 1977.

[21] Ibid., p. 289. The best historical account of this entire period is contained in David McCullough's *The Path between the Seas* (New York: Simon and Schuster, 1977). McCullough argues that the United States itself did not threaten to withdraw its support from Panama in the event of nonratification; rather, it was Bunau-Varilla who fanned Panamanian fears of an American withdrawal of protection.

ments to Panama, but no flexibility on the sovereignty question. In 1936 negotiations produced the Hull-Alfaro Treaty, which increased the annual payment to $430,000 and made clear that the United States had no right to intervene in the internal affairs of Panama. In 1955 the payment was raised again, to $1,930,000 (see Table 5.2). But these concessions were not enough. Panamanian nationalism was growing rapidly in the 1950s, and it spilled into violence in 1959 when a group of young Panamanians tried to parade the Panamanian flag through the Canal Zone. After they were turned back by the U.S. police, small-scale rioting broke out. Although there were no casualties, the 1959 flag riots did cause a stir in Washington. President Dwight D. Eisenhower ordered that the Panamanian flag be allowed to fly at one location in the Canal Zone as a sign of Panama's titular sovereignty, and he was not dissuaded by the fact that the House voted 380-12 against such an action.

There was an uneasy truce in U.S.-Panamanian relations until January 1964, when a group of American students in the Canal Zone hauled down the Panamanian flag and replaced it with an American flag. When news of this incident reached Panama City, a crowd of some two thousand marched on the Canal Zone, throwing rocks and

TABLE 5.2
U.S. Payments under the Various Panama Canal Treaties, 1903–77

Payments to the French Consortium	
Inventories and Salvage Credits	$ 1,282,664
Railroad Capital Stock	7,000,000
Reimbursement for Rights to the Canal	31,391,320
Miscellaneous	326,016
Total Payments to the French Consortium	$40,000,000
Payments to the Republic of Colombia	
Indemnification for the Loss of Panama	$25,000,000
Payments to the Republic of Panama	
Initial Payment	$10,000,000
Annuity Payments, 1913–20	2,000,000
Annuity Payments, 1921–51	10,990,000
Annuity Payments, 1952–76	43,610,992
Total Payments to the Republic of Panama	$66,600,992

Source: U.S. Congress, Senate, Committee on the Judiciary, Subcommittee on the Separation of Powers, *The Panama Canal Treaties*, 95th Cong., 2d sess., 1978, pt. 2:2603–2604.

bottles. The police responded with tear gas and then with bullets, and in the days of violence that followed, twenty-four Panamanians and three Americans were killed.[22]

In the ensuing months, President Lyndon Johnson staunchly said that the United States would never negotiate under pressure, but that he was willing to undertake an extensive review of the canal treaty and begin a new round of bargaining with Panama. To a great degree, Johnson's willingness to open new negotiations was spurred by the belief that it was in America's interest to build a new sea-level canal in Panama that would accommodate the new generation of aircraft carriers and would be less vulnerable to sabotage and military attack because it would not have any locks. Johnson had come to believe that nuclear excavation technology could make the construction of such a canal both feasible and cost-effective.[23] On June 26, 1967, Johnson announced that the United States and Panama had agreed to a new draft treaty. It eliminated both the perpetuity clause in the original treaty and the extraterritorial nature of the Canal Zone; but it also gave the United States exclusive rights to build a new canal and provided for American military domination of the canal area until 2067.[24] Such a recipe was acceptable neither in Panama nor in Washington, and even before the full terms of the treaty were announced, there was a storm of opposition. President Johnson canceled the signing ceremony and postponed submission to the Senate until after the 1968 elections; Panamanian president Marco Robles did not even speak on behalf of the treaty when it came before the Panamanian parliament; and it was quietly withdrawn and shelved.[25]

On October 11, 1968, the Panamanian National Guard staged a coup and replaced the newly elected president, Arnulfo Arias, with Brigadier General Omar Torrijos, the guard commandant. One month later, the citizens of the United States elected Richard Nixon as their new president. For Nixon, Panama was a remote issue filled with po-

[22] William Jorden, *Panama Odyssey* (Austin: University of Texas Press, 1984), pp. 43–63.

[23] Jorden, who had access to Johnson's personal papers on the canal issue, writes that "Lyndon Johnson had always seen the Panama problem as a two-sided affair. One part was doing something positive about Panamanian grievances that caused periodic eruptions in our affairs. The other part was to arrange to dig a new canal at sea level, a waterway that would accommodate the largest ships in the world and be much less vulnerable in wartime." (Ibid., p. 98)

[24] Congressional Research Service, *Background Documents*, pp. 1148–1371.

[25] There has been speculation that Johnson was merely using the treaty negotiations as an effort to put off Panamanian demands and that he did not truly desire a new treaty. But the matter is far from clear. See Stephen Rosenfeld, "The Panama Negotiations: A Close-Run Thing," *Foreign Affairs* 54 (October 1975): 2.

litical problems; thus American negotiators were instructed to take a harsh stance in future bargaining. The administration's stand toughened still further when the commission that Johnson had appointed to study the feasibility of a new sea-level canal reported back that nuclear excavation was technologically untested and that the cost of building such a canal through conventional means would be prohibitive. The idea of a new canal that would be far less vulnerable to attack had been a fundamental prerequisite for Johnson's willingness to relinquish the Canal Zone, and the finding that such a canal was unfeasible severely undercut the United States' ability to cede control of the Zone to Panama while guaranteeing the safety of the canal in time of crisis.[26] Thus during negotiations between the United States and Panama in 1971 and 1972, the American negotiators demanded almost unilateral control of the canal operations well into the twenty-first century; moreover, the Americans demanded that any new treaty relationship should be "without a fixed termination date but subject to periodic review and change by mutual agreement."[27] The Panamanian negotiators, who had come to the bargaining table with instructions to *improve* upon the terms of the 1967 pacts, could not find any constructive middle ground with the American team; and as 1972 ended, the renegotiation of the Panama Canal treaty of 1903 seemed hopelessly deadlocked.

TORRIJOS AND THE UNITED NATIONS: THE INTERNATIONALIZATION OF THE ISSUE

Omar Torrijos, Panama's head of government, was faced with a dilemma in late 1972. Despite the fact that the canal issue was causing constant political ferment within Panama, and despite the fact that Panamanian negotiators had continually warned the United States that a failure to alter the status of the Canal Zone might lead to riots and sabotage against the canal, the American bargaining position remained firm: the United States would retain its military rights and the control of the canal until the middle of the next century. Torrijos had to find a way to put sufficient pressure on the United States to bring about a major shift in its bargaining position. "To resolve a problem, the first thing you have to do is *make* it a problem," Torrijos later told U.S. ambassador William Jorden.[28] Torrijos decided to make the canal issue a problem for the United States.

The opportunity came because of a special meeting of the United

[26] Congressional Research Service, *Background Documents*, pp. 1379–1380.
[27] Jorden, *Panama Odyssey*, p. 154.
[28] Ibid., p. 176.

Nations Security Council that took place in Addis Ababa in 1972 to deal with the problems of colonialism and security in Africa. This was the first meeting of the Security Council outside of New York, and it was devoted to a regional theme. Torrijos saw a precedent in the Addis Ababa session, and in January 1973 he invited the members of the Security Council to hold a special meeting in Panama to deal with the topic of "measures for the maintenance and strengthening of international peace and security in Latin America in conformity with the provisions and principles of the Charter."[29] George Bush, the American ambassador to the UN, correctly believed that the Panamanians would use the special session to focus on the canal treaty, and he attempted to sidetrack the resolution. But most nations felt that they could hardly refuse to hold a session in Latin America after they had held one in Africa, and so the council accepted Panama's invitation for a meeting in Panama City in March 1973.

The special Security Council meeting in Panama was the centerpiece of a diplomatic offensive launched by Torrijos in order to internationalize the canal issue. As one Panamanian official later recounted:

> General Torrijos understood that a struggle for national liberation carried out only at the bilateral level was a struggle without a future for the very simple reason that it was the struggle of a very small country against the major power of the world. Thus he decided . . . that the problem of Panama, the Canal Problem, would not be a real problem until it became a problem of the American continents and of the world.[30]

From the very opening of the special session in Panama, Torrijos attempted to make the canal problem a problem of the world. In his message of greeting, he departed from protocol to make Panama's case to the United Nations, and he made that case in the language of colonialism:

> Panama understands full well the struggle of peoples that are suffering the humiliation of colonialism, of other peoples that, like us, are suffering restrictions and subjection, of those men that do not allow political power to be exercised by a foreign Government over the territory of their birth, of those generations that are struggling and will continue to struggle to root out from their country the presence of foreign troops, placed there without the consent of the occupied nation. . . . [For Panama], which seventy years ago opened its arms for the benefit of the merchant fleet of the

[29] UN Security Council, *Official Records*, March 1973, 1695th meeting, p. 1.
[30] George Moffett, *The Limits of Victory: The Ratification of the Panama Canal Treaties* (Ithaca: Cornell University Press, 1985), p. 38.

world, it becomes extremely difficult to understand how a country whose hallmark has been not to be colonialist insists on maintaining a colony in the very heart of my country. Surely for that people this must be a shame, since they were a colony and they knew how degrading it was to be so, and they struggled heroically to achieve their freedom. I say to the representatives of the United States that it is more noble to redress an injustice than to perpetuate an error. From the world which is represented here today we ask for moral support in this struggle engaged in by the weak. This struggle can triumph only when it is assisted by the conscience of the world, and our people is already reaching the limit of its patience.[31]

The Torrijos speech set off a firestorm in the Security Council, and the overarching agenda of Latin American security became lost in the debate over the American presence in Panama. The predictable condemnations of U.S. colonialism came from China and the Soviet bloc. But when attacks upon the U.S. negotiating position began to come from friendly nations, the American delegation started to become very uneasy. Kenya cited all of the anticolonial resolutions passed by the UN in the 1950s and 1960s, and it urged that these resolutions be the new basis for negotiations between Panama and the United States.[32] Honduras supported the Panamanian demands as an effort to achieve a new treaty that "the law of civilization of the last part of the twentieth century requires."[33] Costa Rica argued that America's failure to surrender sovereignty in Panama raised questions about whether the United States had fully abandoned the imperialist diplomacy of 1903.[34] Austria proposed that any new negotiations should be based upon the principle of territorial integrity and sovereignty, while Australia urged the United States to adopt a negotiating stance that would "bring the treaties up to date with present day realities and international concepts."[35]

John Scali, the newly appointed American ambassador to the UN, tried to put the best light on the U.S. negotiating position. He stated that America was willing to negotiate a new treaty, that the perpetuity clause would be removed, that a significant part of the Canal Zone could be returned, and that a formula could be developed to provide a gradual increase of Panamanian jurisdiction within the Zone.[36] Scali

[31] UN Security Council, *Official Records*, March 1973, 1695th meeting, pp. 1–3.
[32] Ibid., 1700th meeting, p. 4.
[33] Ibid., 1700th meeting, p. 20.
[34] Ibid., 1698th meeting, p. 10.
[35] Ibid., 1700th meeting, p. 6; 1699th meeting, p. 14.
[36] Ibid., 1701st meeting, p. 17.

also tried to negotiate a joint draft resolution with the Panamanians in order to head off a more radical resolution that Panama was considering introducing to the Security Council. But the Panamanians, seeking maximum leverage from the council meeting in Panama, refused to compromise.[37] Juan Antonio Tack, the Panamanian foreign minister, introduced a resolution sponsored by Panama, Peru, Yugoslavia, Guinea, Kenya, the Sudan, India and Indonesia. It called for an end to the Canal Zone, the transfer of responsibility for the operation of the canal to Panama, and the termination of all American jurisdictional rights within Panama.[38] In support of the resolution, Tack argued: "A treaty cannot be new and modern if it does not satisfy our legitimate aspirations effectively to exercise sovereignty over our entire national territory, to exercise sovereignty over our natural resources, to do away with the existence of a government within another government, to put an end to the colonial enclave which gives rise to the present dispute."[39]

In the ensuing debate, the central question became whether the members of the Security Council were willing to vote to sustain the principle of decolonization, as reflected in the 1960 UN General Assembly Resolution on Non-Self-Governing Peoples: "Any attempt aimed at the partial or total disruption of the national unity and territorial integrity of a country is incompatible with the purposes and principles of the United Nations Charter."[40] When the vote came, thirteen nations voted in favor of the resolution, the United Kingdom abstained, and the United States used its veto for only the third time in the history of the UN. Among those voting against the United States were such longtime allies as Australia, France, Kenya, and Canada. The message for the United States was clear: no nation was willing to stand with it on the issue of Panama.

When Scali returned to Washington, he was called before joint hearings of the House to explain why the United States had been maneuvered into the position of having to exercise its veto. Congressman Richard Bowen asked Scali the question that the hearings had been designed to answer:

[37] Scali later told Congress that the negotiations on a compromise resolution were progressing smoothly until the Panamanians suddenly broke off the talks and insisted on their own more hard-line resolution. (U.S. Congress, House, Committee on Foreign Affairs and Committee on Maritime Affairs, *Hearings on the Special Session of the United Nations Security Council in Panama*, 93d Cong., 2d sess., 1973 [Washington: U.S. Government Printing Office, 1973], p. 4.)

[38] UN Security Council, *Official Records*, March 1973, 1698th meeting, p. 13.

[39] Ibid., 1702d meeting, p. 2.

[40] UN Department of Political Affairs, *Decolonization*, p. 10.

BOWEN: We find ourselves very decisively outmaneuvered, outplanned in this instance. Apparently Panamanian diplomacy has been more skillful than American in a matter affecting our vital interests. . . . What might you have to say on this matter?

SCALI: Congressman, we first of all have to start with the issues. The Panama Canal to those who study it superficially looks like the classic example of colonialism in the Western hemisphere. . . . So at a time when you have nationalism sweeping the world, it looks like a case that you could very easily sell if you are a lesser developed country. And you have 132 countries as your potential allies in the United Nations.[41]

Congress was not the only branch of government that was stunned by the outcome of the Security Council session. Henry Kissinger, national security advisor and secretary of state, immediately convened a high-level interagency task force to deal with the Panamanian issue and with Latin American relations in general. As Kissinger's Latin American specialist at the National Security Council recalled: "What really made Kissinger understand he was sitting on a potential powder keg was the U.N. Security Council meeting. . . . It was, after all, a gathering not of the Western Hemisphere but of the world. Votes against the United States came not only from Panama and Peru, but also from the Soviet Union and China and even France. That was enough to awaken any geopolitician."[42]

During the months following the Security Council meeting, General Torrijos mobilized the leaders of Latin America to keep pressing for a resolution of the "colonial situation" in Panama, and when Kissinger attempted to organize a dialogue with Latin America, the Latin foreign ministers stated that the Panama issue should receive the highest priority in any such dialogue.[43] Kissinger concluded that the United States should reopen substantive negotiations with Panama on a higher level and should sharply reduce American demands.[44] Veteran ambassador Ellsworth Bunker was appointed to represent the

[41] House Committee on Foreign Affairs and Committee on Maritime Affairs, *Hearings on the Special Session*, p. 13.

[42] Jorden, *Panama Odyssey*, pp. 206–207.

[43] Congressional Research Service, *Background Documents*, pp. 1475–1476.

[44] The primary and secondary accounts of this episode are unanimous in viewing the reputational damage that the United States suffered at the Security Council meeting in Panama as the impetus for new and intensive interest in the canal issue on the part of Henry Kissinger and the American foreign-policy establishment. See William L. Furlong, *The Dynamics of Foreign Policymaking* (Boulder, Colo.: Westview Press, 1984), p. 65; Moffett, *Limits of Victory*, pp. 38–40; Rosenfeld, "Panama Negotiations," p. 4; Michael J. Hogan, *The Panama Canal in American Politics* (Carbondale: Southern Illinois Press, 1986), pp. 84–85; and Jorden, *Panama Odyssey*, pp. 175–223.

United States in the negotiations, and in October 1973, Kissinger and Bunker met with Foreign Minister Tack in New York. By February 1974, the two sides had reached agreement on a series of principles that would guide negotiations on the future of the canal. Kissinger flew to Panama with the Senate majority and minority leaders to initial what came to be called the Kissinger-Tack agreement. It provided that

1. The treaty of 1903 and its amendments would be abrogated.
2. The concept of perpetuity would be eliminated.
3. There would be a termination of United States jurisdiction over Panamanian territory that would take place in accord with terms specified in the treaty.
4. The Panamanian territory in which the canal is situated would be returned to the jurisdiction of the Republic of Panama. The Republic of Panama, as territorial sovereign, would grant to the United States for the duration of the new canal treaty the right to use the lands, water, and airspace necessary to operate the canal.
5. The Republic of Panama would have a just and equitable share of the benefits derived from the operation of the canal.
6. The Republic of Panama would participate in the administration of the canal.
7. The Republic of Panama would participate with the United States in the protection and defense of the canal.[45]

The Kissinger-Tack principles were joyously received in Panama. Torrijos had received from the United States a commitment to provide an entirely new basis for the American role in Panama, one that gave full recognition to Panamanian sovereignty and that provided for joint operation of the canal at an early date. The strategy of internationalization had worked. As *Washington Post* reporter Stephen Rosenfeld concluded in his analysis of the negotiating process, "The propaganda and political beating administered in the United Nations helped transform the issue within the U.S. government from a modest regional matter, which could safely be left in a state of stagnation, into a major priority."[46] And the way that Torrijos had accomplished this transformation in the importance of Panama for America's foreign-policy agenda was by mobilizing international support around the norm of decolonization. As the members of the Security Council realized, as John Scali realized, and as Henry Kissinger came to realize, the United States found itself isolated on the issue of Panama because the

[45] Congressional Research Service, *Background Documents*, pp. 1478–1479.
[46] Rosenfeld, "Panama Negotiations," p. 4.

Panama Canal looked like, in Scali's words, "a classic example of co-lonialism in the Western hemisphere." And no country was willing to side with the United States if it meant appearing to side against the norm of territorial decolonization.

The events of 1973 thus bear out the notion that international moral norms can have important reputational effects. For Torrijos had mo-bilized support around the international moral norm of decolonization and by doing so had accomplished three objectives. First of all, he had enlisted parties formerly uninterested in the question of the Canal Zone; thus he had broadened his coalition of support. Second, Torrijos had elevated the Panama issue on the American foreign-policy agenda; the reputational damage that the United States suffered in Panama City made the American foreign-policy establishment sit up and take notice.[47] Finally, Torrijos had succeeded in changing the configuration of American interests that would weigh in any decision about transferring the canal. For he had injected a significant new factor into the calculation of national interest: the belief that the canal issue would continue to be read by the Third World in general and Latin America in particular as an indication that the United States continued to operate from a colonialist mentality. Henry Kissinger was willing to initial the Kissinger-Tack principles because he did not want the reputational damage that the United States was suffering over the canal question to be a continuing irritant in relations with less-developed countries.

From Principles to a Treaty

The Kissinger-Tack principles had established the framework for what would become the Panama Canal treaties, but much hard bar-gaining had to occur before these principles could be developed into a full-blown agreement. This bargaining was complicated by the fact that the U.S. Defense Department wanted to take a hard-line stance with the Panamanians on the issue of continuing defense rights after the transfer of the canal.[48] So Ellsworth Bunker patiently negotiated with the Panamanians in the fifteen months following the signing of the Kissinger-Tack principles, while Kissinger waged intramural war-fare within the Ford administration. The Department of Defense vig-orously fought against any effort to limit American rights to defend

[47] John Kingdon labels such a phenomenon a "focusing event," one that attracts the attention of top policymakers and lifts an item onto the policy agenda. See Kingdon, *Agendas, Alternatives, and Public Policies* (Boston: Little, Brown and Company, 1984), pp. 99ff.

[48] *New York Times*, November 28, 1975.

the canal, and the Joint Chiefs were willing to scrap the treaty negotiations rather than give in. But President Gerald Ford, who was becoming increasingly impatient with his administration's inability to reach a common strategy, finally sided with the State Department and ordered the chiefs to accept substantial limitations in the proposed time frame for the American presence in Panama.[49] Meanwhile, Torrijos was mobilizing the Latin American heads of state to keep up the pressure on the Panama issue. In March 1975, he organized a communique from the presidents of Colombia, Costa Rica, and Venezuela calling upon Washington to end the colonialism of the Canal Zone and proposing that a Latin American summit meeting be held in Panama in 1976 to focus on the canal issue.[50] In July, Torrijos and Mexican president Luis Echeverría pledged their continuing support for a quick resolution of the canal issue and proclaimed it to be the linchpin of U.S.–Latin American relations.[51] And throughout 1975, the Panamanian leader made the canal issue a center of attention at the Organization of American States.

As the bargaining continued, it became apparent that a treaty could not be submitted to the Senate before 1976, which was an election year. And as the White House knew quite well, this was too controversial an issue to be prudently brought to Congress in the heat of a campaign. In May 1975, Senator Strom Thurmond had collected thirty-seven signatures on a resolution urging the United States to retain ownership of the canal and the Canal Zone. In June the House of Representatives passed an amendment to the defense appropriations bill that prohibited funding for negotiations designed to transfer the canal to Panama; the vote was 246-164.[52] A June poll by the Opinion Research Corporation found that only 12 percent of the American people favored turning the ownership of the canal over to Panama, while 66 percent favored keeping it.[53] And conservative political leaders were arguing that it would be a highly immoral act to surrender the canal to a leader like Torrijos, who routinely violated human rights. Reading the signs that the canal treaties would be difficult to sell to the Senate, the White House decided that the issue of Panama would best be postponed until 1977. The Panamanians agreed with this strategy, and so it was decided that formal negotiations would be sus-

[49] Rosenfeld, "Panama Negotiations," pp. 7–12. Actually, the final language of the agreement terminated American rights to the Canal Zone bases in 1999, but did not preclude the United States from negotiating with Panama for additional bases.

[50] *New York Times*, March 26, 1975, p. 24.

[51] *New York Times*, July 6, 1975, p. 13.

[52] Moffett, *Limits of Victory*, p. 42.

[53] Ibid., p. 209.

pended until after the election but that the negotiating teams would continue to meet informally so that the outline of an agreement would be ready when formal negotiations resumed.[54]

The decision to suspend negotiations did not prevent the issue of the Panama Canal from surfacing in the presidential election campaign. For candidate Ronald Reagan surprised even himself with the strong reaction he got from audiences when he uttered his soon-to-become-famous line "We bought it, we paid for it, it's ours!" in New Hampshire one night.[55] And as Reagan's popularity increased, President Ford took an increasingly hard line on the Panama issue, causing consternation in Panama. U.S. negotiators assured the Panamanians that the treaty negotiations would still be on track after the electoral campaign, but the tone of Ford's campaign rhetoric and the ambivalent nature of Democratic nominee Jimmy Carter's position on Panama made even the State Department unsure about the future of the agreements. With Carter's victory in November, the Kissinger Department of State no longer had to worry about the future of the canal issue, and Panama began to seek signals from the new administration about how it would approach the impending treaty.

In January 1977, President Carter met with his foreign-policy team to formulate the priorities of the new administration. All those present felt that Carter should publicly endorse the Kissinger-Tack principles and designate the settling of the Panama Canal issue as a primary objective of Carter's foreign policy. The participants fully recognized that the ratification of the canal treaties would be an extremely difficult task, given the congressional and public opposition to a transfer of the canal. But the Carter team believed that despite these obstacles the issue of the Canal Zone had to be faced head-on, and that it should be resolved in the first year of the administration. Essentially, there were three reasons why the president and his advisors gave such a high priority to what had only four years before been a backwater issue.

The first reason concerned the symbolic importance that the canal issue had taken on in U.S.–Latin American relations as a result of Torrijos's efforts to internationalize the question. Just four days before Carter's inauguration, Torrijos had persuaded the presidents of twelve Latin American nations to write to the new president stating that the resolution of the sovereignty issue in the Canal Zone had become the *sine qua non* of good hemispheric relations.[56] Sol Linowitz, whom

[54] Furlong, *Foreign Policymaking*, p. 81.

[55] Thomas J. McIntyre, *The Fear Brokers* (New York: Pilgrim, 1979), p. 56.

[56] Juan de Onis, the *New York Times* correspondent in Buenos Aires, wrote that "the outcome of the Panama Canal Treaty negotiations will serve for Latin America as a

Secretary of State Cyrus Vance had tapped to be the administration's point man on Panama, told President Carter at the January meeting on Panama policy that the canal question was no longer a bilateral issue; rather, it had come to take on a significance that went far beyond the borders of Panama:

> The Panama Canal issue involves far more than the relationship between the U.S. and Panama. It is an issue which affects all U.S.–Latin American relations, for all the countries of Latin America have joined with Panama in urging a new treaty with the United States. In their eyes, the Canal runs not just through the center of Panama, but through the center of the Western Hemisphere. Indeed the problem significantly affects the relationship between this country and the entire Third World, since the nations of the Third World have made common cause on this issue—looking upon our position on the Canal as a last vestige of a colonial past which evokes bitter memories and deep animosities.[57]

Linowitz's comments were seconded by Vance and National Security Advisor Zbigniew Brzezinski.[58] Thus the president came to the conclusion that a failure to endorse the Kissinger-Tack principles and to move quickly for a treaty would subject the United States to reputational damage that would impede other foreign-policy objectives:

> Our failure to act on the treaty was driving a wedge between us and some of our best friends and allies among the other American nations. They were being forced to take sides between us and Panama, and they were not supporting us. In a way not of our choosing, this issue had become a litmus issue throughout the world, indicating how the United States, a superpower, would treat a small and relatively defenseless nation that had always been a close partner and supporter.[59]

---

major test of the kind of relations the incoming Democratic Administration wants with the countries south of the U.S. border." De Onis attributed this fact to "the attention focused on the Canal issue in Latin America by Panama's persistent diplomatic campaign for regional support." (*New York Times*, January 16, 1977, sec. 4, p. 5.)

[57] Moffett, *Limits of Victory*, p. 67.

[58] See Cyrus Vance, *Hard Choices* (New York: Simon and Schuster, 1983), p. 143; and Zbigniew Brzezinski, *Power and Principle* (New York: Farrar, Straus and Giroux, 1983), p. 134.

[59] Jimmy Carter, *Keeping Faith: Memoirs of a President* (New York: Bantam Books, 1982), p. 186; and George Moffett, memorandum on interview with Sol Linowitz, box 3, Moffett Papers, James Earl Carter Presidential Library. It is interesting to note that Carter describes the canal issue as a "litmus issue" of America's intentions; for in describing the role of moral norms in the international system, Robert Keohane uses the term "litmus test" to describe the reputational role that moral norms may play in the international system.

The second reason that the president and his advisors decided to press for a new canal treaty was to insure the continued safe operations of the canal itself. Ever since the 1964 riots in Panama City, the United States had been aware that Panamanian nationalism, if left to simmer, could lead to acts of sabotage against the canal. Secretary of State Vance, who had been dispatched to Panama by Lyndon Johnson during the 1964 uprising, had come to the conclusion that the best way to protect the operation of the canal in the future was to make sure that the Panamanian government did not undertake a campaign of sabotage or military action against the canal:

> There was little question in my mind that sooner or later Panama would resort to major violence, even to the point of destroying the Canal. Defending the canal would be an extremely difficult task. It could be closed by the simplest act of sabotage. We could and would defend it by force if necessary, but the cost in human life and the economic loss would be high for both countries, and the United States would be condemned by world opinion for perpetuating a morally objectionable "colonial" relationship.[60]

Vance's concerns were shared by Defense Secretary Harold Brown and by Brzezinski.[61] They pointed to the great vulnerability of the system of locks and to the jungles that surrounded the canal and could provide haven to saboteurs; the Joint Chiefs estimated that it might take up to 100,000 troops to defend the waterway against a full-scale Panamanian attack. For these reasons, President Carter concluded that "the Canal could not be defended permanently unless we were able to maintain a working partnership and good relationship with Panama."[62]

The final reason that the Carter administration decided to place the Panama Canal treaties at the top of its foreign-policy agenda had to do with the president's personal conception of the role of morality in American foreign policy. As Brzezinski remembers those first weeks in the Carter White House:

[60] Vance, *Hard Choices*, p. 141.

[61] Brzezinski, *Power and Principle*, p. 155. In a speech at the University of Notre Dame in June 1977, Carter outlined his conception of a just and equitable foreign policy: "Our policy is based on a historical vision of America's role. Our policy is derived from a larger view of global change. Our policy is rooted in our moral values, which never change. Our policy is reinforced by our material wealth and our military power. Our policy is designed to serve mankind." (*Department of State Bulletin*, June 13, 1977, p. 625.)

[62] Carter, *Keeping Faith*, p. 186.

Each new President tries to imprint a distinctively new stamp on foreign policy. For Eisenhower, it was to replace containment with proclamations of liberation; for Kennedy, it was to "move America forward again" and in the process to make it more appealing to the developing world; for Nixon, it was to free America from the paralysis induced by the Vietnam War. When Jimmy Carter assumed office, U.S. foreign policy appeared to him and to his team to be stalemated on the level of power and excessively cynical on the level of principle. The new Administration therefore decided to move on a broad front and to tackle several key issues at once while the President's prestige was at its highest. We were determined to demonstrate the primacy of the moral dimension of foreign policy.[63]

The Panama Canal question was one of these "key issues" through which the administration sought to emphasize the role of morality in international affairs.[64] Thus, in part, Carter's decision to seek an early ratification debate on the canal treaties was an effort to educate the public about the need to correct injustices through an equitable foreign policy.[65]

The president instructed Bunker and Linowitz, his designated negotiators, to make the deal with Panama "generous, fair, and appropriate."[66] From May until August, the American team bargained with their Panamanian counterparts in order to turn the Kissinger-Tack principles into a full-blown treaty. It was agreed that the Canal Zone would be dissolved immediately; that 60 percent of the existing Zone territory would immediately be transferred to Panama; and that other segments of the former Zone would be transferred to Panama over a twenty-two-year period. All court and police powers in the former Canal Zone would be shifted to Panama, and Panamanian law would be recognized throughout the whole country. The operations of the canal

[63] Brzezinski, *Power and Principle*, p. 81.

[64] It is always necessary to use memoir literature with caution, especially in delving into the reasons why a particular administration decided to embark upon a foreign-policy endeavor. But there are several reasons for confidence in asserting that the Carter administration sought a new Panama Canal treaty because of the three reasons given above. The first reason for confidence is that the various memoirs are consistent in their presentation of the reasons behind the decision to press ahead on Panama. The second is that historians' oral interviews with large numbers of Carter White House staffers have confirmed the reasoning presented in the memoirs (see particularly Moffett, *Limits of Victory*, pp. 48–71). The final reason for confidence lies in the fact that contemporaneous news accounts of decision making in the early Carter White House point to the above-mentioned three reasons as the basis for the green light on Panama.

[65] See Joseph Kraft, "Righting Our Foreign Wrongs, and Beyond," *Washington Post*, March 10, 1977, p. A23.

[66] Sol Linowitz, *The Making of a Public Man* (Boston: Little, Brown and Company, 1985), p. 152.

itself would be progressively shifted to Panamanian hands, and in 1999 U.S. rights to operate the canal would terminate. Panama would receive $50 million per year in shipping tolls, in addition to some $30 million in other annual benefits. On the thorny issue of U.S. defense rights, it was decided that American rights to bases in Panama would terminate in the year 2000, but that the United States would still remain a codefender of the neutrality of the canal against external threats after that time.

In reviewing the factors that brought the Carter administration from Inauguration Day to the signing of the Panama Canal treaties, it is interesting to note how significant a role the international decolonization norm played in the forging of American foreign policy toward Panama. It was General Torrijos's continuing ability to use the decolonization norm to mobilize Latin American and Third World support for the Panamanian position that led the White House to conclude that a failure to restructure U.S.-Panamanian relations would subject the United States to significant reputational damage. It was the strength of the decolonization norm in the international system and in the American tradition that made President Carter see in the canal issue a truly fitting beginning for his effort to give morality a more prominent place in U.S. foreign policy. And the decolonization norm even accentuated the security risks associated with the canal, since, as Cyrus Vance noted in his assessment of the dangers associated with refusing to negotiate with Panama, a full-scale defense of the canal by U.S. troops would be vehemently condemned by world opinion because of its colonialist overtones.[67] Thus in answering the question of why the Carter White House moved so quickly and so forcefully to negotiate and ratify the Panama Canal treaties, it is important to take into account the very prominent role played by the moral norm against colonization.

THE FIGHT FOR RATIFICATION

Soon after the signing of the Panama Canal treaties, the White House prepared for a massive and intensive public-relations campaign designed to gain the necessary support for the new agreements in the Senate. The administration realized that this task would be far from easy, since polling data consistently showed a two-to-one majority op-

[67] For the CIA's estimate of how the colonial aspects of the Canal Zone would leave the United States diplomatically isolated in the event it was necessary to defend the canal against Panama, see Senate Committee on Foreign Relations, *Hearings on the Panama Canal Treaties*, 1:146.

posed to the canal treaties and the emergent New Right was gearing up for a major antitreaty campaign. Sensing that it would be easier to win over the elite segments of American society than the citizenry as a whole, the Carter strategy focused not upon a reversal of public opinion, but rather upon an effort to convince opinion leaders in the United States that the canal treaties were sound public policy. In Carter's words, "[we] sought not to build up an absolute majority of support among all citizens, but to convince an acceptable number of key political leaders in each important state to give their senators some running room."[68]

The first step in generating such "running room" was the construction of a wide-ranging coalition of opinion leaders who would speak out on behalf of the treaties and isolate the New Right opposition. Accordingly, the White House organized the Committee of Americans for the Canal Treaties (COACT) to press for ratification. The committee's leadership read like a who's who of politically active American society: former president Ford, Mrs. Lyndon Johnson, Nelson Rockefeller, John McCloy, Clark Clifford, Douglas Dillon, Melvin Laird, Paul Nitze, Eugene Rostow, Elmo Zumwalt, Matthew Ridgeway, McGeorge Bundy, Brent Scowcroft, George Meany, Theodore Hesburgh, UAW chief Douglas Fraser, IBM president Thomas Watson, and DuPont chairman Irving Shapiro. As the Boston *Phoenix* noted in admiration of the White House campaign, the faces on the committee's roster sheet constituted "three decades of *Time* magazine covers and evening news broadcasts."[69] COACT sought to build up a national coalition in support of the canal treaties by using the same three arguments that had originally led the Carter administration to push for a new agreement with Panama: the new treaties were vital for improving U.S. relations with Latin America; they would enhance the safe operation of the canal by insuring that Panama remained supportive of the canal's continued operation; and they would correct a historic inequity that contradicted the moral heritage of the United States.[70]

[68] Carter, *Keeping Faith*, p. 162. George Moffett, who conducted interviews with more than fifty Carter administration officials involved in the protreaty effort, concluded that the White House strategy was from the beginning consciously aimed at domestic elites, because the administration felt that it had the best chance of building support with opinion leaders. (Moffett, *Limits of Victory*, pp. 81–82) Many historical accounts of the drive for ratification have noted how ironic it is that a president who came to Washington on a populist platform regarding foreign policy turned to the foreign-policy establishment rather than to the general public for support.

[69] Moffett, *Limits of Victory*, p. 83.

[70] Hamilton Jordan, "Panama Canal Treaties," January 25, 1978, box 50, Files of Hamilton Jordan, White House Central Files, James Earl Carter Presidential Library;

For the foreign-policy establishment in the United States, the key reason for supporting the treaties was the belief that a failure to ratify would subject the United States to continual reputational damage in its relations with Latin America and the Third World. In a coordinated executive-branch response to the Senate Foreign Relations committee about the consequences of nonratification, the administration predicted that

> rejection of the treaties would impair our relationship with Latin America and the Third World and would lead to considerable criticism from developed countries as well. Panama would bring pressure to bear on us in international forums where we would find virtually no support for our position. Even our closest allies believe the time has come for a change in the arrangements.[71]

Henry Kissinger confirmed the White House analysis in Senate testimony, arguing that rejection of the treaties would label the United States as colonialist and would thereby limit America's future ability to build cooperative relationships in Latin America:

> One of the strongest arguments in favor of ratification is in fact its impact on cooperative Western Hemisphere relationships. . . . No government and no public opinion in any of the countries of this hemisphere would be willing to support us if we now refuse to modernize the canal relationship. We would witness a gradual deterioration of our relationships even when some leaders might prefer to retain constructive ties. If the treaties are accepted, on the other hand, our many friends in the hemisphere will be enabled to cooperate in the development of a constructive Western Hemisphere policy.[72]

---

and *Washington Post*, August 4, 1977, p. A7. It is necessary to separate arguments that were presented on behalf of the canal treaties from the rebuttals to arguments that were made against the treaties. COACT and the White House spent much of their time responding to claims that the treaties would severely damage U.S. interests by endangering the security of the canal or by creating the image of the United States as a "paper tiger." But these responses were not arguments *for* signing the canal treaties; they were offered to *counter* arguments about how much signing the treaties would cost the United States. The three arguments that the White House consistently advanced in order to show why the new treaties should be signed concerned U.S.–Latin American relations, the enhanced safety of the canal that would accrue from a transfer to Panama, and the injustice of continuing a colonial enclave in the heart of Panama.

[71] Senate Committee on Foreign Relations, *Hearings on the Panama Canal Treaties*, 3:671; and Memorandum, "White House Briefings on Panama Canal Treaties," January 6, 1978, box 9, Moffett Papers.

[72] Senate Committee on Foreign Relations, *Hearings on the Panama Canal Treaties*, 3:527.

And William Rogers, former assistant secretary of state for Latin American affairs and the chairman of COACT, argued that the colonial nature of the Canal Zone made the treaties a symbolic test of America's ability to lead the West in a manner that respected the independence of other nations:

> What the new treaty relationship with Panama will do is to open the way for us to exercise the responsibilities of leadership which are thrust upon us by our own power, prestige and resources and which no other nation in the world is equipped to discharge. Panama, in this sense, is a symbolic issue, testing in a way which other nations cannot fail to notice the sort of nation we are in this last quarter of the twentieth century. . . . In a material sense these treaties do much for Panama and little that is tangible for the United States. What we do gain, however, is an enhancement of our stature in the world. This is an action which will say to others that we can be sensitive to their needs, that we are prepared to promote our vision of a world order of nations and respect the rights and interests of others, that our policy is cooperation and not domination or confrontation, and that we have the self-confidence and inner strength to apply these principles to our future conduct throughout the world.[73]

In rendering its final report, the Senate Foreign Relations committee concluded that

> the opportunity presented by the treaties is akin to a double edged sword: Acceptance of the treaties will evidence our firm commitment to the peaceful and equitable settlement of international disputes. Acceptance of them will evidence our firm commitment to international cooperation among all nations, big or small, rich or poor, developed or undeveloped. Acceptance of them will evidence our firm commitment to independence and self-determination for all peoples. Acceptance of them will evidence our firm commitment to a foreign policy based on preserving the national interest without sacrificing our nation's principles, values, or honor. These are important commitments. If we do not honor them fully, the sword will cut the other way and our adversaries will exploit the situation to the maximum extent possible.
>
> They will charge that the U.S. talks a good game, that we espouse the principles set forth in the U.N. Charter, that we speak of independence, self-determination and human rights, but that when our interests are on the line we move from the realm of the theoretical to the realm of the practical, that nothing is changed. The U.S., they will say, is playing the same old shell game in the Western Hemisphere that it has played for years. The name of the game is Manifest Destiny, backed up by gunboat

[73] Ibid., 4:458–459.

diplomacy, economic penetration, and political subjugation. In a word, imperialism. And for evidence of all this they will point to Panama and the Canal Zone.[74]

Omar Torrijos's effort to mobilize international support around the norm of decolonization had substantially altered the calculation of U.S. interests in Panama in the minds of America's leading foreign policy makers. For the question of Panama had become an international litmus test of America's foreign-policy intentions, and the reputational damage that the United States would sustain if the treaties were rejected convinced many key opinion leaders that it was now in the best interests of the United States to transfer the canal.

The second argument presented by protreaty forces in order to mobilize elite support concerned the continued safe operation of the canal itself. Cyrus Vance had been an articulate proponent of the proposition that by giving the canal to Panama, the United States would guard against future sabotage to the canal by insuring Panamanian support for its continued operation. Secretary of Defense Harold Brown presented this argument in stark terms to the Senate Foreign Relations Committee:

> Use of the Canal is more important than ownership. Efficient operation of the canal in the years ahead is more important than nostalgia for a simpler past. Ability to defend and control access to the canal is essential, but the issue is how that ability can best be assured—by a cooperative effort with a friendly Panama or by a garrison amid hostile surroundings.[75]

Brown and the Joint Chiefs, together with retired Chief of Naval Operations Elmo Zumwalt, forcefully argued that the continued operation and safety of the canal could best be guaranteed through ratification of the new treaties. They predicted that repelling a full-scale assault by Panamanian forces on the canal would require massive intervention, and that not one U.S. ally could be expected to give even rhetorical support to the United States if it tried to defend its position in Panama.[76]

The third reason for ratification offered by proponents of the treaties concerned the ethics of continuing to hold the canal and Canal Zone against Panamanian wishes. As William Rogers stated in his testi-

[74] U.S. Congress, Senate, Committee on Foreign Relations, *Report on the Panama Canal Treaty and the Neutrality Treaty*, 93d Cong., 2d sess., 1978 (Washington: U.S. Government Printing Office, 1978), pp. 20–21.

[75] Senate Committee on Foreign Relations, *Hearings on the Panama Canal Treaties*, 1:23.

[76] Ibid., p. 146.

mony to the Senate, "We should not support the treaties out of fear. We should support the treaties because they are right." William Jorden, the U.S. ambassador to Panama, framed the ethical issues of the treaties in starkly colonial terms, as did other proponents who spoke to the morality question:

> The issue . . . is the presence in a friendly country of a zone governed by the United States. It is an area over which Panama—the country in which it is located—has absolutely no control of any kind. You and I can well imagine what the reaction would be of Americans faced with such a situation. Suppose that history had dictated that the Mississippi River and a strip on each side were controlled by a foreign power. Suppose that in going from Illinois to Missouri, or from Louisiana to Texas you had to cross that strip. And imagine, if you will, that you broke the law in some fashion—by speeding or having a tail light out, or whatever—and you were arrested by a French gendarme or a Mexican policeman. It does not take great imagination to know what our reactions would be.[77]

Treaty proponents cited extensive sources from the early history of Panama to show that the Canal Zone had never been legitimately granted to the United States. They were careful not to condemn Theodore Roosevelt and the Americans of 1903 for having violated international ethical standards that had evolved only in the postwar era. But they clearly maintained that the moral standards of the contemporary world and the American tradition required that the Canal Zone should return to Panamanian sovereignty and the canal to Panamanian control.[78]

These "ethical" arguments in favor of the treaties brought three significant constituencies to the proratification side: (1) organized labor, with its grass-roots and direct-mail strength; (2) the religious communities of the United States, who helped to increase significantly the number of opinion leaders who were in favor of the treaties; and (3) a group of influential conservatives, including William Buckley, John Wayne, and George Will, who prevented treaty opponents from arguing that the only supporters of the canal treaties were those who accepted the retreat of America from its interests in promoting freedom in the world.[79]

[77] Ibid., p. 281. This quotation was used extensively in the COACT literature and in White House briefings on Panama in order to emphasize the colonial nature of the Canal Zone and the legitimacy of Panamanian demands.

[78] For a discussion of how delicately the White House had to handle the ethical issues of colonialism so as not to seem to be condemning the America of the past, see Hogan, *Panama Canal*, pp. 145–150.

[79] Hamilton Jordan, "Memorandum to the President Re: Labor and the Treaties," Au-

In the end, the Senate ratified the two Panama Canal treaties with one vote to spare. Certainly there were many reasons why the senators who joined the protreaty coalition voted as they did. A few were offered political inducements by the White House to support the treaties. For many in the coalition, the reputational damage that would have accrued to the United States in the event of rejection was the decisive factor. For some, the security threats to the canal argued in favor of ratification. And for a few, the colonial nature of the Canal Zone offered reason enough to vote for the treaties. But for all the protreaty senators, the White House effort to rally elite support behind the new pacts provided what President Carter had called "running room": the belief that a protreaty vote would be supported by substantial elements of the political establishment of both parties and by opinion leaders within the country.

CONCLUSIONS

Certainly any understanding of the process that led the United States to transfer the canal and Canal Zone to Panama must take into account the general attrition of American power in the world in the 1970s, an attrition that made the United States more cognizant of its need to nurture positive relations with Latin America and the Third World. And in this sense, the realist approach to international relations provides the context within which the saga of the canal treaties unfolded. But a realist approach cannot explain why Panama became the focus of international concern in the 1970s, why there was such a sudden surge in international support for the Panamanian cause between 1972 and 1977, or why the domestic configuration of elite American support for the treaties looked as it did. An appreciation of the role of moral norms in international affairs can help to address such questions and can lead to a better understanding of the timing, sequence, and course of events that led from the stalled U.S.-Panamanian negotiations of 1972 to the ratification of the Panama Canal treaties in 1978.

First of all, the existence of international moral norms can explain the odd coalition of support that Omar Torrijos assembled at the special UN Security Council meeting in 1973. There were no common interests that united all of the nations that sided with Panama against the United States except the reputational interest of appearing to side

gust 30, 1977; Jordan, "Memorandum to the President Re: Meeting with Religious Leaders," January 21, 1978; and Jordan, "Memorandum to the President Re: Update on Panama Canal Treaties 11/10/77," box 36, Files of Hamilton Jordan, White House Central Files; and *Washington Post*, October 25, 1977, p. A19.

with the international moral norm of decolonization. The nations that voted against the United States at the Panama City meeting included Canada, Australia, France, and Kenya, all longtime U.S. allies. They were united in support for Panama on the canal issue because they knew that a failure to support the Panamanian resolution could make them appear to be weak on the issue of territorial colonialism. Similarly, an appreciation of the importance of international moral norms can help explain why the White House was able to bring to the pro-treaty coalition certain important domestic groups: religious groups who generally resisted realist arguments; conservatives who showed little care for Third World opinion of the United States on other for-eign-policy issues; and the labor movement, which had strong reasons to oppose the treaties because thousands of American jobs were going to be lost in the Canal Zone. These groups were attracted to the pro-treaty coalition because of their personal or historical dedication to the principle of anticolonialism. The presence of an international moral norm against territorial colonialism thus helps to explain why the in-ternational and domestic coalitions looked as they did at several im-portant stages of the negotiating and ratification process.

In addition, the existence of international moral norms can help to explain how the Panama Canal rose in importance on the foreign-pol-icy agenda of the United States between 1972 and 1978. It was the reputational damage from the UN Security Council meeting in 1973 that led Henry Kissinger to deal personally with the issue of Panama. And it was the fear of continuing reputational damage and the desire to elevate the role of morality in foreign policy that led Jimmy Carter to assign an extremely high priority to the Panama Canal negotiations when he came into office.

Finally, the international moral norm against territorial colonialism can help to explain the calculation of interests that led U.S. policy-makers to decide that it was best to transfer the canal to Panama in spite of the fact that the Panama Canal remained in 1977 a significant U.S. military and economic asset. The most important reason for the American acceptance of the Panama Canal treaties can be found in the belief of the Carter administration and the foreign-policy establish-ment as a whole that the benefits of retaining the canal were out-weighed by the fact that the canal issue promised to be a continual irritant between the United States and the Third World. As American foreign-policy experts recognized, the reputational damage accruing to the United States over the question of Panama arose from the "co-lonial" nature of the canal and Canal Zone, and they believed that that reputational damage was severe enough to make transferring the ca-nal in the best interests of the United States.

Thus the hypotheses about international moral norms outlined in chapter 2 are supported by the case of the Panama Canal treaties. Omar Torrijos was able to mobilize an international coalition around the norm of decolonization, and he skillfully used that coalition to raise the position of Panama on America's foreign-policy agenda and to dramatically alter the configuration of U.S. interests in the canal issue. Domestic support for the international norm against colonialism brought important constituencies to the ratification coalition and convinced many that retaining the canal was less important than ending American territorial colonialism. And personal ethical convictions led President Carter to place the canal issue high on the foreign-policy agenda and led both the president and some senators to press for ratification in order to correct an injustice against the people of Panama.

Chapter Six

THE LIMITS OF MORAL NORMS:
THE BOMBING OF DRESDEN

THE PREVIOUS THREE case studies have focused upon instances where the existence of an international moral norm led U.S. decision makers to act in a norm-observant manner. In the case of the Russian famine in 1921, the tenets of the famine-relief norm led Herbert Hoover and the Harding administration to send massive relief supplies to the Soviet Union despite the fact that such a relief effort might stabilize the Bolshevik government. In the case of U.S. policies on chemical and biological weapons, a group of prominent American scientists, journalists, and politicians worked together in 1969 to forge a domestic coalition in support of the international moral norm against chemical and biological warfare; because of pressure from this coalition, President Nixon dramatically reversed existing U.S. policies in a series of decisions that shape American CBW policy to this day. And in the case of the Panama Canal treaties, Panamanian leader Omar Torrijos effectively used the international norm against colonialism in order to pressure the United States into giving up a valuable strategic and economic asset. These three case studies lend strong support to the notion that vibrant international moral norms do exist and that they can play an important role in the formulation of foreign policy through the pathways of individual conscience, domestic politics, and international reputation.

But what of cases where the existence of a strong international moral norm does *not* lead to norm observance in foreign policy? What conditions militate against compliance with moral norms in the international system? This chapter seeks to address these questions by exploring the United States' decision to launch terror-bombing raids against the city of Dresden in 1945. Dresden had no major war industries and was remote from the eastern front. Yet in February 1945, the United States Air Forces launched a series of massive raids upon the city of Dresden, killing sixty thousand people and destroying 90 percent of the homes in the Saxon capital. How could this have occurred when there existed in 1945 a strong international moral norm prohibiting the direct targeting of civilian centers in warfare? The norm of noncombatant immunity is one of the oldest moral norms in the international system; moreover, the United States had repeatedly accepted the tenets of this norm as binding on its combat operations. Why did the norm of noncombatant immunity fail to dissuade American decision makers from launching terror-bombing raids on Dresden, and what does this failure have to say about the operation of moral norms in the international system? In order to find the answer to these questions, it is necessary to look first at the structure of the norm of noncombatant immunity itself, and then at the series of steps by which the United States drifted from a commitment to the immunity of civilian targets to an endorsement of the terror bombing of urban centers.

THE PRINCIPLE OF NONCOMBATANT IMMUNITY

The principle that noncombatants should not be subject to direct military attack is rooted in classical antiquity. Plato argued that violence and destruction in war should be limited to those who were actually guilty of breaking the peace, rather than being inflicted upon the whole population of a region.[1] Similarly, the Roman tracts on warfare endorsed a series of restraints on combat that arose from the principle that only the "guilty"—those who actually bear arms or directly support the war effort—should be targets of attack.[2] Against this background of Greek and Roman thought on the limits to war, Saint Augustine in the fourth century formulated a doctrine of "just war" that was to be the framework within which the principle of noncombatant immunity developed during the next fifteen hundred years.

Augustine began his reflection on the nature of war with the *prima facie* assumption that the taking of human life was wrong; so high a value must a Christian place upon human life, he argued, that a follower of Jesus could not even kill another person in self-defense. But living in an age when civilization, human life, and social order were threatened by German invasions, Augustine reasoned that there were some instances in which a Christian could take a human life in order to defend the lives and rights of others. In such cases, it was moral for Christians to engage in a war to redress injustice, as long as that war was being waged merely to redress the original injustice and to restore peace.[3] Even in these limited cases of just warfare, Augustine pro-

---

[1] Plato, *The Republic*, ed. Francis Cornford (Oxford: Clarendon Press, 1941), p. 170.

[2] Richard Shelly Hartigan, "Non-Combatant Immunity: Reflections on Its Origins and Present Status," *Review of Politics* 29 (1967): 204.

[3] Augustine, *Questiones in Heptateuchum* 6.10; and Richard Shelly Hartigan, "Saint Augustine on War and Killing: The Problem of the Innocent," *Journal of the History of Ideas* 27 (April–June 1966): 195–204.

posed that there were clear restrictions on the tactics that could morally be employed in combat; thus there could be no wanton violence against noncombatants, no lootings, massacres, or conflagrations.[4]

The effort to restrict the legitimate targets of warfare continued and intensified during the Middle Ages, spurred by the desire to limit the bloodshed resulting from the private feudal wars that proliferated in Europe after the disintegration of the Roman Empire. Through a series of decrees, canons, and conciliar pronouncements, the Church erected a code of conduct in war that came to be known as the "Peace of God."[5] Essentially, the Peace of God proscribed armed attacks upon all those who did not directly participate in the conduct of war: clerics, women, merchants, peasants, travelers, and shepherds.[6] While these exemptions were not uniformly honored throughout the medieval period, they were surprisingly well observed, and they greatly aided in the formation of a European cultural consensus that civilians were not legitimate targets of warfare. Widespread recognition of noncombatant immunity was further enhanced by the code of chivalry, which saw war fighting as strictly a battle between soldiers and which viewed the injuring of women, children, or peasants as cowardly and dishonorable.[7] Thus through a fusion of Church sanctions, chivalric oaths, and common military practice during the late medieval period, war fighting came to be seen as strictly limited in scope, and the principle of noncombatant immunity became a consensual moral norm within Europe.

The formalization of the principle of noncombatant immunity into the language and categories that are utilized in the present day can be traced to the writings of Francisco de Victoria and Hugo Grotius. Victoria, a neo-Scholastic theologian at the University of Salamanca who pioneered many of the concepts of international law during the period of Spanish hegemony, outlined four principles that should

[4] Roland Bainton, *Christian Attitudes toward War and Peace* (New York: Abingdon Press, 1960), p. 97.

[5] The Peace of God pertained to the categories of people who were to be exempt from attack during wartime. It is to be contrasted with the "Truce of God," a series of Church codes that limited the days and seasons during which battles could be undertaken.

[6] There were several different versions of the exemptions embodied in the Peace of God, since these exemptions evolved over a period of some seven centuries. But the lists contained in the decrees of the Council of Narbonne and the canonical decree *De truega et pace* were the most widely accepted versions of the Peace and contained the exemptions enumerated here. See James Turner Johnson, *Just-War Tradition and the Restraint of War* (Princeton: Princeton University Press, 1981), pp. 127–128; and Bainton, *Christian Attitudes*, p. 110.

[7] James Turner Johnson, *Ideology, Reason, and the Limitation of War: Religious and Secular Concepts, 1200–1740* (Princeton: Princeton University Press, 1975), p. 71.

guide the targeting of civilians in a just war: (1) certain classes of an enemy population are immune from direct attack—women and children, foreigners and travelers, agricultural workers and the rest of the civilian population; (2) this immunity is granted because these individuals do not participate actively in material aggression; (3) this immunity is not an absolute one; that is, there are instances in which civilians will be indirectly killed during attacks aimed at legitimate military targets; and (4) the indirect killing of civilians should be kept to a minimum and should be proportionate to the military value of the target being attacked.[8] Grotius, acknowledging his intellectual debt to Victoria, transmitted the neo-Scholastic doctrine of noncombatant immunity into modern international law through the principle of "moderation" in warfare. Quoting Cicero, Grotius argued, "There are some good offices to be performed, even to those who have injured us; there is also some moderation to be used even in revenge and punishments. And even in the sharpest War, there ought to be some grains of mildness and clemency."[9] In Grotius's view, this principle of moderation in warfare demanded that the traditional categories of women, children, agricultural workers, merchants, and other civilians be immune from direct attack because they do not bear arms.[10] And the destruction wrought by acts of warfare should be proportionate to the military value of such acts.

The principle of noncombatant immunity, as formulated by Victoria and Grotius, became a centerpiece of the international law of war that was formalized in the late nineteenth and early twentieth centuries. And as strategic bombardment became an ever more prominent part of modern warfare, the nations of the world signaled their willingness to apply the principle of noncombatant immunity to the issue of bombing civilian targets. The Brussels Conference of 1874 condemned the bombing of "open towns, agglomerations of dwellings, or villages which are not defended" as a war crime and a violation of international moral standards.[11] The Hague Convention of 1907 stated that "the attack or bombardment, by whatever means, of towns, villages, dwellings, or buildings which are undefended is prohibited" and demanded that in any bombardment every effort be taken to limit civil-

---

[8] Hartigan, "Non-Combatant Immunity," pp. 215–216; and Johnson, *Ideology, Reason*, pp. 196–197.

[9] Hugo Grotius, *The Most Excellent Hugo Grotius His Three Books Treating the Rights of War and Peace*, trans. William Evats (London: Thomas Basset and Ralph Smith, 1682), bk. 2, chap. 11, p. 497.

[10] Ibid., pp. 506–509.

[11] Dietrich Schindler and Jiri Toman, eds., *The Laws of Armed Conflicts* (Geneva: Henry Dunant Institute, 1973), p. 29.

ian casualties, spare historic buildings, and warn the populace before the bombardment begins.[12] And the 1922 Hague Rules of Air Warfare specified clear limits to aerial bombardment based upon the principle of noncombatant immunity. Thus by the beginning of World War II, there was a clear international moral norm that applied the principle of noncombatant immunity to aerial bombardment: the direct attacking of nonmilitary targets was prohibited, and the collateral civilian death and destruction resulting from raids against military targets had to be outweighed by the purely military value of those targets.

The United States government subscribed wholeheartedly to these moral constraints on the waging of war. During World War I, Woodrow Wilson rejected all plans for indiscriminate bombing of noncombatants, saying, "I desire no sort of participation by the Air Service of the United States in a plan . . . which has as its object promiscuous bombing upon industry, commerce or populations in enemy countries dissociated from obvious military needs to be served by such action."[13] When the Japanese were poised to bomb Nanking in 1937, the State Department warned that "this government holds the view that any general bombing of an extensive area wherein there resides a large population engaged in peaceful pursuits is unwarranted and contrary to the principles of law and humanity."[14] And in response to the Russian bombing of Helsinki in 1939, President Franklin D. Roosevelt termed the action barbaric, saying that "the American government and the American people have for some time pursued a policy of wholeheartedly condemning the unprovoked bombing and machine-gunning of civilian populations from the air."[15] The international moral consensus against indiscriminate attacks upon civilians during wartime had broad and deep support within the United States, and as America was poised on the threshold of World War II, it was with a view of warfare shaped in no small part by the norm of noncombatant immunity.

U.S. BOMBING POLICY: 1942–44

By the late 1930s, technological advances in aviation and weaponry had made possible a new dimension of modern warfare—the ability to

[12] Ibid., p. 78.

[13] Harvey de Weerd, *President Wilson Fights His War: The American Military Experience in World War I* (New York: Macmillan Company, 1968), p. xx.

[14] Lester Nurick, "The Distinction between Combatants and Noncombatants in the Law of War," *American Journal of International Law* 39 (1945): 692.

[15] Ronald Schaffer, *Wings of Judgment: American Bombing in World War II* (New York: Oxford University Press, 1985), p. 32.

bypass the front lines of a war and bomb the home territory of opponents in order to destroy their ability and will to fight. Strategic bombing, as it came to be called, sought to identify and destroy those vital industries that supplied an enemy's war machine, with the hope of drying up supplies of vital spare parts, fuel, and new weapons.[16] It was the belief of air-force planners in Great Britain, Germany, Italy, and the United States that strategic bombing could radically alter the nature of modern warfare by making the battle lines mere holding actions that would allow the nation with air superiority to win future wars by strategically bombing its opponent's vital war industries until submission was inevitable.[17]

The doctrine of strategic bombing greatly expanded the breadth of the traditional battlefield, but it did not necessarily violate the traditional principle of noncombatant immunity. The just-war theory had long recognized that arms depots and arms-manufacturing plants constituted legitimate targets of attack, and these were precisely the sort of objectives that the new theory of strategic bombing seemed to emphasize. But the concept of strategic bombing did open the door to a gradual erosion of the norm of noncombatant immunity, since the strategy of using heavy bombing raids to cripple a nation's ability and will to fight invited an ever-widening definition of which industrial targets were war-related. Moreover, certain versions of strategic-bombing doctrine explicitly sought to undermine civilian morale in an enemy country by making the common man and woman feel that their lives were in danger. Most clearly articulated by Italian strategist Giulio Douhet and American aviation pioneer Billy Mitchell, these more extreme versions of strategic-bombing theory advocated the bombing of population centers in order to terrorize the civilian population so that they would press their government for peace.[18]

Upon the United States' entry into World War II, the American and British Combined Chiefs of Staff adopted a war plan that clearly recognized the importance of strategic bombing. The chiefs did hew to tradition in underscoring the importance of air forces for ground sup-

[16] Technically, strategic bombing could also include bombing in support of some ground-force objectives; but it was generally used to apply to the bombardment of targets not directly related to action on the ground. See David MacIsaac, *Strategic Bombing in World War II* (New York: Garland Publishing, 1976), pp. 5–7.

[17] Haywood Hansell, *The Strategic Air War against Germany and Japan* (Washington: U.S. Government Printing Office, 1961), pp. 9–10.

[18] Douhet was the primary exponent of unlimited strategic bombing in the late 1930s, and his works were widely read, though not endorsed, in the U.S. Air Corps Tactical School. Mitchell did not advocate the bombing of population centers while he was in the Air Corps, but he expressed these views after he left the military service in 1926. See Schaffer, *Wings of Judgment*, pp. 20–34.

port, but they also committed a significant portion of their air forces to "the progressive destruction and dislocation of the German military, industrial, and economic systems, the disruption of vital elements of lines of communications, and the material reductions of air combat strength by the successful prosecution of the combined bomber offensive from all convenient bases."[19] This "progressive destruction and dislocation" was intended to weaken Germany in preparation for the final invasion; only die-hard advocates of air war believed that strategic bombing itself could constitute the final blow against the Nazi homeland. The targets contemplated for strategic attack during 1942 and 1943 were limited in scope, reflecting the Allied view that the best path to victory lay in a "high degree of destruction in a few really essential industries."[20] Thus U.S. and British bombers were dispatched to destroy fighter and bomber assembly plants, submarine yards, the German rail system, and production facilities for synthetic rubber, synthetic oil, and aluminum.[21]

Early in the strategic-bombing effort, a debate broke out between the American and British forces over the best way to accomplish the bombing objectives upon which they had agreed. The British had originally entered the war with a precision daylight-bombing strategy designed to hit only the specific military and industrial targets against which the bombers had been dispatched. But during the early raids against Germany and German-held territory, the Royal Air Force suffered enormous casualties from the Luftwaffe. It seemed that strategic-bombing theory had sharply overestimated the ability of heavy bombers to escape strafing from enemy aircraft. As a consequence, the RAF turned to nighttime attacks. The British radar systems were extremely primitive early in the war, so it was impossible to hit targets in night raids with any significant degree of accuracy. Thus the Royal Air Force's bombing strategy became one of "area raids" aimed at the general vicinity of significant military or industrial targets; as a con-

---

[19] Memorandums from the Joint Chiefs, November 5, 1943 and February 13, 1944, box 36, the Richard Anderson Papers, Hoover Institution Archives, Stanford University. (Richard Anderson was the deputy chief of operations for the U.S. Strategic Air Force in Europe from 1943 to 1945.) The United States had formulated contingency plans for war even before the bombing of Pearl Harbor, and these plans advocated devoting significant resources to strategic bombing of Germany and German-held territory. The joint British-U.S. plan, which was to guide the Allied bombing strategy for most of the war, was adopted at the Casablanca Conference in January 1943. See Hansell, *Strategic Air War*, p. 59; MacIsaac, *Strategic Bombing*, pp. 14–15.

[20] Memorandum from the Combined Chiefs of Staff, November 5, 1943, box 36, Anderson Papers.

[21] Hansell, *Strategic Airwar*, pp. 58–59.

sequence, there was little effort to limit the collateral damage to civilians.[22]

The Americans from the first refused to adopt British "area bombing" tactics. A central reason was the use of the sophisticated Norden bombsight on American B-17s, which allowed the U.S. planes to conduct precision daylight raids from altitudes above twenty thousand feet. But the greater effectiveness of American precision bombing was not the only factor that led the U.S. to resist British arguments on behalf of area bombing. For many in the leadership of the U.S. Army Air Forces[23] believed that the moral tradition against indiscriminate bombing of civilians argued strongly for the adoption of a precision strategy. In a 1943 memo to his top commanders, Air Forces chief Henry Harley ("Hap") Arnold contended that precision bombing represented a morally superior way of attaining American objectives. In addition, Arnold believed that a seeming American disregard for civilian German casualties during the bombing raids might poison America's postwar relations with Germany and other nations, as well as jeopardize postwar American domestic support for the Air Forces. So as a "spur to conscience," the Air Forces chief of staff urged his top lieutenants to make sure that U.S. planes bombed as accurately as possible during their strategic raids.[24]

THE DEBATE ON TERROR BOMBING: JUNE–SEPTEMBER, 1944

Soon after the successful Allied landing at Normandy, American Air Forces planners began to pursue the question of how best to use strategic bombing to force the final capitulation of Germany. It was at this

[22] MacIsaac, *Strategic Bombing*, pp. 12–13; and Max Hastings, *Bomber Command* (New York: Dial Press, 1979), pp. 106–140. As the war progressed, area bombing became de facto the indiscriminate bombing of Germany's major cities. And while the effectiveness of the German air defenses had much to do with the British decision to resort to area bombing, the fact that the United Kingdom had itself been the target of indiscriminate German bomb attacks also heavily influenced Royal Air Force policy. In addition, the British believed that area attacks were simply more efficient than precision attacks, because there was greater certainty that the major target in the bombed area had indeed been hit if bombs were dropped wholesale upon the vicinity.

[23] During the 1930s, the U.S. air forces were called the Army Air Corps and were part of the Army. In 1941 the name was changed to Army Air Forces, and this division of the Army was given greater independence. In 1942 the Air Forces were given still more independence, and the commanding general of the Army Air Forces became a member of the Joint Chiefs of Staff. Under the terms of the National Security Act of 1947, the independent U.S. Air Force was created. For simplicity, the term *Air Forces* is generally used in this work. See Monro MacCloskey, *The United States Air Force* (New York: Frederick Praeger, 1967).

[24] Schaffer, *Wings of Judgment*, p. 61.

juncture that the issue of terror bombing came to the fore. The theories of strategic bombing that had been formulated by Douhet and Mitchell in the 1920s had envisioned the modern bomber as the ultimate weapon of war that could carry the battle directly to civilians and force them to press their government to surrender. During the early stages of World War II, U.S. planners had thought it unlikely that terror bombing would force the capitulation of Germany, since the Nazi apparatus held such complete control over the mechanisms of power in the Reich that citizen dissatisfaction was judged to be unlikely to influence government policy. But the landing at Normandy, and the relatively slow progress of Allied troops in the weeks after D-Day, once again raised the issue of whether strategic bombing aimed at terrorizing the German civilian population could generate a swift collapse of the Nazi regime.

On June 9, 1944, General Carl Spaatz authorized the formulation of a series of planning options that would entail terror bombing in order to break the general morale of the German population. Colonel Lowell P. Weicker, the deputy director of intelligence for the U.S. Strategic Air Force (a division of the U.S. Army Air Forces), devised a plan called Operation Shatter that sought to maximize the impact of terror bombing by spreading it across a hundred cities and towns within Germany. Operation Shatter would target urban areas precisely on the basis of their freedom from previous attack and their distance from logical military objectives; thus no German citizen would feel free from the specter of bombing, and there would be maximum pressure on the German government to surrender.[25]

The opposition to Operation Shatter was led by Colonel Richard Hughes, the chief target-selection officer of the U.S. Strategic Air Force. Hughes challenged Weicker's claims that terrorizing German civilians would end the war more quickly, and he maintained that precision bombing of oil facilities, military production plants, and key military depots continued to represent the most effective deployment of U.S. strategic air forces during the final part of the European campaign. In addition, Hughes argued that Operation Shatter was immoral and betrayed the moral heritage of the United States, which "rightly . . . represented in world thought an urge toward decency and better treatment of man by man."[26] Hughes warned of a significant negative reaction at home to such a campaign of indiscriminate bomb-

[25] Memorandum from Colonel Lowell P. Weicker, June 26, 1944, box 32, Anderson Papers.
[26] Schaffer, *Wings of Judgment*, p. 76.

ing, and he predicted that the future of the U.S. Air Forces might be jeopardized by any association with terror-bombing techniques.[27]

Weicker responded that it was indeed repugnant to harass civilians, but that "you cannot always use the Marquis of Queensberry's rules against a nation brought up on doctrines of unprecedented cruelty, brutality, and disregard of basic human decencies."[28] Weicker emphasized that the most important moral consideration that should guide U.S. planners was the desire to save Allied lives and end the war more quickly. In his eyes and those of his supporters on the strategic planning staff, the regard for the norm of noncombatant immunity was a noble impulse, but one that was blind to both the realities of war and the evil of the Nazi regime.

The ultimate fate of Operation Shatter was decided by General Charles Cabell, the U.S. Strategic Air Force director of planning. Cabell accepted the fact that the proposed bombing could deliver a stinging blow against Germany and cause widespread despair about the Reich's ability to protect its citizenry. But he saw three major reasons for rejecting the plan: (1) Operation Shatter would divert air resources from the campaign against the oil facilities and war-production plants that were much more directly related to the German war effort; (2) the terror bombing of civilians would be used by the Germans to portray the United States internationally as a barbaric nation; and (3) such bombing would do significant damage to the future reputation of the Air Forces within the United States.[29] Because of these drawbacks, Operation Shatter was shelved in July 1944, and it appeared that the Air Forces had rejected the concept of terror bombing.

But just as General Cabell was burying Operation Shatter, the British chiefs of staff were formulating a plan of their own for the terror bombing of Germany. In a note to the prime minister in early July 1944, the British chiefs stated that "the time might well come in the not too distant future when an all-out attack by every means at our disposal on German civilian morale might be decisive. . . . The method by which such an attack might be made should be examined and all possible preparations made."[30] The method of attack on which the British planning staff eventually settled was a series of terror-bombing raids, code-named Operation Thunderclap, which were designed to bring fear and despair into the hearts of the German man and woman in the street. The memorandums proposing Thunderclap pointed out that the actual danger to a German civilian of being killed in previous

[27] Ibid.
[28] Ibid., p. 77.
[29] Ibid., p. 78.
[30] Hastings, *Bomber Command*, p. 301.

Allied raids was quite small; even the use of incendiary bombs by British bombers had not generally yielded high percentage rates of civilian casualties in targeted cities.[31] For this reason, the Thunderclap proposal went on, the terrorizing of the German population could be accomplished only by a new targeting strategy aimed directly at the maximization of civilian casualties:

> The attack must be delivered in such density that it imposes as nearly as possible a one hundred percent risk of death *to the individual* in the area to which it is applied.
>
> The target chosen should be one involving the maximum association, both traditional and personal, for the population as a whole. Considerations of economic destruction must not be permitted to influence the selection of the target.
>
> Subject to [the above], the area selected should embrace the highest density of population.
>
> Attacks of this nature are likely to have the maximum effect when the population has become convinced that its Government is powerless to prevent a repetition.[32]

Berlin, as the historical and political center of the Reich, was considered to be the ideal target under these criteria, and the British Air Ministry estimated that concentrated bombing raids aimed at the center of the German capital would yield 220,000 casualties out of a population of 300,000.[33] The justification for this major shift in Allied bombing policy was that such raids would bring about the capitulation of the German high command. "If the operation should succeed in curtailing the duration of the war by even a few weeks, it would save many thousands of Allied casualties and would justify itself many times over."[34]

Since Operation Thunderclap had to rely heavily upon the accuracy of the American heavy-bomber fleet in order to generate the desired concentration of bombing, the British had to secure U.S. approval for the plan. But from the beginning, the leadership of the American Air Forces was resistant to the British proposal. Generals Arnold and

[31] A significant exception was noted in the bombing of Hamburg, which the memorandums on Thunderclap label as abnormal in Allied bombing practices. (Record of telephone conversation between General Anderson and Lt. General James Doolittle, August 21, 1944, Thunderclap Files, box 37, Anderson Papers; Memorandum from General Laurence S. Kuter to General Richard Anderson, September 4, 1944, Thunderclap Files, box 37, Anderson Papers; and Royal Air Force, Proposal for Operation Thunderclap, August 15, 1944, Thunderclap Files, box 37, Anderson Papers)

[32] Royal Air Force, Proposal for Operation Thunderclap.

[33] Hastings, *Bomber Command*, p. 301.

[34] Royal Air Force, Proposal for Operation Thunderclap.

Spaatz had long been skeptical of claims that terror bombing would bring a rapid capitulation by the German high command, and they believed that it was more important to concentrate upon the military-related targets that had long been the priority for strategic bombing. Moreover, much of the Air Forces leadership was repelled by the moral implications of Operation Thunderclap and viewed it as an RAF effort to implicate the United States in the indiscriminate bombing that had for some time characterized British area raids. Spaatz protested to Arnold that the British wished to see the U.S. Air Forces "tarred with the morale bombing aftermath, which we feel will be terrific."[35] Cabell labeled the British proposal a repugnant "baby-killing scheme" and said: "It would be a blot on the history of the Air Forces and of the U.S. We should strongly resist being sucked into such a plan. It gives full rein to the baser elements of our people and [to the baser elements] of the character of our good people."[36] General Laurence S. Kuter, the director of planning, contended that it was "contrary to our national ideals to wage war against civilians" and that the Air Forces should continue its policy of precision bombing solely against military targets.[37] After much review, Spaatz wrote to General Dwight D. Eisenhower formally recommending a rejection of the British proposal: "The U.S. bombing policy, as you know, has been directed against precision military objectives, and not morale. I am opposed to this operation as now planned."[38] Operation Thunderclap was shelved, and there emerged a consensus within the U.S. military leadership that U.S. forces would "continue to be employed exclusively against critical military objectives," at least until there might come a time "when it is broadly accepted that morale attacks including the killing of civilians will tip the scales causing the cessation of hostilities."[39]

THE DRIFT TOWARD TERROR BOMBING AND THE RAIDS ON DRESDEN: 1945

In late 1944, the Allied offensive against Germany began to stall, slowed by the Nazi offensive in the Ardennes forest and the tenacious

---

[35] Schaffer, *Wings of Judgment*, p. 84.

[36] Ibid., p. 83.

[37] Memorandum from Kuter to Anderson, September 4, 1944, p. 3, Thunderclap Files, box 37, Anderson Papers.

[38] Memorandum from General Carl Spaatz to General Dwight D. Eisenhower, August 24, 1944, Thunderclap Files, box 37, Anderson Papers.

[39] Kuter to Anderson, September 4, 1944; and Kuter to Anderson, February 13, 1945, Thunderclap Files, box 16, Anderson Papers.

refusal of the German armed forces to collapse despite the seeming inevitability of defeat. The U.S. War Department began to fear that the final offensive against Germany itself might be slower and more arduous than they had originally expected, with much higher Allied casualties. Air Forces leaders, who had for years been boasting that modern bombing techniques would change the face of warfare and sap the enemy's ability to resist, were finding themselves under increasing pressure to show that strategic bombing could indeed provide the breakthrough that the Allies needed. As General Arnold complained to his chief commanders:

> We have a superiority of at least 5 to 1 now against Germany and yet, in spite of all our hopes, anticipations, dreams, and plans, we have not yet been able to capitalize to the extent which we should. We may not be able to force capitulation of the Germans by air attacks, but on the other hand, it would seem to me that we should get much better and more decisive results than we are getting now.[40]

The search for alternatives capable of breaking the back of German resistance intensified both in the War Department as a whole and within the Air Forces, and in this context the question of terror bombing emerged once again.

Operation Thunderclap had been rejected for three reasons: (1) many members of the Air Forces leadership were skeptical about the possibilities of terror bombing breaking German morale; (2) many Air Forces leaders viewed with repugnance the operation's blatant attempt to maximize civilian casualties in order to induce terror; and (3) many American decision makers felt that Thunderclap might damage the reputation of the United States and the U.S. Air Forces. When the debate on terror bombing arose again in early 1945, the proponents of terror bombing chose to address all three of these issues—by citing new psychological data to reinforce claims for the effectiveness of terror bombing, by creating a terror-bombing strategy that did not rely so heavily on civilian casualties for its effectiveness, and by producing plans that combined terror bombing with elements of "legitimate" military targeting so that it was difficult to identify where selective targeting left off and terror bombing began.

During the fall of 1944, the War Department had asked Harvard psychologist Gordon Allport to consult with leading members of the psychological community in the United States about the likely effects of strategic bombing upon general civilian morale. Although the results of Allport's consultation were far from unanimous, they did point

[40] MacIsaac, *Strategic Bombing*, p. 80.

to a very significant probability that sustained bombing of German cities could generate a massive terror that would cause the collapse of German society and the German ability to resist.[41] These findings put great pressure on the opponents of terror bombing, for in the search for "quick-fix" avenues for forcing a German surrender, the psychological data seemed to indicate that the general bombing of civilian areas for the purpose of breaking civilian morale offered the best chance for an end to the war in Europe.

But there remained the moral question and its attendant ramifications for the future reputation of the U.S. Air Forces. Thunderclap, with its objective of maximizing civilian casualties by concentrating massive firepower on a single urban area, so grossly violated the norm of noncombatant immunity that a large part of the Air Forces hierarchy had rejected it. The bombing proposals that were put forward in early 1945 took an entirely different tack. They did not seek to create terror by maximizing civilian casualties; rather, these newer plans sought to terrorize the general German populace by spreading Allied firepower over the entire country and hitting specific "military" targets in urban areas throughout Germany. In this way, proponents argued, it would be possible to generate terror by showing complete Allied mastery over German airspace, while not engaging in bombing that was exclusively terroristic in nature.[42] Thus the benefits of morale bombing could be obtained without the reputational risks or moral dilemmas that Thunderclap had entailed.

The principal terror-bombing plan that emerged in early 1945 was Operation Clarion, a product of the Air Forces strategic-planning staff. The avowed purpose of Clarion was "to outline a coordinated attack against strategic targets, particularly transportation, by all available American Air Forces."[43] But the Clarion proposal was quick to point out the impact that such massive and widespread raids would have upon civilian morale throughout Germany:

A widespread attack of over seven thousand aircraft, extending over Germany as a whole and attacking lightly defended or non-defended transportation targets, will bring home the effects of the war upon German industry and the German people as no other method could do. The in-

[41] Schaffer, *Wings of Judgment*, pp. 90–91.

[42] These proposals, which came to be known as the Quesada Plan, aimed for breadth of bombing rather than concentration in bombing in order to generate terror among the populace of Germany. See the Quesada Plan File, box 17, Anderson Papers.

[43] "General Plan for Maximum Effort Attack against Transportation Objectives," December 17, 1944, Operation Clarion Files, box 37, Anderson Papers.

creasing instability of the German people and German industry may be pushed over the brink by these attacks.[44]

In reading the proposal for Operation Clarion, it is difficult to tell whether it was primarily a plan for destroying the German transportation network or a plan for terrorizing the civilian population so as to break German morale and force capitulation. And the proponents of Clarion relied heavily upon this ambiguity.

Several members of the Air Forces leadership saw Clarion as no different from Thunderclap in its moral dimensions. General Cabell wrote, "This is the same old baby killing plan of the get-rich psychological boys, dressed up in a new kimono."[45] And General Ira C. Eaker, the commander of air forces in the Mediterranean theater, protested that "Clarion would absolutely convince the Germans that we are the barbarians they say we are, for it would be perfectly obvious to them that this is primarily a large scale attack on civilians as, in fact, of course it is."[46] But other members of the Air Forces leadership saw Clarion as quite different from Thunderclap because Clarion relied for its effectiveness upon a demonstration of massive U.S. force rather than upon a huge civilian death toll and because Clarion was technically aimed at "military" targets within each city. As pressure began to build upon the Air Forces to aid in breaking the back of the German resistance, the American chiefs of staff came more and more to see Clarion as a way to save American lives and shorten the war. On January 30, 1945, the chiefs decided to approve Clarion, and General George Marshall ordered the operation to begin as soon as weather permitted. In relaying this instruction to his commanders, General Spaatz, commander of U.S. air forces in Europe, reminded them that "special care should be taken against giving any impression that this operation is aimed, repeat aimed, at civilian populations or intended to terrorize them."[47]

The city of Dresden was not generally considered to be a significant military target. A cultural center that based its economy on theaters, museums, crafts, and home industries, Dresden had become famous for its artistic endeavors, not its military or industrial capacity. While there were some optical plants and gas-mask production facilities located in the outer suburbs of Dresden, the city itself was considered so unlikely a focus of Allied bombing that its small defensive artillery

[44] Ibid.
[45] Schaffer, *Wings of Judgment*, p. 92.
[46] Ibid.
[47] Ibid., p. 94.

had largely been transferred to other, more prominent centers of military value. It is true that there were some regional transportation hubs in Dresden, and the postal network for much of eastern Germany ran through the city. But Dresden constituted a "virgin" target in 1945; there had been no major raids on the city itself, and there was little expectation among the inhabitants that they would soon be the object of repeated and concentrated Allied raids.[48]

The event that made Dresden an ideal target for terror bombing was the success of the Russian offensive in Silesia in the winter of 1945.[49] The Russians advanced swiftly and forcefully through eastern Germany in late December and early January, and some 1.4 million refugees fled from Silesia to Saxony, more than doubling Dresden's population of 650,000. The British chiefs of staff, spurred by Winston Churchill, sought to demonstrate British and American support for the Russian advance by disrupting the lines of communication and transportation in eastern Germany and by increasing pandemonium in the cities flooded by evacuees.[50] Spaatz, as commander of the U.S. air forces in Europe, was charged with responding to the British proposal for bombing Berlin, Dresden, Chemnitz, and Leipzig. Spaatz wished to insure that American planes targeted the transportation systems in these cities, since these at least represented objectives somewhat related to the war effort on the eastern front. But in keeping with the philosophy of Operation Clarion, Spaatz was very supportive of the British desire to disrupt the evacuation of refugees from the eastern front by creating massive terror and destruction in the cities of eastern Germany.[51] As a result, the "virgin" city of Dresden became a target for concentrated U.S. bombing.

The attacks upon Dresden were delayed for several days because of weather, but on February 13 the British and U.S. air forces launched a series of bombing raids that killed more than sixty thousand people and left most of the city's population homeless. Of the twenty-eight thousand homes in the central quadrant of the town, more than

[48] David Irving, *The Destruction of Dresden* (New York: Holt, Rinehart and Winston, 1964), pp. 69–85.

[49] Technically, the bombing of Dresden was not a component of Operation Clarion. But the Dresden raids did grow directly out of the principles that the Joint Chiefs relied upon in adopting Clarion—namely, that the bombing of "virgin" cities in order to create mass terror was an acceptable tactic as long as it was tied to the targeting of at least marginally military objectives, such as urban transportation systems.

[50] Hastings, *Bomber Command*, pp. 340–342.

[51] Report of Combined Strategic Targets Committee, February 7, 1945, p. 1; Memorandum of Air Ministry, Whitehall, to Headquarters, U.S.S.T.A.F., February 8, 1945, box 14, Anderson Papers; and Irving, *Destruction of Dresden*, pp. 93–94.

twenty-five thousand were totally destroyed.[52] The transportation and postal systems were thoroughly smashed, and the sheer immensity of the carnage and destruction bred a hopelessness and despair among the populace of the city. Thus the Dresden mission seemed to have succeeded in all of its aims: it largely demolished the "military" targets of transportation and communications; it disrupted the evacuation of Silesia by making uninhabitable a major evacuation center; and it terrorized a region of Germany that had been largely free from the specter of strategic bombing.

But the story of Dresden did not end with the bombing raids themselves. For an Associated Press correspondent, misinterpreting an official communique distributed to reporters in London, reported that Dresden represented a new departure in Allied bombing practices, a departure in which the British and Americans had initiated "deliberate terror bombing of German population centers as a ruthless expedient to hasten doom."[53] The British censors managed to suppress the report, but it was printed in U.S. papers before the implications of the story were recognized by American censors; as a consequence, questions arose in the United States about the parameters and morality of Air Forces bombing practices.[54] General Arnold publicly cabled a message to Spaatz, asking to know the distinction between "morale bombing" and attacks on transportation targets in urban areas. Spaatz publicly replied that the Dresden raids were aimed at vital transport targets and that the Air Forces "had not departed from the historic U.S. bombing policies in Europe." In response, Arnold pronounced himself satisfied that the norm of noncombatant immunity had not been violated.[55] On February 22, Secretary of War Henry Stimson held a press conference on the subject and asserted, "Our policy has never been to inflict terror bombing on civilian populations. . . . Our efforts are still confined to the attack of enemy military objectives. The transportation and communication centers we attack become our objective in that they feed the front on which our Allied armies are now engaging the German armies."[56] For most Americans, this was reassurance enough that the norm of noncombatant immunity still guided

[52] The bomber pilots were given lists of targets in the city, but the raids were so massive, the targets so many, and the precision of the bombers so poor by modern standards that none of the mission planners could realistically have had any expectation other than the complete devastation of the central quadrant of the city.

[53] Hastings, *Bomber Command*, p. 343.

[54] Schaffer, *Wings of Judgment*, pp. 99–100.

[55] Memorandum from Spaatz to Maxwell, February 14, 1945, Diaries, box 14, Anderson Papers.

[56] Forrest Pogue, *George C. Marshall*, vol. 4, *Organizer of Victory* (New York: Viking Press, 1967), pp. 545–546.

American bombing policy and that the United States was not directly targeting civilians in Europe.[57]

DRESDEN AND THE NORM OF NONCOMBATANT IMMUNITY

The decision to bomb Dresden was not made in isolation. Rather, it constituted the end product of a drift in American policy toward the indiscriminate bombing of civilians. Upon America's entry into World War II, the U.S. military leadership had been committed to precision bombing of military and industrial targets in Germany that were closely tied to the Nazi war effort: fighter and bomber assembly plants, submarine yards, the German rail system, and production facilities for synthetic rubber, synthetic oil, and aluminum. While the rather primitive "precision" bombing techniques of the 1940s made it impossible to conduct raids against even these targets without widespread civilian casualties, the casualty rates were relatively small compared to those of the Dresden and Berlin raids of 1945. Thus American bombing policy from 1942 to 1944 consciously rejected the indiscriminate bombing of civilian populations, in part because the leadership of the U.S. Air Forces had serious reservations about the effectiveness of morale bombing, and in part because of concerns about the morality of terror bombing and the effects it would have upon the reputation of the Air Forces. But in early 1945 a shift occurred, and the United States accepted terror bombing as a legitimate military tactic. What led the same military leadership that had rejected Operation Thunderclap in the summer of 1944 to accept the terror bombing implicit in Operation Clarion in January 1945? The answer lies largely in three factors that can help to illuminate the general problem of compliance with moral norms in the international system: the structure of the norm of noncombatant immunity; the increasingly compelling security incentives for the United States to initiate terror-bombing raids; and the clash of moral imperatives that American planners faced in making their strategic choices on bombing targets.

By 1945 the norm of noncombatant immunity had had a long history, and in the course of that history it had gained wide acceptance in the international system. But the structure of the norm of noncom-

---

[57] The debate that broke out in the aftermath of the Associated Press story was rather short-lived. But as wartime censorship ended and more and more evidence came out about the extensiveness of the destruction in Dresden, the nonmilitary nature of the city itself, and the relatively minor "military" targets that the Air Forces cited to legitimate the raids, the bombing of Dresden came to be a symbol of disregard for the norm of noncombatant immunity. See Irving, *Destruction of Dresden*, "The Aftermath."

batant immunity contained two glaring ambiguities that were exacerbated by the advent of strategic bombing and modern warfare: (1) The norm demands that civilian targets be immune from direct attacks. But the difficulty of defining what is a civilian target and what is a military target has become enormous in an age when whole societies become mobilized for war production. The definition of military and civilian targets has an inherent elasticity that can be detected in the drift in U.S. targeting posture from a focus upon airplane-production plants to a focus upon general transportation facilities in major urban areas. Because of this inherent elasticity, it is difficult to identify clear boundaries between civilian and military targets, and thus it is difficult to know when the norm of noncombatant immunity has been violated. (2) The norm of noncombatant immunity puts great stress upon the distinction between direct and indirect attacks. But essentially this distinction is one of intentionality and is therefore not easily observable to third parties. It was this ambiguity of intention that lay at the heart of Operation Clarion and the Dresden raids: were they principally aimed at terrorizing a civilian populace or at hitting transportation targets? Not even the U.S. military leadership that approved these plans was sure. As a result, the debate on the morality of Clarion and Dresden became very unfocused within the armed forces, and in the aftermath of the raids the military could effectively claim that they were undertaken because of the military value of the transportation systems that had been targeted.

The second factor that accounted for the shift in U.S. attitudes toward terror bombing in early 1945 was the set of increasingly compelling incentives for the United States to launch terror-bombing raids. The slowdown of the Allied advance in the winter of 1944–45 raised the possibility of a protracted ground campaign that would cost tens of thousands of American lives; if air power could break the German resistance, then these lives could be saved and the war dramatically shortened. Moreover, the data that Gordon Allport had collected on the effectiveness of morale bombing increased the confidence of U.S. officials that terror bombing could actually break the spirit of the German army and people and thus bring about a quick surrender. Finally, Air Forces officials recognized that despite an immense commitment of resources to strategic bombing during 1943 and 1944, the German war machine had not collapsed, as the architects of strategic bombing had predicted. The initiation of terror bombing constituted the last chance for the Air Forces to show that air power could be decisive in modern warfare.

The final factor that helps to explain the U.S. decision to bomb Dresden in 1945 lies in the clash of moral imperatives that American policymakers faced in making their key decisions on bombing targets. Opponents of terror bombing constantly cited the principle of noncombatant immunity in pressing the Air Forces to reject strategies that targeted civilian populations. But proponents of terror bombing cited the moral imperatives of saving Allied lives, ending the war at the earliest opportunity, and toppling the German dictatorship. In the minds of key American decision makers, there was a genuine clash of moral imperatives that made the decision on bombing targets a difficult one, even when considered from a purely ethical perspective. This clash points to an important element in the operation of moral norms in the international system: moral imperatives, like imperatives of strategic interest, seldom fall all on one side of a policy discussion. Opponents of terror bombing found it more difficult to protect the principle of noncombatant immunity because their adversaries could cite potent moral claims in support of the need to end the war at the earliest possible opportunity, by any means possible.

Thus while the norm of noncombatant immunity did help to shape early U.S. bombing decisions in World War II, it failed to prevent the initiation of terror-bombing raids against Dresden and other German cities in early 1945. The ambiguities inherent in the norm, together with the increasingly compelling state incentives to initiate terror bombing and the clash of moral imperatives faced by American decision makers, led U.S. planners to conclude that raids aimed against civilian morale should be launched. The case of Dresden testifies to the fact that the mere existence of a strong international moral norm does not guarantee norm compliance, and that there are specific conditions that contribute to or militate against compliance in the international system.

Chapter Seven

CONCLUSIONS

ONE OF THE MOST significant debates in the field of international relations concerns the degree to which state behavior is influenced by the presence of norms and institutions in the international system. Traditional realists continue to stress the importance of state power and interests in determining the politics of nations, and they argue that efforts to generate more elaborate conceptions of state behavior based on institutions and values will only sacrifice analytic clarity while yielding little additional explanatory power.[1] Advocates of a more institutional approach to the international system point to patterns of behavior in the state system that realism cannot explain, and they argue that a recognition of the importance of power and interests in the politics of nations cannot be allowed to obscure the existence of continuing and identifiable behavioral rules in the international system that are at least partly independent of the existing distribution of power and interests and that have a substantial impact upon state behavior.[2]

The hypotheses about international moral norms outlined in chapter 2 and explored in the four case studies are an outgrowth of this

[1] The most powerful presentation of this viewpoint can be found in Kenneth Waltz, *Theory of International Politics* (New York: Random House, 1979).

[2] Stephen Krasner's *International Regimes* (Ithaca: Cornell University Press, 1983) constitutes a compendium of many of the most important works on this subject, although a thorough overview of the regime literature would also have to include Robert Keohane's *After Hegemony: Cooperation and Discord in the World Political Economy* (Princeton: Princeton University Press, 1984); Ernest Haas, "Why Collaborate? Issue Linkage and International Regimes," *World Politics* 32 (April 1980): 357–405; Oran Young, "International Regimes: Toward a New Theory of Institutions," *World Politics* 39 (October 1986): 104–122; Friedrich Kratochwil and John Ruggie, "International Organization: A State of the Art on the Art of the State," *International Organization* 40 (Autumn 1986): 753–775; and Raymond Cohen, "Rules of the Game in International Politics," *International Studies Quarterly* 24 (March 1980): 129–150. Important insights into the role of norms in the international system and in various societal settings can be found in Robert Axelrod, "An Evolutionary Approach to Norms," *American Political Science Review* 80 (December 1986): 1095–1111; Friedrich Kratochwil, "The Force of Prescriptions," *International Organization* 38 (Autumn 1984): 703–708; Karl Dieter Opp, "The Evolutionary Emergence of Norms," *British Journal of Social Psychology* 21 (1982): 139–149; and Francesca Cancian, *What Are Norms?* (Cambridge: Cambridge University Press, 1975).

institutional argument that there exist specific rules of behavior that affect state action and that cannot be seen as mere projections of state power and interests. International moral norms are identifiable behavioral rules that oblige states to undertake some actions and avoid others. International moral norms have been formed by transnational cultural and political networks and have been consensually subscribed to by the great majority of the world's nation-states. And international moral norms have a significant and discernible effect upon the behavior of states. By reviewing each of the cases investigated in this work, it is possible to see that the existence of international moral norms can account for significant instances of state behavior that traditional realist approaches cannot explain. It is also possible to see that international moral norms operate in a variety of ways to influence state decision makers, and that some preliminary conclusions can be drawn about the role of moral norms in the international system.

The first of the cases treated in this work is the U.S. decision to send massive amounts of food and medical supplies to the Soviet Union during the devastating Russian famine of 1921. Why was this relief sent, and why did the American government devote more than 1 percent of its federal budget to Russian famine relief in 1921 during a period of economic uncertainty in the United States? Traditional realist approaches to foreign-policy decision making cannot supply an answer to this question. Indeed, traditional approaches to foreign-policy decision making point to a host of reasons why the United States should *not* have sent aid to Russia. The Bolshevik campaign to undermine the capitalist governments of Central Europe, the confiscation of American and other foreign investments in Russia, and the precedent created by the Soviet repudiation of Russia's international debts all constituted a serious threat to U.S. interests. Because of this threat, the Harding administration fashioned its foreign policy in order to isolate the Soviet Union and destabilize the Bolshevik regime: normal U.S. government credits were not extended, the Commerce Department pressured leading banks not to make loans to Russian enterprises, and the Treasury Department even refused to accept Russian gold in payment for the American goods that the Soviet Union desperately needed for postwar reconstruction. Yet in spite of this consistent campaign to destabilize the Soviet regime, when the onset of a devastating Russian famine in the winter of 1921 led even Lenin to conclude that the Soviet government would fall without outside relief, the United States did not allow its animosity toward the Bolshevik regime to deter it from sending aid to Russia. Why?

Interest-based explanations are wholly unconvincing. The American food-relief effort cannot be attributed to a desire to restore trade relations with Russia, because both during and after the famine-relief effort the Harding administration consistently refused to take any steps to end the economic isolation of the Soviet Union. Similarly, the U.S. decision could not have been shaped by a desire to reduce American food surpluses, since government purchasing patterns for famine relief indicate that Russian dietary and planting needs, rather than U.S. market conditions, determined the timing of purchases and selection of grains for shipment to Russia. In fact, the Harding administration was even willing to purchase certain Canadian grains for Russian famine relief because those types of grain had been sold out on the U.S. market and were best fitted to the Russian climate.

The only convincing explanation for the U.S. decision to send massive relief to the USSR is that leading American decision makers, principally Herbert Hoover, believed in the principles of the international famine-relief norm that had emerged in the wake of World War I—namely, that nations with an abundance of food have a moral obligation to assist starving countries even at the expense of important foreign-policy objectives. Hoover was convinced that America's food wealth imposed upon it a humanitarian duty to come to the rescue of the Russian people, and he was able to convince President Harding, Secretary of State Hughes, and the leading members of Congress that the normal interests of foreign policy should be set aside because of the moral issue at stake. Thus the case of famine relief to Soviet Russia in 1921 is an instance where leading state decision makers had internalized the tenets of an international moral norm and were driven by conscience to follow that norm.

The second case study concerns an instance in which domestic political support for an international moral norm led state decision makers to act in a norm-observant manner. In November 1969, President Nixon announced a series of policy decisions dealing with the issue of chemical and biological warfare. Nixon stated that the United States would unilaterally destroy its stockpiles of biological weapons, formally pledge not to initiate the use of lethal chemical weapons in war, and begin ratification proceedings on the Geneva Protocol of 1925, which forbade the first use of either chemical or biological weapons in combat. Traditional interest-based approaches to international relations have great difficulty in accounting for this major about-face in U.S. policy. During the discussions that led up to the 1969 decision, the Joint Chiefs of Staff had consistently opposed such steps because they would deprive the United States of potentially significant weapons systems and because the unilateral no-first-use pledge on chemical and biological weapons might well constitute a precedent that other nations would demand be applied to other classes of weapons (e.g., nuclear weapons). Thus the preponderance of interests defined in the traditional terms of power and security argued for retaining flexibility for the U.S. chemical and biological arsenal and scrapping the no-first-use proposal.

But the existence of a strong international moral norm against the use of these weapons allowed a small group of scientists, journalists, and congressional representatives to generate substantial domestic political pressure upon the Nixon administration to alter U.S. policy. The use of tear gas by American troops in Vietnam and significant increases in U.S expenditures on the development and production of chemical and biological weapons in the late 1960s had created in the mind of the American public an image of the United States as a very reluctant participant in the worldwide effort to limit the spread of chemical weapons. Opponents of U.S. CBW policy seized upon this image to argue that the United States was faced with a fundamental moral choice in 1969—whether to alter its policies in order to bring them into line with the letter and the spirit of the international moral norm against chemical and biological warfare that had grown up in the wake of World War I, or to continue its historical reluctance to endorse, both in treaty and in practice, that norm. Faced with this perceived need to choose for or against the international moral norm proscribing CBW, both elite public opinion and congressional majorities came to favor a substantial change in U.S. policies.

The Nixon administration, which was already facing questions about its moral credibility because of the war in Vietnam, felt that it could enhance its moral reputation by altering U.S. CBW policies. In addition, the administration recognized that a failure to change American chemical and biological weapons practices would leave it open to continuing charges of disregarding an issue that had a deep resonance within the American public. As one participant in the crucial 1969 National Security Council meeting on chemical and biological weapons remembers: "President Nixon made the changes in chemical and biological weapons policies because he wanted to make clear to the American people that the administration's foreign policy had an ethical side to it."[3] Thus the United States' policies on CBW during the last twenty years have been shaped by a decision that was influenced by domestic political support for the international moral norm on chemical and biological weapons and that can most convincingly be explained by an approach to international relations that accords room to the existence and ramifications of international morality.

[3] Author's interview with Phillip Farley, acting director of the Arms Control and Disarmament Agency in 1969, May 16, 1989.

The third case treated in this work is the U.S. decision to ratify the Panama Canal treaties of 1978. For more than sixty years, the United States had enjoyed quasi-sovereign control over a ten-mile-wide strip running across the center of Panama and had owned and operated the Panama Canal. While the economic and military importance of the canal had decreased during the late 1960s, the waterway still remained an enormous commercial and strategic asset of the United States. More than fifteen major trade routes critical to the U.S. economy passed through the Panama Canal, and virtually every major U.S. war plan in existence in the mid-1970s demanded that the canal be open and in friendly hands for channeling ships and war supplies between the Atlantic and the Pacific. Yet in 1977–78, the United States negotiated, signed, and ratified two new treaties that ended American control over the canal and the Canal Zone. Why did the United States agree to surrender this substantial military and economic asset to a small and unstable country such as Panama?

Approaches to international relations that ignore the role of international moral norms would point to the vulnerability of the canal to Panamanian sabotage and argue that the United States agreed to surrender the canal and Canal Zone to the Panamanians in order best to guarantee the future security of the canal. But such an argument ignores the fact that the military, which had the greatest interest in guaranteeing the future security of the canal, was deeply opposed to transferring the canal to Panama. In 1975 President Ford had to order the Joint Chiefs of Staff to cease their opposition to the continuing Panama Canal negotiations and accept his decision to turn the canal and Canal Zone over to Panama. And retired members of the Joint Chiefs of Staff, who were not obliged by the duties of their office to support the policy decisions of Presidents Ford and Carter, almost to a man registered strong and vocal objections to the entire concept of seeking to guarantee the security of the canal by turning it over to Panama. In addition to encountering significant difficulties in explaining the continuing military opposition to the Panama Canal treaties, approaches to international relations that ignore the role of international moral norms are hard put to account for the timing and sequence of the key events that led to the negotiation and ratification of the Panama Canal treaties. If fear of Panamanian unrest and sabotage was the governing motivation for the U.S. decision, why were the treaties accepted by the United States in the 1970s, when Panamanian violence was quite muted, rather than during the bloody mid-1960s, when violent riots engulfed the Canal Zone? And why did the issue of the Panama Canal suddenly become a "live" foreign-policy question for the United States in 1975?

An approach to international relations that recognizes the existence and importance of international moral norms encounters none of these problems. It can point to the fact that General Omar Torrijos, the Panamanian head of government, managed to place the canal issue high on the U.S. foreign-policy agenda by skillfully arguing in a series of carefully chosen international forums that American rule in the Canal Zone constituted a violation of the international moral norm against colonialism. Torrijos forced the major nations of the world to choose publicly between the United States and anticolonialism, and all of America's closest allies deserted the United States on crucial votes because they refused to be seen as supporting territorial colonialism in the late 1970s. As a result of these debates, Third World countries were coming to see the United States as a defender of territorial colonialism, and the foreign-policy community in the United States became alarmed that future cooperation with the Third World would be harmed by the continued American control of the Canal Zone. It was this reputational pressure upon the United States, pressure that arose from the fact that U.S. control over the canal and Canal Zone violated the norm against territorial colonialism, that was the largest single factor behind U.S. acceptance of the Panama Canal treaties of 1978.

Of course, there were other factors that also militated in favor of transferring the canal to Panama; and several of these also arose because of the existence of an international moral norm against territorial colonialism. President Jimmy Carter came to office in 1977 deeply committed to formulating a more forthrightly moral foreign policy for the United States, and he was willing to devote enormous energy and political capital to the ratification of the canal treaties because he saw them as the linchpin for his campaign to return American foreign policy to its roots of support for freedom, human rights, and anticolonialism. In addition, several key constituencies in the coalition that supported the canal treaties during the long and arduous ratification campaign were motivated by a belief that continued American control of the canal and Canal Zone did constitute colonialism and was therefore morally repugnant. Thus the case of the Panama Canal treaties demonstrates three different pathways from international moral norms to foreign-policy decision making: President Carter's conscience-driven dedication to a more moral American foreign policy; domestic political pressure upon the Senate, generated by the adherence of key interest groups to the norm of anticolonialism; and the ability of General Torrijos to use the anticolonial norm to form a coalition of nations that brought serious reputational pressure on the United States to alter its policies on Panama.

The U.S. decision to send famine relief to the Soviet Union in 1921, the Nixon administration's decision in 1969 to alter radically U.S. policies on chemical and biological weapons, and the U.S. negotiation and ratification of the Panama Canal treaties in 1978 all point to the fact that morality does play a substantive role in international affairs. All three cases indicate the existence of a set of clearly identifiable moral norms that have been formally agreed to by essentially all of the world's nations and that have been internalized by large numbers of people on every continent. The existence of these international moral norms provides an opportunity for morality to affect the making of foreign policy through three pathways: personal conscience, domestic politics, and reputational pressure generated by the collective action of states.

State decision makers are subject to the imperatives of conscience, as are ordinary citizens. There will be differences among state leaders in their degree of moral development and sensitivity, just as there are differences among citizens in society at large. But the internalization of moral norms by state decision makers will often create a *prima facie* motivation to respect those norms in formulating foreign policy. This pathway of conscience can be seen in Herbert Hoover's unswerving commitment to mount an American relief effort to Russia and in the willingness of President Harding and Secretary of State Hughes to accept Hoover's argument that the United States had a moral obligation to come to the aid of the starving Russian people. The pathway of conscience can also be seen in President Carter's willingness to place the issue of the Panama Canal at the top of his foreign-policy agenda in large part because of his personal commitment to forging a more moral American foreign policy free of territorial colonialism.

The second pathway from international moral norms to norm-observant foreign-policy decisions is domestic politics. Domestic public opinion is certainly not a consistent monitor and enforcer of international morality. But the ability of domestic pressure groups and public opinion to mobilize in support of a particular international moral norm can produce significant pressure upon Congress and the president to change American foreign policy. The CBW case is an example of the way in which conscience-driven adherence to an international moral norm can lead citizens and domestic elites to join coalitions that seek to change a norm-violating policy. When such a coalition becomes strong enough, then the president and Congress will have political incentives to follow the behavior indicated by the international moral norm.

The third pathway from moral norms to norm-observant foreign policy springs from the desire of nations to establish and maintain a reputation as a reliable partner for future cooperative relationships. Violating an international moral norm can significantly undermine a nation's reputation for equity, especially when there is continuing international focus on the norm violation. Thus it is profitable at times for a nation that is suffering from the violation of an international moral norm to mobilize third parties around the norm and force them to take a public stand against the violating country. The Panama Canal case is a classic example of a successful employment of this strategy. General Torrijos used the consensual acceptance of the norm against territorial colonialism to forge a coalition against continued American control of the canal and Canal Zone. The resulting reputational pressures upon the United States led American foreign policy makers to conclude that a refusal to renegotiate the Panama Canal treaties would label the United States as "colonialist" and lead to a lessening of Third World cooperation with the United States. This continuing reputational damage was viewed as more harmful to American interests than a decision to surrender the canal, and as a result the treaties were renegotiated.

While the three cases of Russian famine relief, the decisions on chemical and biological weapons, and the Panama Canal treaties all emphasize the important role that moral norms can play in the international system, the bombing of Dresden in 1945 underscores the fact that the mere existence of a strong international moral norm does not guarantee that that norm will consistently be followed in foreign-policy decision making. The norm of noncombatant immunity was one of the oldest moral norms in the international system, and it had been publicly reaffirmed by the United States throughout the period leading up to World War II. Yet in the winter of 1944–45, the leadership of the United States Air Forces authorized a series of terror-bombing raids upon German cities, raids that flagrantly violated the norm of noncombatant immunity by targeting German civilians and civilian morale. Why did the Air Forces endorse such raids in 1945, after having rejected the idea of terror bombing at several earlier stages in the war? In part, the American about-face was influenced by new psychological studies that indicated that terror bombing actually could break the morale of the German civilian population. In part, the Dresden decision resulted from the slow advance of the Allied forces during the winter of 1944–45 and from the possibility that the ground offensive in Europe would turn out to be much more protracted and more costly than had been anticipated. And, in part, the decision to authorize terror-bombing raids in 1945 resulted from ambiguities in the structure of the norm of noncombatant immunity itself, ambiguities that made it difficult to tell exactly when the norm was being violated. The bombing of Dresden demonstrates that there are significant limitations to the ability of international moral norms to mold foreign policy and that norm compliance is influenced by competing pressures of power and security that often favor violating an international moral norm.

CONCLUDING HYPOTHESES

This work seeks to supplement more traditional approaches to international relations by identifying a significant pattern of behavior in international affairs that is inexplicable using traditional categories. The three cases of Russian famine relief, American policies on chemical and biological weapons, and the Panama Canal treaties speak to the relevance of moral norms in the study of international relations. These cases provide significant support for the claim that international morality influences state behavior and that it operates through the pathways of conscience, domestic politics, and international reputation. The case of the bombing of Dresden, in contrast, points to the limits of moral norms in influencing state behavior and to the need to undertake further work designed to identify those conditions that favor compliance with international moral norms. Even without further work, it is possible to draw several important conclusions about the role of morality in the international system.

The clarity of the behavioral prescriptions attached to a particular international moral norm affects compliance with that norm.

Every international moral norm is a specific behavioral prescription that either demands or proscribes particular actions by nation-states. But since moral norms, like other norms in the international system, are rules designed to limit or encourage rather complex state activity, it is often difficult to formulate the norm in a manner that clearly demarcates what is acceptable conduct and what conduct goes beyond the line of moral acceptability.[4] Since the extent of pressures for com-

[4] Much of the social-science literature that deals with this issue of the boundaries of moral norms utilizes the concept of *scope*, which emerged in treatments of power and society during the 1950s. Oran Young has advanced a particularly helpful definition of scope: "The term scope applies to contextual limitations associated with behavioral prescriptions or to the appropriate circumstances in which the relevant actions are to be performed. Some prescriptions are broad with respect to scope in the sense that the required actions are to be carried out in virtually every situation (for example, there are relatively few contexts in which the taking of human life is morally or legally justifiable), whereas other prescriptions demand the performance of the specified actions only under highly restricted circumstances. Of course there are also cases in which serious controversies arise precisely with regard to the proper contextual limitations to be as-

pliance with an international moral norm (arising from conscience, domestic politics, or collective international action) depend upon the ability of an observer to determine when that norm has been violated, ambiguities in the demands of the norm can dramatically undercut state compliance. Thus the clearer the behavioral demands of a moral norm, the greater the compliance with that norm.

The contrast between the case study on the bombing of Dresden and the case studies on CBW policies and the Panama Canal treaties illustrates this reality. One of the most important factors contributing to the gradual drift toward terror bombing in U.S. Air Forces policies was the lack of clear boundaries to the norm of noncombatant immunity. That norm demands that civilians not be the direct targets of aerial attacks. But in an era of total war, there is an inherent elasticity to the notion of what constitutes a civilian, and this elasticity is detectable in the ever-widening American definitions of legitimate military targets: first aircraft plants, then major railroad crossings, and finally urban transportation networks were determined to be "noncivilian" targets that contributed materially to the German war effort. This ambiguity in the boundaries established by the norm of noncombatant immunity was further increased by the norm's willingness to allow the indirect destruction of civilian targets. For directness is an attribute of intentionality, which makes it very difficult for a third-party observer to tell when the norm of noncombatant immunity has been violated. Since the pressures upon Air Forces leaders to comply with the norm (e.g., the fear of international attacks upon the United States and the fear of endangering the future of the Air Forces by linking them with "baby killing" in the mind of the American public) largely depended upon the ability of third parties to discern when moral standards had been violated, the ambiguity of the norm of noncombatant immunity severely undermined its usefulness as a constraint upon U.S. policymakers.

The Nixon decisions on chemical and biological weapons in 1969 and the Panama Canal treaties of 1978 provide a vivid contrast with the Dresden bombing case and indicate how important clarity in an international moral norm can be to compliance with that norm. The United States did not use poison gas in Vietnam; it only utilized tear gas against enemy troops in order to clear them out from caves and foxholes. But the boundaries of the moral norm against chemical and biological warfare are so clear and strong that even this usage of

---

sociated with a particular behavioral prescription." (Oran Young, *Compliance and Public Authority: A Theory with International Implications* [Baltimore: The Johns Hopkins University Press, 1979], p. 3)

chemicals in war subjected the United States to massive international criticism and allowed domestic opponents of American CBW policies to rally the U.S. public around a radical change in the U.S. stance on these weapons. Part of the reason that the norm against CBW has been so well respected during the past sixty years is that it is an absolute norm that proscribes any use of chemical and biological weapons; thus it is easy for third parties to tell when the norm has been violated. Similarly, the anticolonial norm that lay at the heart of the Panama Canal case specifies clear boundaries for state conduct. The United States was castigated for its reluctance to end the Canal Zone because that enclave clearly constituted a "disruption of the national unity and territorial integrity" of Panama by an outside power.[5] And General Torrijos was able to force America's usual allies to vote to condemn the United States because they recognized that the moral norm against territorial colonialism clearly applied to the canal and Canal Zone. Thus clarity in an international moral norm enhances compliance with that norm because it allows state decision makers, as well as domestic publics and other nations, to recognize easily when a norm has been violated.

International moral norms vary in their period of gestation and in the sources that contribute to their formation, but this variation does not affect compliance with a particular moral norm.

The moral norms that lie at the foundations of the four case studies in this work testify to the fact that there is no typical length of gestation or source of development for an international moral norm. The norm of noncombatant immunity evolved over a period of some fifteen centuries and was shaped by ecclesiastical law, the code of chivalry, the fledgling science of international law, and technological breakthroughs such as the use of aviation in warfare. The international proscription of chemical and biological warfare, on the other hand, was a "shock-induced" moral norm that formed very rapidly. The experience of gas warfare during World War I had been so hideous that the major nations of the world were quite willing to accept a moral ban on all forms of chemical and biological warfare by 1925, and the major source for this norm was general public opinion during the early 1920s. The famine-relief norm also emerged in the immediate aftermath of World War I, but it resulted from the immense hunger that beset Central Europe in 1918; and the guiding force for the formation of the famine-relief norm was the International Red Cross, rather than

---

[5] United Nations, Department of Political Affairs, *Decolonization* 2, no. 6 (December 1975), p. 10.

general public opinion. The anticolonialism norm, which was crucial to the U.S. decision to renegotiate the Panama Canal treaties, took approximately fifty years to develop and become accepted in the international system. The guiding force behind the anticolonialism norm is a particularly interesting one, because although the philosophical roots of the norm can be traced to Europe, the application of those philosophical principles to the problem of territorial colonialism was largely spurred by the emerging leaders of the Third World. Thus even for the four norms treated in this work, the period of formation varies from four years to fifteen centuries, and the primary sources for the norms vary from Saint Augustine to Nehru to the Washington arms conference to the Red Cross.

Despite this great variation among international moral norms in their sources and periods of gestation, compliance with an international moral norm does not depend upon the length of time that that norm has existed or upon the avenue through which it came into existence. The United States complied with the famine-relief norm less than two years after it had been generally accepted by the leading nations of the world. But the United States was also willing to acknowledge the legitimacy of the norm against CBW in 1969 and is still willing to acknowledge the binding force of that norm today, some sixty years after its creation. Once an international moral norm has come to be accepted as a legitimate moral imperative in the international system, the particular cultural sources of its formation become irrelevant to international compliance with that norm, and the pressures for compliance depend not upon the length of time that the norm has been in existence, but upon the degree to which the norm is accepted as a morally binding behavioral precept by the collectivity of states, by domestic publics, and by the consciences of individual state decision makers.

"Norm entrepreneurs" play a critical role in bringing about compliance with an international moral norm.

In each of the three cases treated here in which the United States acted in compliance with an international moral norm, there was an identifiable individual or group of individuals who were instrumental in placing the issue on the American foreign-policy agenda and in generating support for norm-observant U.S. behavior. In the case of famine relief to Soviet Russia, Herbert Hoover was the prime mover behind the U.S. decision to send aid. Hoover interceded with President Harding and Secretary of State Hughes in order to convince them that America had a moral duty to help the Russian people; he organized a massive publicity campaign in the United States in order to make the general public aware of the drastic situation in the Soviet Union; and he lobbied key congressional representatives in order to persuade them that despite economic uncertainty in the United States, the American government had an ethical responsibility to appropriate $25 million for Russian relief. Similarly, in the case of the 1969 decisions on CBW, leading members of the scientific community, aided by journalist Seymour Hersh and Congressman Richard McCarthy, orchestrated the campaign to portray existing U.S. policies as antithetical to the moral norm against the use of chemical and biological weapons in warfare. This leadership coalition provided the scientific expertise, the journalistic contacts, and the political skills necessary to place the issue on the American foreign-policy agenda and to pressure the Nixon administration to alter radically the U.S. attitude toward chemical and biological weapons. Finally, in the Panama Canal case, General Torrijos functioned brilliantly as a "norm entrepreneur" who arranged a series of international forums designed precisely to force U.S. allies to make a choice between anticolonialism and their loyalties to the United States. By continually emphasizing the colonial nature of the American enclave in Panama, Torrijos succeeded in making the canal issue a major irritant in U.S.–Third World relations and led American policymakers to conclude that it was better to transfer the canal than to continue to jeopardize future cooperation with the Third World by retaining the waterway in perpetuity.

It is important to note that "norm entrepreneurs" operate out of a variety of motives. Herbert Hoover sought to rally support for the famine-relief norm because he believed wholeheartedly in the norm and altruistically concluded that the United States had an ethical obligation to come to the aid of the Russian people. General Torrijos, on the other hand, was acting not out of altruism, but out of his country's interest in regaining control over the canal and Canal Zone; one would look in vain for other instances in which Torrijos devoted such time and energy to the prosecution of an anticolonial cause. In the CBW case, professors Matthew Meselson and Joshua Lederberg acted out of a profound conviction that the moral norm constituted humankind's best defense against the specter of hideous and widespread chemical and biological warfare. Congressman McCarthy and his liberal Democratic allies in the House largely shared this view, but they were also motivated to attack America's use of tear gas in Vietnam and America's weapons-procurement programs because doing so would embarrass the Nixon administration and would particularly weaken the administration in its contention that it was pursuing a moral course in Vietnam. Thus while successful mobilizations in favor of compliance with a moral norm must involve the presence of identifiable "norm entrepreneurs," it is not necessary that the entrepreneurs operate from wholly altruistic motives. The work of these entrepreneurs in rallying support for norm-observant behavior is successful not because they themselves necessarily believe in the norm, but because there are state decision makers or domestic publics or other states who do subscribe to the moral norm at issue and thus can be successfully appealed to.

Moral language frequently serves a purely ideological function in the formulation of foreign policy. At the same time, substantive moral norms can and do affect the direction of major foreign-policy decisions. The study of international relations should recognize both of these realities.

Hans Morgenthau's critique of the supposed role of morality in foreign policy relied heavily upon the fact that what purports to be morality in the formulation of foreign policy often turns out to be ethical ideology, that is, the use of ethical language to justify a position taken for reasons wholly unrelated to moral concerns. And even the cases treated in this work confirm Morgenthau's contention that ethical ideology is a frequent ingredient in foreign-policy decision making. The argument put forth by Panama Canal treaty opponents that the United States should not transfer the canal because General Torrijos was a violator of human rights was ethical ideology. And ethical ideology was utilized in the effort to defend the U.S. stockpiling of chemical and biological weapons, when military planners contended that those stockpiles should be retained because CBW was the most moral and humane form of combat for the twentieth century. Ethical ideology is an ever-present ingredient in the foreign-policy decision-making process, and the scientific study of international relations should always view with a certain skepticism appeals rendered in moral language in the formulation of foreign policy.

But the frequent use of ethical language to justify interest-based foreign-policy decisions does not mean that substantive morality does not significantly influence the foreign-policy decision-making process. The cases treated in this work reveal that moral norms can function as independent variables in foreign-policy decision making. They can function as independent variables when state decision makers have internalized a moral norm and as a result follow their conscience in formulating national policies. Moral norms can function as independent variables when domestic interest groups or the general public subscribe to a moral norm and as a result bring pressure upon their government to come into compliance with that norm. And moral norms can function as independent variables when nations coalesce around a moral norm to bring reputational pressure upon a norm-violating state and thus alter that state's policies. One goal of empirical investigations into the role of morality in international relations should be to better understand when morality, rather than ethical ideology, is at work in the process of foreign-policy decision making.

The phenomenon of moral conflict is frequently present in major foreign-policy decision making. But while this means that the international system is a domain of moral complexity, it does not mean that it is a domain of moral ambiguity.

The phenomenon of moral conflict is present when significant moral claims fall on both sides of a policy decision. The Russian-famine case and the bombing of Dresden constitute two such instances. Opponents of famine relief to the Soviet Union argued with legitimacy that a U.S. decision to provide foodstuffs to the Russian people might well insure the stability and continuation of the Bolshevik regime; they complained that such a course of action was actually the less moral course because it would subject the Russian people to greater suffering in the long run. In the case of the bombing of Dresden, many in the U.S. military command structure claimed that it was morally preferable to bomb German cities rather than to continue a war that was taking an increasingly large toll of American soldiers and delaying the United States from focusing its energies on Japan. These are situations of genuine moral conflict; the objections made to following the international moral norm in question reflect significant moral claims and should not be dismissed as ethical ideology.[6]

But the fact that moral conflict is present in foreign-policy decision making does not mean that foreign-policy decisions are morally neutral or morally ambiguous. An analogy with state interests is helpful here. In most major policy decisions facing a nation, some significant claims of state interest fall on either side of the issue being debated. This means that the interpretation of where the nation's interest lies in the issue at hand is a complex exercise; but it does not mean that it is meaningless to ask in which course of action the nation's interest lies. So it is in cases of moral conflict. Moral claims will be legitimately

---

[6] In part, such situations of moral conflict embody a conflict between international moral norms and local or national moral norms. The case against providing food aid to the Soviet Union had more legitimacy within an American context because the Bolshevik system semed particularly to repudiate the American values of freedom and individualism. In the case of the bombing of Dresden, U.S. military planners were in part motivated by their special moral duty to protect American soldiers. For a discussion of how different levels of moral obligation interact within the universe of ethical discourse, see Michael Walzer, *Spheres of Justice* (New York: Basic Books, 1983).

raised on both sides of a policy question; the task of the decision maker or citizen interested in following the moral course of action is to weigh these moral claims carefully and decide where they come down on balance.

When the military or economic security of a state would be genuinely endangered by compliance with an international moral norm, the existence of such a norm will not generate norm compliance. But in those much more frequent instances of significant foreign-policy decision making where the military or economic security of the state is not put in jeopardy by following an international moral norm, the existence of such a norm can prove decisive in determining state behavior.

In his classic treatment of morality and foreign-policy decision making, Arnold Wolfers proposed that there is a continuum of pressures that operate upon state policymakers. At one end of the continuum lie decision-making situations where one alternative clearly insures the military or economic security of the state, while all other alternatives put that security in jeopardy. One might label this the *pole of necessity*. At the other end of the spectrum lie those far more frequent situations where the military or economic security of the state is not at risk, or where no one alternative clearly insures the security of the state. This can be called the *pole of choice*. In those instances that are very close to the pole of necessity, the existence of international moral norms will not significantly influence state decision making. But in those many instances involving an international moral norm where the situation is closer to the pole of choice, the pathways of conscience, domestic politics, and international reputational pressure can be capable of producing norm-observant behavior.[7]

Once again, the cases treated in this work are instructive. The bombing of Dresden illustrates a situation very close to the pole of necessity. By January 1945, proponents of terror bombing were able to argue with ever-increasing credibility that terror bombing had the potential to end the war far more quickly, thus saving tens of thousands of American lives and preventing a stalemate of German

[7] This argument draws heavily from Wolfers's argument that most situations in the foreign-policy decision-making process are not instances where the state is gravely threatened; thus moral choice is possible on many occasions. The terms *pole of choice* and *pole of necessity* as used here are quite distinct from Wolfers's "pole of power" and "pole of indifference," although they were inspired by his use of polar terminology to describe the dilemma in which decision makers may find themselves. See Arnold Wolfers, *Discord and Collaboration* (Baltimore: The Johns Hopkins University Press, 1962), pp. 47–66; 81–102; 233–252.

and Allied forces on the ground. The sooner the United States could end the war in Europe, the sooner it could shift massive amounts of war materiel to the Pacific theater. Thus vital state interests favored the initiation of terror bombing in early 1945, and the influence of the moral norm of noncombatant immunity was swept aside in favor of seeking a quick end to the war.

The other three cases are much closer to the pole of choice, and thus incentives flowing from the existence of relevant international moral norms could directly and substantially affect the outcomes. In the case of the 1969 decisions on chemical and biological warfare, the United States had interest-based incentives to maintain its freedom of action in the further production of chemical and biological weapons, but these incentives were not particularly strong. Thus President Nixon felt free to enhance his "moral" reputation in foreign policy by accepting the Geneva Protocol, destroying America's biological-weapons arsenal, and giving a unilateral no-first-use pledge. In the case of Russian famine relief, America's incentives to violate the norm were much stronger, since the Soviet regime did constitute a substantial threat to U.S. interests in the world. But these incentives did not arise from America's vital security interests, and thus Herbert Hoover and the other members of the Harding administration felt free to provide famine relief even at the risk of stabilizing the Bolshevik regime. The Panama Canal was important to America's national security, but less so than it had been in the past. Moreover, the reputational damage that General Torrijos was able to inflict upon the United States using the anticolonialism norm was also a very significant U.S. interest. For this reason, American state interests cut both ways in the Panama Canal case, and President Carter felt free to follow the state interests that were linked to the anticolonialism norm. Thus the realm of choice, as Arnold Wolfers proposed thirty years ago, occurs quite frequently and for many different reasons in international affairs. And when the realm of choice exists, there is an opportunity for morality to shape major foreign-policy decision making in crucially important ways.

SELECTED BIBLIOGRAPHY

ARCHIVAL RESOURCES

Archives of the Hoover Institution on War, Peace, and Revolution, Stanford, California. The Papers of the American Relief Association (Russian Operations). This collection contains the internal documents related to the American effort to relieve the Russian famine of 1921, including correspondence between Herbert Hoover and the White House, correspondence between Hoover and the American relief representatives in the Soviet Union, and the reports of ARA activities within Russia.

Archives of the Hoover Institution on War, Peace, and Revolution, Stanford, California. The Richard Anderson Papers. General Richard Anderson was deputy chief of operations for the U.S. Strategic Air Force from 1943 to 1945, and his papers include the daily correspondence that went through his office pertaining to all of the major policy decisions about strategic bombing during the war.

The James Earl Carter Presidential Library, Atlanta, Georgia. Papers of the White House Central Files and Papers of Hamilton Jordan. The Carter and Jordan papers contain strategy documents outlining the Carter administration's approach to securing support for the Panama Canal treaties within the United States. Some declassified papers regarding the administration's decision to negotiate and sign the treaties are also available, but most documents on this topic are still classified.

GOVERNMENT DOCUMENTS

League of Nations. *Official Journal of the League of Nations.* Geneva, 1921.
———. *Records of the Second Assembly.* Geneva, 1922.
United Nations. *Chemical and Bacteriological (Biological) Weapons and the Effects of Their Possible Use: A Report to the Secretary General.* New York: United Nations, 1969.
———. *The United Nations and Disarmament, 1945–1970.* New York: United Nations, 1970.
———. Department of Political Affairs. *Decolonization* 2, no. 6 (December 1975).
———. Security Council. *Official Records.* 1973.
U.S. Arms Control and Disarmament Agency. *1968 Report.* Washington: U.S. Government Printing Office, 1968.
Congressional Research Service. *Background Documents Relating to the Panama Canal.* Washington: U.S. Government Printing Office, 1977.
———. *Senate Debate on the Panama Canal Treaty.* Washington: U.S. Government Printing Office, 1979.

U.S. Congress. *Congressional Record.* 67th Cong., 2d sess., 1921. Vol. 62. Washington: U.S. Government Printing Office, 1921.

U.S. Congress. House. Committee on Foreign Affairs. *Hearings on Conditions in Russia.* 66th Cong., 3d sess., 1921. Washington: U.S. Government Printing Office, 1921.

U.S. Congress. House. Committee on Foreign Affairs, Subcommittee on National Security Policy and Scientific Developments. *Hearings on Chemical-Biological Warfare: U.S. Policies and International Effects.* 91st Cong., 2d sess., 1969. Washington: U.S. Government Printing Office, 1970.

U.S. Congress. Senate. Committee on Foreign Relations, Subcommittee on Disarmament. *Chemical-Biological-Radiological Warfare and Its Disarmament Aspects.* 86th Cong., 2d sess., 1960. Washington: U.S. Government Printing Office, 1960.

U.S. Congress. Senate. Committee on Foreign Relations. *Hearings on Chemical and Biological Warfare.* 91st Cong., 1st sess., 1969. Washington: U.S. Government Printing Office, 1969.

————. *Hearings on the Panama Canal Treaties.* 95th Cong., 1st sess., 1978. Washington: U.S. Government Printing Office, 1978.

————. *Report on the Panama Canal Treaty and the Neutrality Treaty.* 93rd Cong., 2d sess., 1978. Washington: U.S. Government Printing Office, 1978.

BOOKS

Beitz, Charles. *Political Theory and International Relations.* Princeton: Princeton University Press, 1979.

Brown, Frederic. *Chemical Warfare: A Study in Restraints.* Princeton: Princeton University Press, 1968.

Bull, Hedley. *The Anarchical Society: A Study of Order in World Politics.* New York: Columbia University Press, 1977.

Butler, Nicholas Murray. *Between Two Worlds.* New York: Charles Scribner's Sons, 1934.

————. *The Family of Nations.* New York: Charles Scribner's Sons, 1938.

Cancian, Francesca. *What Are Norms?* Cambridge: Cambridge University Press, 1975.

Carr, E. H. *The Twenty Years' Crisis: 1919–1939.* London: Macmillan and Company, 1956.

Cohen, Marshall, Thomas Nagel, and Thomas Scanlon, eds. *War and Moral Responsibility.* Princeton: Princeton University Press, 1974.

Cookson, John, and Judith Nottingham. *A Survey of Chemical and Biological Warfare.* New York: Monthly Review Press, 1969.

Dickinson, G. Lowes. *The European Anarchy: 1904–1914.* London: Swarthmore Press, 1916.

Durand, Andre. *History of the International Committee of the Red Cross.* Geneva: Henry Dunant Institute, 1978.

Emerson, Rupert. *From Empire to Nation.* Boston: Beacon Press, 1960.

Filene, Peter G. *Americans and the Soviet Experiment, 1917–1933.* Cambridge: Harvard University Press, 1967.

Fisher, Hugh. *The Famine in Soviet Russia*. New York: Macmillan Company, 1927.

Friedrich, Carl J., ed. *The Philosophy of Kant*. New York: Random House, 1949.

Hansell, Haywood. *The Strategic Air War against Germany and Japan*. Washington: U.S. Government Printing Office, 1961.

Hare, J. E., and Carey Joynt. *Ethics and International Affairs*. London: Macmillan Press, 1982.

Hare, R. M. *Freedom and Reason*. Oxford: Oxford University Press, 1963.

Henkin, Louis. *The Age of Rights*. New York: Columbia University Press, 1990.

Hersh, Seymour. *Chemical and Biological Warfare: America's Hidden Arsenal*. Indianapolis: Bobbs-Merrill Company, 1968.

Hoffmann, Stanley. *Duties beyond Borders: On the Limits and Possibilities of Ethical International Politics*. Syracuse: Syracuse University Press, 1981.

———. *The Political Ethics of International Relations*. New York: Carnegie Council on Ethics and International Affairs, 1988.

Hogan, J. Michael. *The Panama Canal in American Politics*. Carbondale: Southern Illinois University Press, 1986.

Johnson, James Turner. *Just-War Tradition and the Restraint of War*. Princeton: Princeton University Press, 1981.

Jorden, William. *Panama Odyssey*. Austin: University of Texas Press, 1984.

Josephson, Harold. *James T. Shotwell and the Rise of Internationalism in America*. London: Associated Press, 1975.

Kegley, Charles, ed. *Reinhold Niebuhr: His Religious, Social and Political Thought*. New York: Pilgrim Press, 1984.

Kennan, George. *American Diplomacy: 1900–1950*. Chicago: University of Chicago Press, 1951.

Keohane, Robert. *After Hegemony: Cooperation and Discord in the World Political Economy*. Princeton: Princeton University Press, 1984.

Killen, Linda. *The Russian Bureau*. Lexington: University of Kentucky Press, 1983.

Kingdon, John. *Agendas, Alternatives, and Public Policies*. Boston: Little, Brown and Company, 1984.

Kohlberg, Lawrence. *The Psychology of Moral Development*. San Francisco: Harper and Row, 1984.

Krasner, Stephen. *International Regimes*. Ithaca: Cornell University Press, 1983.

Lefever, Ernest. *Ethics and United States Foreign Policy*. Cleveland: Meridien Books, 1967.

Lickona, Thomas, ed. *Moral Development and Moral Behavior*. New York: Holt, Rinehart and Winston, 1976.

McCarthy, Richard. *The Ultimate Folly*. New York: Alfred A. Knopf, 1969.

MacIsaac, David. *Strategic Bombing in World War II*. New York: Garland Publishing, 1976.

Moffett, George. *The Limits of Victory: The Ratification of the Panama Canal Treaties*. Ithaca: Cornell University Press, 1985.

Morgenthau, Hans. *In Defense of the National Interest*. Washington: University Press of America, 1982.

———. *Politics among Nations*. New York: Alfred A. Knopf, 1956.

———. *Scientific Man versus Power Politics*. Chicago: University of Chicago Press, 1962.

Murray, Gilbert. *Liberality and Civilization*. London: George Allen and Unwin, 1938.

———. *Liberality and Progress*. London: George Allen and Unwin, 1938.

———. *The Ordeal of This Generation*. New York: Harper and Brothers, 1929.

———. *The Problem of Foreign Policy*. Boston: Houghton Mifflin, 1921.

———. *Tradition and Progress*. Boston: Houghton Mifflin, 1922.

Nardin, Terry. *Law, Morality, and the Relations of States*. Princeton: Princeton University Press, 1983.

Niebuhr, Reinhold. *Moral Man and Immoral Society*. New York: Charles Scribner's Sons, 1960.

———. *The Nature and Destiny of Man: Human Nature*. New York: Charles Scribner and Sons, 1943.

Nye, Joseph. *Nuclear Ethics*. New York: The Free Press, 1986.

Pettmann, Ralph, ed. *Moral Claims in World Affairs*. New York: St. Martin's Press, 1979.

Russell, Frederick. *The Just War in the Middle Ages*. Cambridge: Cambridge University Press, 1975.

Schindler, Dietrich, and Jiri Toman, eds. *The Laws of Armed Conflicts*. Geneva: Henry Dunant Institute, 1973.

Schuman, Frederick. *American Policy toward Russia since 1917*. New York: International Publishers, 1928.

Schaffer, Ronald. *Wings of Judgment: American Bombing in World War II*. New York: Oxford University Press, 1985.

Shotwell, James. *On the Rim of the Abyss*. New York: Macmillan Company, 1936.

———. *War as an Instrument of National Policy*. New York: Harcourt, Brace, 1929.

Singer, Hans. *Food Aid*. Oxford: Clarendon Press, 1987.

Stockholm International Peace Research Institute. *The Problem of Chemical and Biological Warfare*. Vols. 1–4. New York: Humanities Press, 1971–75.

Surface, Frank M., and Raymond Bland. *American Food Aid in the World War and Reconstruction Period*. Stanford: Stanford University Press, 1931.

von Albertini, Rudolph. *Decolonization*. Translated by Francesca Garvie. Garden City: Doubleday and Company, 1971.

Wallace, G., and A. D. M. Walker, eds. *The Meaning of Morality*. London: Methuen and Company, 1970.

Waltz, Kenneth. *Theory of International Politics*. New York: Random House, 1979.

Walzer, Michael. *Just and Unjust Wars: A Moral Argument with Historical Illustrations.* New York: Basic Books, 1977.

Weissman, Benjamin. *Herbert Hoover and Famine Relief to Soviet Russia: 1921–1923.* Stanford: Hoover Institution Press, 1974.

Williams, Howard. *Kant's Political Philosophy.* New York: St. Martin's Press, 1983.

Williamson, Oliver. *The Economic Institutions of Capitalism.* New York: The Free Press, 1985.

Wolfers, Arnold. *Discord and Collaboration.* Baltimore: The Johns Hopkins University Press, 1962.

Zimmern, Alfred. *America and Europe.* New York: Oxford University Press, 1929.

―――. *Europe in Convalescence.* New York: G. P. Putnam's Sons, 1922.

―――. *The League of Nations and the Rule of Law: 1918–1935.* London: Macmillan and Company, 1939.

―――. *Nationality and Government.* New York: Robert MacBride and Company, 1918.

―――. *The Study of International Relations.* Oxford: Clarendon Press, 1931.

ARTICLES

Axelrod, Robert. "An Evolutionary Approach to Norms." *American Political Science Review* 80 (December 1986): 1095–1111.

Barry, Brian. "Can States Be Moral? International Morality and the Compliance Problem." In *Ethics and International Relations,* ed. Anthony Ellis, pp. 70–81. Manchester: Manchester University Press, 1986.

Blasi, Augusto. "Bridging Moral Cognition and Moral Action: A Critical Review of the Literature." *Psychological Bulletin* 88 (1980): 1–45.

Cohen, Marshall. "Moral Skepticism and International Relations." *Philosophy and Public Affairs* 13 (Fall 1984): 299–346.

Cohen, Raymond. "Rules of the Game in International Politics." *International Studies Quarterly* 24 (March 1980): 129–150.

Donnelly, Jack. "International Human Rights: Regime Analysis." *International Organization* 40 (Summer 1986): 599–632.

Dore, Ronald. "The Prestige Factor in International Affairs." *International Affairs* 51 (April 1975): 407–424.

George, Alexander. "Case Studies and Theory Development." Paper presented to the Second Annual Symposium on Information Processing in Organizations, Carnegie-Mellon University, October 15–16, 1982.

―――. "Domestic Constraints on Regime Change in U.S. Foreign Policy: The Need for Policy Legitimacy." In *Change in the International System,* ed. Ole Holsti, pp. 233–262. Boulder, Colo.: Westview Press, 1980.

Goldberg, Victor. "Toward an Expanded Theory of Economic Contract." *Journal of Economic Issues* 10 (March 1976): 45–61.

Hartigan, Richard Shelly. "Non-Combatant Immunity: Reflections on Its Origins and Present Status." *Review of Politics* 29 (1967): 199–215.

Heyman, Philip. "The Problem of Coordination: Bargaining and Rules." *Harvard Law Review* 86 (March 1973): 797–897.

Klein, Benjamin, and Keith Leffler. "The Role of Market Forces in Assuring Contractual Performance." *Journal of Political Economy* 89 (1981): 615–641.

Kratochwil, Friedrich. "The Force of Prescriptions." *International Organization* 38 (Autumn 1984): 685–708.

Kreps, David. "Corporate Culture and Economic Theory." Paper prepared for the Second Mitsubishi Bank Foundation Conference on Technology and Business Strategy, August 1984.

Lipjhart, Arend. "The Comparable-Case Strategy in Comparative Research." *Comparative Political Studies* 8 (July 1975): 158–177.

———. "Comparative Politics and the Comparative Method." *American Political Science Review* 65 (September 1971): 682–693.

Macneil, Ian. "Contracts: Adjustment of Long-Term Economic Relationships under Classical, Neoclassical, and Relational Contract Law." *Northwestern University Law Review* 72 (1977–78): 854–906.

Meyer, John. "The World Polity and the Authority of the Nation-State." In *Studies of the Modern World System*, ed. Albert Bergeson, pp. 109–138. New York: Academic Press, 1980.

Monroe, Alan. "Consistency between Public Preferences and National Policy Decisions." *Political Science Quarterly* 7 (January 1979): 3–19.

Opp, Karl Dieter. "The Evolutionary Emergence of Norms." *British Journal of Social Psychology* 21 (1982): 139–149.

Page, Benjamin, and Robert Shapiro. "Effects of Public Opinion on Policy." *American Political Science Review* 77 (March 1983): 175–191.

Primack, Joel, and Frank von Hippel. "Matthew Meselson and the United States Policy on Chemical and Biological Warfare." In *Advice and Dissent: Scientists in the Political Arena*, ed. Joel Primack, pp. 143–164. New York: Basic Books, 1974.

Quandt, William. "The Electoral Cycle and the Conduct of Foreign Policy." *Political Science Quarterly* 101 (November 1986): 825–837.

Rosenfeld, Stephen. "The Panama Negotiations: A Close-Run Thing." *Foreign Affairs* 54 (October 1975): 1–14.

Wren, Thomas. "Social Learning Theory." *Ethics* 92 (April 1982): 409–424.

INDEX